James Harrison Kennedy

Early Days of Mormonism, Palmyra, Kirtland, and Nauvoo

James Harrison Kennedy

Early Days of Mormonism, Palmyra, Kirtland, and Nauvoo

ISBN/EAN: 9783337297824

Printed in Europe, USA, Canada, Australia, Japan

Cover: Foto ©Lupo / pixelio.de

More available books at **www.hansebooks.com**

Early Days of Mormonism

PALMYRA, KIRTLAND, AND NAUVOO

BY

J. H. KENNEDY

EDITOR OF THE MAGAZINE OF WESTERN HISTORY

NEW YORK
CHARLES SCRIBNER'S SONS
1888

PREFACE.

AMONG the many books that have been written upon Mormonism, there is not one that purports to be a plain, concise, complete, and unbiased history of the early days of the Mormon Church, where no tinge of personal interest existed, and no theory was to be advanced or defended. The main body of writers upon polygamy and Salt Lake, have only referred incidentally to the days of Palmyra, Kirtland, and Nauvoo, that they might properly introduce and explain the main topics it was their purpose to discuss. In these pages the author has simply told the story of the inception and growth of that remarkable body of misleading and misled men, from the birth of Joseph Smith to his tragic death in Carthage jail,—a story so full of incident and interest that it becomes worthy of narration by itself, as detached from the final journey across the wilderness, and the founding of Brigham Young's empire in the valley of Salt Lake.

The gathering of material upon which this narrative is based has not been the hurried work of a few weeks or months, but has been carried through years of unusual opportunity. While all available authorities who speak in print have been carefully searched and freely used, their statements have been supplemented or corrected by many personal interviews, by search of musty records in county courthouses, and the examination of files of newspapers published in the days of Joseph Smith. In deference to the modern conclusion that even theological history should not be controversial, no attempt has been made at argument; no statement of fact has been shaded to the color of a personal belief; no open question has been decided *perforce* against the Mormon creed; and no conclusion has been reached that the facts of the case did not seem to warrant. There has been but one aim in mind: to tell the story as directly and truthfully as it can be told; and to leave the issues that make Mormonism one of the problems of the age, to those who have studied it from the moral, religious, or political point of view.

The universal interest of the American people in all that pertains to Mormonism, and the fact that no such narration as this exists in print, seem to warrant its appearance at this date.

CONTENTS.

		PAGE
I.—A Rapid Growth in Fruitful Soil,	1
II.—The Evolution of the Book,	19
III.—Sidney Rigdon and the Kirtland Haven,	60
IV.—The Life of the Transplanted Tree,	88
V.—Miracles, and the Gift of Tongues,	111
VI.—Kirtland Stake of Zion, and Brigham Young,	131
VII.—Enemies Without and Within,	153
VIII.—The Army of Zion,	174
IX.—Far West and Nauvoo,	189
X.—At the High-Tide of Power,	210
XI.—Downfall and Death,	233
XII.—The Scattered Flock,	254
Appendix,	265

EARLY DAYS OF MORMONISM.

I.

A RAPID GROWTH IN FRUITFUL SOIL.

THERE was no premeditated preparation for the advent of Mormonism, yet none the less was the way made straight before it, and all the conditions to insure its life abundantly supplied. Smith its creator, Rigdon its evangelist, and Young who saved it in its supreme hour of fate at Nauvoo, held no divine commission for the founding of a creed, yet each was well equipped by nature and circumstances in all the essentials for the part he was to play. Had the first failed at Palmyra, the second at Kirtland, or the third on the banks of the Mississippi, the complex and dangerous problem of the Salt Lake valley would not now demand solution at the hands of the nineteenth century.

The outlines of this great drama of human life and human folly were unconsciously prepared long before the lines were written or the parts assigned. The atmosphere in which Joseph Smith was reared was saturated with ignorant superstition. The ease with which his parents and himself were duped, proved to his low cunning that others could be duped as well. The phases of social and religious life with which he was surrounded were such as to nourish within him the grossest germs of spiritual thought with which he had been endowed. His mother dreamed strange dreams, had visions, and sold to others the knowledge of the future which she believed she had received from celestial sources. For many years she had repeated the announcement that a seer was to be born of her family, and upon Joseph this doubtful honor was at last laid. He passed through childhood and into youth under the burden of this annunciation, and whether or not he wholly believed it in his heart, it must have colored his mental vision to some degree, and he was shrewd enough to see that it was not unheeded by many about him, and that it might be made to serve him in material things. It became one of the currents of impulse along which he at last drifted into the creation of a creed. I use the word drifted advisedly, as all the evidence obtainable shows that the Mormon scheme grew from one small fraud set upon another, and that no definite and determining intention held control in the heart of Smith, until he saw by experience the amount of nonsense that fanatical ignorance would enable mankind to accept and digest.

That this crude and cumbersome religion should find such ready root, can only be accounted for by an analysis of the soil in which it was set. The early years of the nineteenth century were filled with doctrinal jousts, in which denomination set itself against denomination, and creed made war upon creed. The religious crusades of new and aggressive churches were waged upon the older organizations with unusual fury, and with that relentless purpose that is possible only to ignorance well armed with zeal. There had been no period yet seen in America, and there has been none since, in which fanaticism and spiritual fervor took so close a hold upon the life and thought of the people. It was a season of revivals, and the spirit that was moving the theologians was felt in the lowest stratum of home and rural life. In illustration it may be noted that the extended era of the great revivalist, Lorenzo Dow, commenced in 1796. The works that for a third of a century came in the wake of his preaching, were possible only in a season when the ignorant and over-wrought fear of the people partook of the surrendering haste that is born of panic. Those remarkable nervous manifestations known as "the falling," "the jerking," "the rolling," and "the dancing" exercises, were yet other evidences of the mood in which certain of the more emotional sections of America were preparing to receive whatever of truth, or alleged truth, might be spoken unto them. Very many of the religious meetings of the day were attended by these remarkable physical and mental phenomena, that were looked upon by the ignorant mass as the moving of a divine power upon the bodies and minds of men.

It was not until 1799 that the great revivals of religion that afterward so stirred and wrought upon the West were inaugurated, and the first of an innumerable series of "camp-meetings" held. This method of reaching men found such favor and became so popular, that by 1801 we are told that over twenty thousand people were at times seen in one open-air gathering. "In consequence of such a vast assemblage of people," says one historian,* "it was impossible for one person to address them; hence they were divided into several groups, and addressed by as many different speakers, while the whole grove at times became vocal with the praises of God, and at others pierced with the cries of distressed penitents. . . . . The effect was peculiarly striking at night. The range of tents; the fires, reflecting light through the branches of the trees; the candles and lamps, illuminating the entire encampment; hundreds of immortal beings moving to and fro, some preaching, some praying for mercy, others praising God—all presented a scene indescribably solemn and affecting. These meetings soon spread through all the settlements in the West, and such was the eagerness of the people to attend, that entire neighborhoods were forsaken, and the roads literally crowded by those pressing forward on their way to the groves."

A striking and grotesque example of frenzied zeal, and of arrogant assumption accepted with humble faith, was furnished by the "Pilgrims" who made their appearance in the valleys of the Ohio and Mississippi in 1817. Commencing with a few fanatics in Canada, they gained in numbers as they moved across Vermont and New York, and from thence drifted into the far Southwest, where they finally dwindled to extinction. They preached a common stock of property; they had a prophet who received advice direct from heaven, and ruled with arbitrary power, and all things great and small were done in

* "Historical Collections of the Great West." By Henry Howe, Cincinnati, 1857, page 205.

direct obedience to the inspired voice; they enjoined penance for sin; wore their garments without changing as long as they would hold together; made of raggedness and uncleanness a virtue; and left their dead unburied where they fell. Yet even they won followers, and many who heard them were persuaded that the message they conveyed was divine.

Isolated evidences of this religious trend of the public conscience and thought might be advanced in abundance. It was only in 1832 that John Jay Shipherd and Philo Penfield Stewart founded the Oberlin Colony in a forest of Northern Ohio, and promulgated the Oberlin Covenant, declaring their purpose above all things to serve God, and to hold no more property than each could manage for His interest. Even such episodes as that of Dylks, the Leatherwood God, were possible, when a mysterious stranger, whose antecedents have not yet been discovered, suddenly appeared in the midst of a Southern Ohio camp-meeting, in 1828, announced himself as the real Messiah, whose coming was the beginning of the thousand years of peace, was soon surrounded by a sect which accepted him as divine, and would hardly be driven from him by exposure and public disgrace.

Rebellion and contention found their way into many of the churches. The Free-Will Baptists began, during the closing years of the eighteenth century, to make their inroads upon the parent church, and their doctrine was preached with spirit and fervor. The Church of God, or Winebrennarian, was growing and preparing for that great revival of 1825 which set its mark upon portions of Pennsylvania, and was felt to the north and west in isolated preachings and conversions. The Disciples, who unwittingly aided in preparing Eastern Ohio for Mormonism, found in this period their field-day of victory over the older creeds. Thomas Campbell and his brilliant son Alexander, had set forth to build up that Christian union which they thought so needed, and of which the Bible alone should be the foundation. It was at Brush Run, Pennsylvania, on September 7, 1810, that they organized their first effort, and set the fire of their fervor running through the West, with results which have left their mark upon the age. The Methodist Church was still feeling the personal influence of Wesley and Asbury, and its fervid and aggressive growth was one of the moving factors of the time. The Reformed Presbyterians had gained a foothold upon these shores. The Restorationists were preaching the doctrine that all men would ultimately become holy and happy; to which Hosea Ballou, in 1818, added that equally pleasant afterthought, that all punishment for sin is confined to this world.

Mother Ann Lee and the Shakers had commenced their work in America, and it was not until 1784 that their leader, who claimed to be the revealed Christ in female form, had departed into that death from which so many of her followers had believed she was to be exempt; but Joseph Meacham and Lucy Wright, to whom she had yielded the keys of her kingdom, used all the power of their strong individuality to hold the society up to the level of its faith, and to add to its membership and influence. It was in 1831, when Mormonism was beginning to gain a hold on the minds of men, that William Miller was preaching the Second Advent and offering to the world that wonderful drama of superstition that has hardly been paralleled in the annals of the world—a movement that strikingly illustrates the grotesque and unresting spirit of the times. Unitarian and Universalist were making their inroads on the older faiths and adding to the theological din and disturbance of the day, and many believed that the Millennial year had already dawned.

A spirit, not so much of inquiry as of positive declaration and assumed revelation, had taken hold upon the people, and through it ran an expectation that the times were ripe for some grand change in man's condition. Whether it should be the second advent of Christ upon the earth, the destruction of the world by fire, or the fulfillment of Daniel or Revelation in the movements of nations or the deeds of men, could not be clearly read by many; but that something strange and marvellous was at hand, was agreed upon by the mass. A declaration of divine power or apostolic commission that to-day would be assigned to the mental derangement or speculative quackery that had been its cause, was at that period in danger of finding enough who would believe it, and be spiritually elated or depressed by the message it conveyed. No surprise need therefore be felt when we see men of shrewd business cunning and fair intelligence in worldly affairs, giving of their faith, influence, and money to set an audacious charlatan upon a pedestal of spiritual power, or listening with rapt attention to the revelations of a youth who was their inferior in every relation of worldly life.

That branch of the Smith family of which Joseph, the founder of Mormonism, was a part, came originally from Scotland, although his immediate ancestors showed few of those strong and industrious qualities to which the sons of Scotia are natural heirs. The origin of the future prophet was sufficiently humble to make his later elevation all the more marked. The obtainable facts concerning his ancestry are meagre; but the following statements can be relied upon, as they are made upon authority that can hardly be gainsaid. "I have recently been upon the ground where Joe Smith first saw the light," writes Daniel Woodward, Judge of the County Court of Windsor, Vermont.* "The house was upon the top of the high ridge of land between Royalton and Sharon; and the buildings were located in Royalton. It is a beautiful place in summer, and is secluded from disturbance by the outside world. Joe's mother was the daughter of Solomon Mack, an infirm man, who used to ride about the country on horseback, using a woman's saddle, or what was termed a side-saddle. Joseph Smith, Sr., was at times engaged in hunting for Captain Kidd's buried treasure; and he also became implicated with one Jack Downing in counterfeiting money, but turned State's evidence and escaped the penalty. The Smith family moved from the old farm farther into Royalton, about one-half or three-fourths of a mile from my father's, and was living there while our house was building, and Joe came to the raising. I think it was in 1812, and Joe was then about eight years of age." Another

---

* *The Historical Magazine*, 1870, p. 316.

authority in the same article states that his recollections of Mr. Mack are very distinct, and that "his business on horseback was selling an autobiography of himself."

The first point of personal interest to which this narrative can with profit attach itself, is found in 1816, when Joseph Smith, Sr., and his wife Lucy Mack, and their family migrated from their Vermont home to Palmyra, New York. Their worldly goods were few and their children many, Joseph coming fourth in a line of six sons and three daughters. Upon reaching their new home in the semi-wilderness of Western New York, the father gave himself to the pursuits that had been a part of the old New England life. Like others who can be found in any new and growing community, he was content to make certain of enough for the day, with no effort toward a better means of livelihood, and no ambition to have part in the material advancement and development going on about him. He gave a day here and there to manual labor as it came to hand, and filled in the intervals by attendance upon a small cake-shop he had found means to open. On rare occasions when the country people were gathered to the town by some holiday or political demonstration, the future Patriarch of the Mormon Church would load his hand-cart with specimens of his art and go forth upon the streets, to find such patronage as might come to hand.

This precarious course of life was followed at Palmyra some two and a half years, when he decided upon a venture that would have been of promise had he and his sons been as well supplied with industry and ambition as they were with skill for the evasion of sustained toil. He moved his family to Manchester, two miles to the south, and took possession of a piece of timbered land which belonged to parties living at a distance. A small log-house was erected, containing two rooms and a loft; and in this the whole family made their residence. After seven years of squatter possession Smith made a nominal purchase of the land upon which he was located, but never paid for it in full, and it passed out of his hands when he followed the fortunes of his son to Ohio, and cast his lot in with the Mormon Church.

The work upon this little farm was done in a careless, half-hearted manner. No serious effort was made for the cultivation of the land, and the forest was cleared away only as there was demand for its product. Wood-chopping, the growing of small crops, the manufacture of baskets and brooms, and the making of maple sugar in season, were interspersed with occasional forays with the peddler's cart. Many intervals of lazy lounging occurred on the part of father and sons, and one keen-eyed neighbor has left on record the declaration that "the proportionate time given by the Smiths to work of any kind was largely exceeded by that devoted to hunting and fishing, trapping muskrats, digging woodchucks, and lounging about the stores and shops of the village." The watchful attention of a neighborhood where goods were few and the absence of even a little was missed, caused special attention to be paid the habits of the Smiths, and it was not long before their half-vagrant course of life laid them under suspicion of all the small thefts of the vicinity. How much of actual guilt belonged to them it would be difficult to determine at this late day, but the life of Joseph and his father in after-years was such as to deprive them of the benefit of the doubt. As one has borne vehement and perhaps biased witness: "The Smith family (at this period) were popularly regarded as an illiterate, whiskey-drinking, shiftless, irreligious race of people," Joseph "being unanimously voted the laziest and most worthless of the generation." *

Joseph, Jr., was born on December 23, 1805, in Sharon, Vermont,† and was well along in boyhood when the family migrated to the West. There is little in his early days of sufficient importance to attract historical attention, except the powerful influence his mother exerted upon him. She was of a morbidly sensitive nature in reference to matters of religion, and was no doubt a fanatic rather than a fraud. She was given to deep reveries, told fortunes, and claimed to have been miraculously cured of a mortal complaint. She felt the influence of the theological discussions that were being carried on about her, but in their complexity she found distraction rather than relief. She could not surrender her heart and obedience to any one doctrine, and the nearest she ever

* "Origin, Rise, and Progress of Mormonism." By Pomeroy Tucker, New York, 1867, p. 16.

† Judge Woodward, in the foregoing statement, locates Smith's birthplace in Royalton; but as Smith himself gives Sharon, and the authorities all follow his lead in that respect, the above will be allowed to stand. The buildings may be in Royalton, but the Smiths always considered themselves as a part of the other township.

came to having a fixed religion was when she allowed herself to be baptized by a minister of the Presbyterian Church, but declined to place her name upon the roll of church membership. She was convinced that one of her daughters had been restored to life by a direct dispensation of divine power, and long before the removal to New York she had announced the advent of a prophet in her family, and on the death of Alvah, the first born, the commission that had been intended for him was laid upon Joseph.*

The entire training of the youth was in the direction of his mother's wish. Perhaps the seed of an actual belief in this destiny was so deeply planted in

*<i>Littell's Living Age</i>, vol. 30, p. 429: "The elder Smith had been a Universalist, and subsequently a Methodist; was a good deal of a smatterer in Scriptural knowledge, but the seed of revelation was sown on weak ground; he was a great babbler, credulous, not especially industrious, a money-digger, prone to the marvellous; and, withal, a little given to difficulties with neighbors and petty lawsuits. . . . . Mrs. Smith was a woman of strong, uncultivated intellect; artful and cunning; imbued with an ill-regulated religious enthusiasm. The incipient hints, the first givings out that a prophet was to spring from her humble household, came from her; and when matters were maturing for denouement, she gave out that such and such ones—always fixing upon those who had both money and credulity—were to be instruments in some great work of new revelation. The old man was rather her faithful co-worker, or executive exponent. Their son Alvah was originally intended or designated, by fireside consultations and solemn and mysterious outdoor hints, as the forthcoming prophet. The mother and the father said he was the chosen one; but Alvah, however spiritual he may have been, had a carnal appetite; ate too many green turnips, sickened and died. Thus the world lost a prophet, and Mormonism a leader. . . . . The mantle of the prophet which Mrs. and Mr. Joseph Smith and one Oliver Cowdery had wove themselves,—every thread of it,—fell upon their next eldest son, Joseph Smith, Jr."

his soul that it bore fruit in all the years of his career, and was never altogether destroyed by the enlarged education and knowledge of later years, giving the key to some things in his character not otherwise made plain. That he was an immense imposition upon the credulity of man, and knew himself to be such, can hardly be questioned; yet under all quackery there usually lies a stratum of self-deception. The boy's education, or rather the rude smattering of learning that went by that name, was but added preparation for that which lay before him; he was not given to books, and the few he was persuaded to read were of vicious tendency, and set his imagination in the wrong direction. His favorites have been described as the "Life of Stephen Burroughs," a scoundrel dressed in the garb of the church, and the autobiography of the pirate Kidd. Smith afterward made confession that the book last named made a deep impression upon him, and owned to a special fascination in these lines found therein:

> "My name was Robert Kidd,
> As I sailed, as I sailed;
> And most wickedly I did,
> God's laws I did forbid,
> As I sailed, as I sailed."

A description of young Smith in these days was afterward written by one who saw him on many occasions: "He was lounging, idle (not to say vicious), and possessed of less than ordinary intelligence. He used to come into the village of Palmyra with little jags of wood from his backwoods home; sometimes patronizing a village grocery too freely; sometimes finding an odd job to do about the store of Seymour Scoville, and once a week he would stroll into the office of the old Palmyra *Register* for his father's paper. How impious in us young dare-devils to once in a while blacken the face of the then meddling, inquisitive lounger, but afterward prophet, with the old-fashioned balls, when he used to put himself in the way of working of the old-fashioned Rammage press. . . . . But Joseph had a little ambition, and some very laudable aspirations. The mother's intellect occasionally shone out in him feebly, especially when he used to help us solve some portentous questions of moral or political ethics in our juvenile debating club, which we moved down to the old red school-house on Durfee street to get rid of the annoyance of critics that used to drop in on us in the village; and subsequently, after catching a spark of Methodism in the camp-meeting away down in the woods, on the Vienna road, he was a very passable exhorter in evening meetings." *

An even less pleasing picture has been drawn by another, who perhaps studied the boy at closer range and from a more intimate personal acquaintance. Between twelve and thirteen years of age he is remembered by this witness as "a dull-eyed, flaxen-haired, prevaricating boy, noted only for his indolent and vagabondish character, and his habits of exaggeration and untruthfulness. . . . . He seldom spoke to any one outside of his intimate associates, except when first addressed by another, and then, by reason of his extravagances of statement, his word was

* "Origin of the Mormon Imposture." *Littell's Living Age*, vol 30, p. 429.

received with the least confidence by those who knew him best. He could utter the most palpable exaggeration or marvellous absurdity with the utmost apparent gravity. He nevertheless evidenced the rapid development of a thinking, plodding, evil-brewing mental composition—largely given to inventions of low cunning, schemes of mischief and deception, and false and mysterious pretensions. . . . . He was, however, proverbially good-natured, very rarely, if ever, indulging in any combative spirit toward any one, whatever might be the provocation." *

As the boy advanced in years he developed a mental aptitude that, amid more favoring circumstances and under the stress of some moral encouragement, might have grown to usefulness. As he grew away from the period in which his fancy yielded to Captain Kidd, the real desire for food of some kind that his mother had bequeathed him, led him into the nearest and most open channel that was before him. He listened to the battle of religious controversy that was then being waged in Western New York, and was controlled by its influence as a boy of 1849 might have been won to the golden fields of California, or one of 1856 to the denunciation or defense of slavery. His reading took a theological turn, and the Bible became a matter of almost daily study. His mind was retentive; he was possessed of a rude eloquence of speech, and had that rare power of expression that to the stranger or the simple would seem the outward form of a sincere belief within. The more mysterious and complex the chapter of Scripture to which he

* "Origin, Rise, and Progress of Mormonism," p. 16.

gave attention, the more open and bold his explanation and application when surrounded by auditors who did not surpass him in knowledge. He was an attendant upon many of the revivals in the churches of the neighborhood, and upon one occasion was so far led as to make a profession of faith, and to join, upon probation, the Methodist church of Palmyra. Whether he took this step through the excitement of the moment or really sought for spiritual light, can hardly be determined, and in either case the result was the same. He abandoned even this slight church connection, and was soon afterward heard denouncing sectarianism as an evil, and to declare that all the churches were built upon a false foundation.

That Joseph was led at an early age to hold a hearty contempt for manual labor, and resolved to make cunning take the place of muscle, is proved by every discoverable portion of his record. There was an almost brutal frankness upon this point by some who thrived upon his scheming, and it has been again and again quoted that even Brigham Young declared that "The Prophet was of mean birth; that he was wild, intemperate, even dishonest and tricky in his youth." We have eminent authority for believing that a prophet is not often honored in his own country, yet it is seldom that a prophet, even of Mormonism, is sent before the world with such certificate of character as was awarded Joseph Smith and his family by eleven of the most prominent and respectable citizens of Manchester, who, under date of November 3, 1833, affixed their names to this emphatic declaration: *

---

* "Mormonism and the Mormons." By Daniel P. Kidder, New York, 1842, p. 20.

"We, the undersigned, being personally acquainted with the family of Joseph Smith, Sr., with whom the Gold Bible, so called, originated, state: That they were not only a lazy, indolent set of men, but also intemperate, and their word was not to be depended upon; and that we are truly glad to dispense with their society."

As if the above did not cover the ground with sufficient force and exactness, a supplemental declaration was made on December 4, 1833, and signed by sixty-two residents of Palmyra:*

"We, the undersigned, have been acquainted with the Smith family for a number of years, while they resided near this place, and we have no hesitation in saying that we consider them destitute of that moral character which ought to entitle them to the confidence of any community. They were particularly famous for visionary projects; spent much of their time in digging for money which they pretended was hid in the earth, and to this day large excavations may be seen in the earth, not far from their residence, where they used to spend their time in digging for hidden treasures. Joseph Smith, Sr., and his son Joseph were, in particular, considered entirely destitute of moral character, and addicted to vicious habits."

Some portion of this may have been dictated by envy, malice, or that form of righteousness which controls men at times when their neighbors have been more successful than themselves, but the allegations had a foundation in fact.

* "Mormonism and the Mormons," pp. 20, 21.

It was by such people, and amid such surroundings, that Mormonism had birth, and was nurtured in its early days. In an extended and honestly intended quest along this line of information, I have been unable to find that one of the Mormon leaders in the early days was an earnest, honest-minded believer in the creed he advocated. Not one of them would have met martyrdom for conscience' sake. There was not one who did not value it for the gain there was to be had of it. This does not hold true of their followers and dupes, among whom were many who beggared themselves that their church might live, and bravely and lovingly met scorn and injustice that their faith might be made manifest in their works. It was through them that the church gained all the stability of which it was possessed; and it was through their efforts that Smith and his co-conspirators were enabled to live in the ease and comfort of which they made such ready use.

II.

THE EVOLUTION OF THE BOOK.

THE first venture made by young Smith in the line of mystification was as a "Water Witch." Armed with the forked hazel rod he moved from point to point over the country, successfully locating some hidden streams, and gaining reputation thereby: and meeting with many failures, of which all mention was discreetly omitted by himself and followers. His father had laid claim to a like power, and contented himself with its practice; but the more ambitious boy soon discovered that a success equal to his expectations must come from enlarged claims and more ample powers.

From locating subterranean veins of water he advanced to the discovery of hidden riches, and was soon practicing the new profession as zealously as he had pursued the old. Of his career as a seeker after hidden wealth many stories have been told, some of which no doubt are pure fabrications, while others may have a narrow foundation in fact. Others are well authenticated. When the Smith family lived at Manchester, Joseph assisted his father in well-digging. In September, 1819, they were engaged in such occupation upon the premises of Clark Chase, near Palmyra, and the famous "Peek Stone" of ante-Mormon fame was brought to light. With the earth thrown to the surface, there appeared a small stone, shaped something like a human foot, opaque, and of a clear, whitish appearance.

The children of Mr. Chase claimed it as a matter of natural possession, but young Joe advanced the claim of discovery, and carried it home in his hands. Under the encouragement of his mother, in whose eyes all things took on a supernatural tinge, the stone became a fossilized miracle that had been awaiting his coming for many years. With a bandage over his eyes he would fall upon his knees and bury his face in the depths of an old white hat, where the stone was already hidden. Out of these oracular depths he would tell his gaping audience where the treasures of Kidd and others lay concealed; locate the trail of wandering flocks; point out the deposit of stolen goods; and perform other wonderful things which only those of that faith which asked no questions could believe. His father and brothers accepted his claims with a confidence suggestive of a charming simplicity of mind, or a purpose of making his cunning of substantial benefit to the family. The cupidity of neighbors was excited, and they were determined that no fault of theirs should compel the wealth of the old buccaneers to longer corrode and rust in the bosom of the earth.

Companies of diggers were organized, and the spade and lantern made nocturnal raids in company. Such faith had arisen in Joseph and the "Peek Stone" that in 1820 he was enabled to raise a small sum of money from his dupes to defray the expense of reaching a vast deposit of wealth he had located during one of his explorations of the wonderful hat. At the mid-hour of the chosen night the little company, with Joseph in the lead, repaired to a small hill near his father's house. A mysterious ceremony was performed by Smith, and the spades were driven sharply into the earth, in the midst of profound silence, stirred only by the nervous excitement of those who were there in obedience to an actual faith. Not a word was spoken, else the magic of those with whom Joseph was in commune and by whose sufferance he was present, should whisk the treasure to some far corner of the earth.

The labor was carried on for two hours, Joseph standing by with a wand in hand, directing along what line the shaft should be sent. As the crisis approached and it was felt that a few strokes more would crown the venture with success and place them all beyond the reach of want, the devil made an inopportune visit and prevailed upon some member of the party to speak. The riches that were so close at hand took unto themselves wings, and were beyond the reach of spade and peek stone forever.

There were those among the skeptical of Manchester who affirmed that one of the Smiths had spoken at the opportune moment, to relieve Joseph of an embarrassing dilemma, but those who had set out to be duped were consistent in their purpose and refuted all counter argument by declaring that there was a heavy odor of brimstone at the moment the speech was heard, and that the very earth vibrated under their feet, as the iron money-chests were magically hurled from beneath them.

One other occasion of like character has been placed on record. After Joseph had pointed out the position of the treasure, it was announced that a black sheep must be slain as a blood-offering, upon the spot, before work could be commenced with any hope of success. By a coincidence that would be remarkable to one who did not know the Smiths, a neighbor, William Stafford, who in early life had been a sailor, and never overcame the superstition of an ocean life, possessed a fine black ewe that he had been fattening for the market. The statement of conditions being made in his presence, he promptly offered the sacrifice, on condition that he should be a sharer in the spoils. When the diggers reached the designated spot a circle was described, the sheep killed, and the blood sprinkled under Joseph's direction. The work went on in silence for some hours, when Satan again made his appearance, and the scheme was frustrated. Stafford was compelled to console himself with the belief that the remains of his sheep had been taken by the Devil as a trophy of war, and the fact that one of the Smiths had disappeared with it some time after the work commenced, may have been suggested to him, although he was discreet enough to hold his peace.

This money-digging fraud of the Smiths was kept up at irregular intervals from 1820 to 1827. The experience Joseph gained in handling his dupes was of great aid to him in the larger operations of later years. He had a natural power over men, and could gain and hold an ascendency in cases where most impostors would have failed. No story that he could invent seemed too wild for belief, and no failure of to-day stood in the way of a ready and willing obedience to-morrow. It was this success that led him on, by gradual stages, to schemes of audacious falsehood that even he would have refused to sanction in the start.

Joseph's own statement as to how he came to turn his attention to spiritual things, widely differs from the facts furnished by those about him. His mind, he says, had been prepared by the incidental reading of a portion of the New Testament during a great revival excitement; and he believed that to ask for heavenly wisdom was to make certain of an answer. The Methodists had inaugurated the movement in the neighborhood, and had received the aid of the other denominations. When the converts that had been made by this union movement began to choose their future church homes, they were naturally confused and perplexed by the special claims of superior right and safety put forward by each. His mother gave a nominal adhesion to the Presbyterians, whither she was followed by two sons and one daughter. Joseph confesses to a leaning on his own side toward the Methodists.

Uncertain as to which way he should go, and torn by conflicting emotions, he was led to retire to a solitary place in the forest, for prayer and meditation. "After I had retired into the place," he writes, "where I had previously designed to go, having looked around me, and finding myself alone, I kneeled down and began to offer up the desires of my heart to God. I had scarcely done so when I was seized upon by some power which entirely overcame me, and had such astonishing influence over me as to bind my tongue so that I could not speak. Thick darkness gathered around me, and it seemed to me for a time as if I were doomed to sudden destruction.

But, exerting all my powers to call upon God to deliver me out of the power of this enemy which had seized upon me, and, at the very moment when I was ready to sink into despair and abandon myself to destruction—not to an imaginary ruin, but to the power of some actual being from the unseen world, who had such a marvellous power as I had never before felt in any being—just at this moment of great alarm, I saw a pillar of light exactly over my head, above the brightness of the sun, which descended gradually until it fell upon me. It no sooner approached than I found myself delivered from the power of the enemy which had held me bound. When the light rested upon me I saw two personages whose brightness and glory defy all description, standing above me in the air. One of them spake unto me, calling me by name, and said, pointing to the other, ' This is my beloved Son—hear him!' "*

Burdened with his difficulty as to which church he should join, he asked his heavenly visitor his duty in the premises, and was told to attach himself to none, as all creeds were an abomination. Darkness then passed upon his vision, and when he came once more to his normal condition he found himself prone upon his back, with his gaze turned heavenward.

Pursuing his narrative, Joseph states that he continued at his farm work, and in three years, on the 21st of September, 1823, was granted another and far more important visit from the upper world. Upon retiring in the evening of the day last mentioned, he betook himself to prayer, asking forgiveness for his

* "The Rocky Mountain Saints." By T. B. H. Stenhouse, New York, 1873, p. 15.

many sins and follies, and also for a manifestation, that he might know of his religious standing. He felt "full confidence" in receiving a response, and while thus in the act of calling upon God, discovered a light in the room, "which continued to increase until the room was lighter than at noonday."

A person appeared at his bedside, "standing in the air, for his feet did not touch the floor. He had on a loose robe of most exquisite whiteness." His hands and feet were naked; his head and neck bare. The youth felt no fear. The visitor called him by name, and said that he was a messenger from God; that God had a work for him to do, and that his name should be had for good or evil among all nations, kindreds, and tongues. He said there was a book deposited, written upon gold plates, giving an account of the former inhabitants of this continent and the source from whence they sprung. That the fullness of the everlasting gospel was contained in it as delivered by the Saviour to the ancient races of the world.

Also that "there were two stones in silver bows (and these stones fastened to a breastplate, constituted what is called the Urim and Thummim) deposited with the plates, and the possession and use of these stones was what constituted seers in ancient or former times, and that God had prepared them for the purpose of translating the book." After relating these things the angel quoted many prophecies of the Old Testament, declaring that they were not yet fulfilled. He afterward told Joseph that when he was given the plates he should not show them, nor the breastplate, to any person excepting to those to whom he should be commanded to show them. If he did he should be destroyed. Twice more during the night the messenger approached in the same manner, rehearsing the same thing, and on the third visit added a caution that Satan, on account of the poverty of the Smiths, would tempt Joseph to get the plates for mercenary uses, but that he must be influenced by no other purpose than a desire to build up a kingdom.

The mental excitement attendant upon this interview was such that when Joseph went to his labor on the following day he was so exhausted that his father insisted upon his returning home. In doing so he attempted to cross a fence, but his strength failed him, and he fell to the ground in an unconscious condition. The first thing he recollected was hearing his name called, and when he looked up he beheld the same messenger standing over his head and surrounded by light. All that had been related during the night was again told him, and he was instructed to tell his father of the visions and the commandments he had received. He returned and did so, and his father replied that it was of God, and bade him go and do as directed. Joseph immediately repaired to the locality where he had been told the plates were deposited, and at once recognized it.

Smith's statement continues: "On the west side of this hill, not far from the top, under a stone of considerable size, lay the plates, deposited in a stone box. This stone was thick and rounded in the middle on the upper side, and thinner toward the edges, so that the middle part of it was visible above the ground, but the edge all around was covered with earth. Having removed the earth and obtained a lever which I got fixed under the edge of the stone, and with a little exertion, raised it up, I looked in and there, indeed, did I behold the plates; the Urim and Thummim and breastplate as stated by the messenger.

"The box in which they lay, was formed by laying stones together in some kind of cement. In the bottom of the box were laid two stones crossways of the box, and on these stones laid the plates, and the other things with them. I made an attempt to take them out, but was forbidden by the messenger. I was again informed that the time for bringing them out had not yet arrived, neither would until four years from that time; but he told me that I should come to that place precisely in one year from that time, and that he would there meet with me, and that I should continue to do so until the time should come for obtaining the plates." *

Joseph obeyed the command of the angel, and every year met him at the appointed spot to receive his instructions as to what the Lord wished done, as well as revelations as to the manner in which His kingdom was to be governed in the latter days.

Joseph's father attempted to describe the beginning

---

*One mile from the Smith residence was the farm of Alonzo Saunders, four miles south of Palmyra. It includes the now famous hill, which rises abruptly to the height of one hundred and fifty feet; the ridge runs almost due north and south, and from the summit thereof beautiful views of the hills surrounding Canandaigua and Seneca Lakes may be obtained. It is known to the present generation as "Gold Bible Hill." To Joseph it was the Hill Cumorah.

of these things, in an interview in 1830,* when the claims of the young man had begun to be noised abroad. He declared that when the son was fourteen years of age, and yet very illiterate, he happened one day to be present when a man was "looking" into a dark stone, and informing people where money and other buried treasures could be found. Joseph asked permission to look also, and when the request was granted, placed his face in the hat where the stone was deposited. It did not prove to be the special seer-stone gauged to his vision, but he was enabled to discern a few things, and among them was the stone that was meant for him, and its location at the time. The place was not far from their house, and under pretence of digging a well, they reached it at the depth of some twenty feet. After this, the father added, Joseph made use of it, and spent a couple of years in the money-searching adventures already described.

Despite the attractive ingenuity of these stories, there is substantial grounds for the belief that the whole fabrication of the golden plates grew out of an impromptu jest on the part of young Smith, which was received in such earnest, that his subtle cunning saw in it a new way to distinction and possible gain. The story is told plainly and fully by Peter Ingersol,† a near neighbor to the Smiths, and at that time one of Joseph's most intimate friends. He declares that one day the future Prophet of Mormonism called

---

* "Interview with the father of Joseph Smith, the Mormon Prophet, forty years ago," by Fayette Lapham.—*The Historical Magazine*, 1870, p. 305.

† "Mormonism and the Mormons," p. 22.

upon him, and that his countenance and manner betrayed evident enjoyment of some hidden jest. Upon being questioned, he made the following statement: "As I was passing yesterday across the woods after a heavy shower of rain, I found in a hollow some beautiful white sand that had been washed up by the water. I took off my frock and tied up several quarts of it and then went home.

"On my entering the house, I found the family at the table eating dinner. They were all anxious to know the contents of my frock. At that moment I happened to think of what I had heard about a history found in Canada called the Golden Bible, so I very gravely told them it was the Golden Bible. To my surprise, they were credulous enough to believe what I said. Accordingly, I told them I had received a commandment to let no one see it; 'for,' says I, 'no man can see it with the naked eye and live.' However, I offered to take out the book and show it to them, but they refused to see it, and left the room. Now," said Jo., "*I have got the d——d fools fixed, and will carry out the fun.*"

And carry it out he did, with results far beyond his own expectations or the imaginings of others. His family may have continued their belief in his story, or discovered its falsity, but in either case the result was the same. They professed their adherence before others, and aided Joseph in the advancement of his claims. Neighbors heard of the wonderful discovery, and came to verify rumor by investigation. Smith was equal to the emergency. He gravely reiterated his declaration that no man but himself could look upon the Golden Book and live. As he saw the impression his invention had made, he took steps to keep it alive. Willard Chase, a neighbor, in after-years made affidavit to the following effect:[*] "In the fore-part of September, I believe 1827, the Prophet requested me to make him a chest, informing me that he designed to move back to Pennsylvania, and, expecting soon to get his Gold Book, he wanted a chest to lock it up, giving me to understand at the same time that if I would make the chest, he would give me a share in the book. I told him that my business was such that I could not make it, but if he would bring the book to me I would lock it up for him. He said that would not do, as he was commanded to keep it two years without letting it come to the eye of any one but himself. I told him to get it and convince me of its existence and I would make him a chest; but he said that would not do, as he must have a chest to lock the book in as soon as he took it out of the ground. I saw him a few days after, when he told me that I must make the chest. I told him plainly that I could not, upon which he told me that I could have no share in the book."

Unable to swindle his neighbor, he fashioned for himself a box of clapboards, in which he deposited whatever he made fill the mission of the golden plates. His mother's memoirs declare that there was not enough money in the family purse to pay for a fitting receptacle, and that Joseph went to well-digging in order to supply the lacking sum.

The excitement created in the neighborhood by the alleged discovery of the young man caused investiga-

---

[*] "Mormonism and the Mormons," p. 23.

tion on the part of some who had no faith in Smith or his claims. The account of a visit paid Smith by two young men * possesses a touch of such genuine human nature, that one cannot hesitate to accept it as true in every detail. It aptly illustrates the crude and clumsy character of the whole swindle. William T. Hussey and Asel Van Druver, young fellows well known for their waggish habits, and intimates of Smith, made their appearance and strongly importuned for at least one glance at the famous and mysterious book. Joseph declared that he could not yield, as even one look would be the end of earth for both.

Their pleading was in vain, as was also their offer to take upon themselves all responsibility for what might occur. Smith offered them what was in his power—they might go with him to the hiding-place of the treasure and look upon its shape through the canvas in which it was wrapped. They accepted and were led to a remote corner of the garret, where Smith solemnly opened the box and showed them a bag hidden within it. As he still persisted in his refusal, Hussey dexterously whipped off the cover with the exclamation, "By ——, I will see the critter, live or die!" and exposed to view a large brick.

Most men would have been abashed when confronted with this ridiculous conclusion. But Joseph was made of readier stuff. He was equal to the emergency. He declared that the supernatural power with which he was endowed had enabled him to see the daring purpose in their minds, and that he

* "Origin, Rise, and Progress of Mormonism," p. 31.

had purposely misled them. But he was of sufficient worldly-mindedness to understand the effect of an exposure before the people, and when the trio had passed down-stairs, he treated his guests liberally to whiskey, and asked them to make no mention of what had occurred.

According to Joseph's narration, it was on September 22,* 1827, that the plates and the instrument by which they were to be deciphered were delivered to him by the angel who had them in charge. They were yielded only upon condition that he would preserve them with the greatest care until their return should be demanded at his hands. His account of the final surrender of the book on the part of its angelic custodian, as related to Willard Chase, was as follows:† "On the 22d of September he arose early in the morning and took a one-horse wagon of some one that had stayed overnight at their house, without leave or license, and together with his wife, repaired to the hill which contained the book. He left his wife in the wagon by the road, and went alone to the hill, a distance of thirty or forty rods from the road. He said he then took the book out of the ground and hid it in a tree-top, and returned home. He then went to the town of Macedon to work.

"After about ten days' time, it having been suggested that some one had got his book, his wife went after him. He hired a horse and went home in the afternoon. Stayed long enough to drink one

---

*This was subsequent to his removal to Pennsylvania, and marriage, as related hereafter.

† A continuation of Chase's statement, related above.

cup of tea, and then went for his book. Found it safe. Took off his frock and wrapped it around it, put it under his arm and ran all the way home, a distance of about two miles. He said he should think it would weigh sixty pounds, and was sure it would weigh forty. On his return home he said he was attacked by two men in the woods, and knocked them both down and made his escape. Arrived safe and secured his treasure."

To this narration Mr. Chase somewhat bitterly adds this choice portion of personal biography: "A few days afterward he told one of my neighbors that he had not got any such book, and never had, but that he had told the story to deceive the d——d fool (meaning me), to get him to make a chest."

The Prophet's mother* has left an elaborate description of the Urim and Thummim,† by aid of

---

* In that unique book, "Biographical Sketches of Joseph Smith, the Prophet, and his progenitors for many generations." By Lucy Smith, mother of the Prophet.

† "'Urim' means 'light,' and 'Thummim' 'perfection.' The mysterious words meet us for the first time, as if they needed no explanation, in the description of the high priest's apparel. . . . . Inside the breastplate, as the tables of the covenant were placed inside the ark, are to be placed 'the Urim and the Thummim'; . . . . and they, too, are to be on Aaron's heart when he goes in before the Lord. Not a word describes them. They are mentioned as things already familiar both to Moses and the people, connected naturally with the functions of the high-priest, as mediating between Jehovah and his people. . . . . In what way the Urim and Thummim were consulted is quite uncertain. Josephus and the rabbis supposed that the stones gave out the oracular answer by preternatural illumination; but it seems to be far simpler . . . . to suppose that the answer was given simply by the word of the Lord to the high-priest . . . . when, clothed with the ephod and the breastplate, he had enquired of the Lord."

which the translation of the golden plates was to be made, and also of the book itself. The former consisted of two transparent stones, clear as crystal, and set in rims of silver. "The plates had the appearance of gold. They were about seven inches wide by eight long, and their thickness was not quite that of an ordinary sheet of tin. Egyptian characters were engraved on both sides of each plate, and the whole was bound in one volume, like the leaves of a book, closed by three clasps. Its thickness was six inches. One portion of the plate was sealed up. On those which were not sealed there were small characters skilfully cut. The breastplate was of bright gold. It had four golden straps, of which two were intended to attach it to the shoulders, and the other two to fix it onto the hips. These straps were exactly the breadth of two female fingers, and were pierced with several holes at the ends, by which to fasten them." This article, the mother declares, was worth at least five hundred dollars.

The chief object had in mind by the Smiths in the early days of the Gold-Bible delusion was the making of money, to which was doubtless added a desire for local notoriety. The foundation of a new sect was an after-thought. When speculation had worked itself to a point where the possibilities of the future began to foreshadow themselves, and the popular belief in his new Bible had so grown that he was filled with the belief that a pretended translation of the plates

---

"Smith's Bible Dictionary," p. 723. Many of the Jews believe that since the captivity of Babylon, God has ceased to make known His will by this means, and that the instrument has disappeared forever. Some look for its reappearance, but others do not.

would sell, Joseph naturally cast about for some one who would furnish the needed capital. Other help he could command in abundance. He seemed to have already been placed in quiet communication with Sidney Rigdon, or some one who had the means of furnishing him with the basis for this great fraud, in the book of Solomon Spaulding, of whom more anon, or in some other manner supplied the literary skill and scholarship he lacked. Other help was at hand in the person of Oliver Cowdery, a schoolmaster of the neighborhood, who was prepared to listen to such overtures as Smith was likely to make.*

How many men of means were approached before the victim was finally secured has not been placed on record by any confession of those concerned. In one case the rebuff was of a character that would have cooled the ardor of a less vehement man than Smith. Calling upon a Mr. Crane, a prominent Quaker, Joseph asked him for the needed assistance, and declared that he was "moved by the Spirit" to make the call. The response was prompt, and to the point. Smith was advised to cease his money-digging and golden-Bible schemes, and to make a living in some honest way, lest the doors of a prison should open to receive him.

The part played by Martin Harris in the Mormon scheme was one of great importance, and had he failed in supplying the funds needed at an important crisis of affairs, Mormonism would probably have found an end in its very beginning. He was a

---

* Oliver Cowdery was born on October 3d, 1806; and the best authority I can discover gives his birth-place as Wells, Rutland County, Vermont.

farmer of Palmyra, and bore the reputation of an honest, hard-working man, who loved money a little too well, and inclined to be too easily moved by any form of religious frenzy that took possession of his mind. He was at first a Quaker, then in turn a Universalist, Restrictionist, Baptist, and Presbyterian. He owned a good farm, and had never been involved in any questionable transaction. He has been described as proverbially peaceful, and it was said of him that he lived as closely to his religion as the conditions about him would allow. This illustration of his character has been placed on record: when he was fully committed to the Mormon-Bible scheme he was "urging the sale of the book with great confidence in the genuineness of its revelations, and fell into a debate about its character with a neighbor of hasty temperament. His opponent became angry and struck him a severe blow on the side of his face. Instantly turning toward his assailant his other cheek, he quoted the Christian maxim, reading it from the book in his hand, 'If thine enemy shall smite thee on the right cheek, turn to him the other also.'"

There were those who gave him a reputation less favorable than that suggested above. One of his neighbors, Jesse Townsend,* speaks of him as a "visionary fanatic," although "an industrious farmer . . . . who had been unfortunate in the choice of a wife, or she had been in that of a husband." "He had whipped his wife," Mr. Townsend adds, "and beaten her so cruelly and frequently that she was

* In a letter written by Jesse Townsend, under date of Palmyra, N. Y., Dec. 24, 1833.

obliged to seek refuge in separation..... He is considered here to this day a brute in his domestic relations, a fool and a dupe to Smith in religion, and an unlearned, conceited hypocrite generally. He paid for printing the Book of Mormon, which exhausted all of his money and most of his property. Since he went to Ohio he has attempted to get another wife, though it is believed he was frustrated in this design by the discovery of his having a wife living here." This was written after the hegira to Kirtland.

Smith seems to have known his man thoroughly, and to have planned the attack with a strategy sure to win. Harris prided himself upon his unassailable honesty, and when Smith approached him with a declaration that the Lord had revealed the fact that Harris and himself were the only two honest men in the world, the battle was half won. By that subtle influence which Joseph exerted to an almost unlimited degree over men of a certain mould, he soon had Harris fully committed to the Gold-Bible scheme. Harris was at that time considered wealthy, while the Smith family possessed practically nothing at all.

When young Joseph was near sixteen years of age, he accompanied his father and a number of others to the village of Harmony, on the north bank of the Susquehanna River, in Northeastern Pennsylvania. Their object was to locate and open a mine which they affirmed had once belonged to Spanish adventurers, and long since abandoned. His stay in this neighborhood was extended from 1821 to 1829, varied by occasional visits to his old home in Northern New York. His reputation among his new associates tallied in a remarkable manner with that he had won in the old home, and we hear him graphically described as "an idle, plausible schemer, who made his living by his wits, was a general favorite with the women, and had considerable influence over a certain class of men."

Upon his first appearance he was compelled perforce to engage in manual labor to a certain extent, but the time was not long distant before he sought an easier road to a maintenance. As he discovered dupes he began the old practice of the Manchester days. He set up as a revelator of hidden riches, and once more brought the famous peek stone into use. He occasionally blessed a neighbor's crops in return for the cash in hand; and when one piece which he had contracted to insure was the only one in the vicinity laid under blight, he adroitly turned the exception to his own advantage by declaring that he had made a mistake and placed the field under a curse rather than a blessing. Men were actually found who believed his professions and made it worth his while to put them into practice.

While here the Smiths and their accomplices in the search for hidden riches, boarded for a time with Isaac Hale, whose daughter Emma afterward became Joseph's wife, and played a part of no small importance in the early days of Mormonism. Mr. Hale, against whose bitter protest the marriage occurred, made a statement under date of March 20, 1834, in which he used the following language, in description of young Smith and the occurrences of which he was a part:

"I first became acquainted with Joseph Smith, Jr., in November, 1825. He was at that time in the employ of a set of men who were called *money-diggers;* and his occupation was that of seeing, or pretending to see, by means of a stone placed in his hat, and his hat closed over his face. In this way he pretended to discover minerals and hidden treasure. His appearance at this time was that of a careless young man, not very well educated, and very saucy and insolent to his father. Smith and his father, with several other money-diggers, boarded at my house while they were employed in digging for a mine that they supposed had been opened and worked by the Spaniards many years since. Young Smith gave the money-diggers great encouragement at first, but when they had arrived in digging to near the place where he had stated an immense treasure would be found, he said the enchantment was so powerful that he could not see. They then became discouraged, and soon after dispersed. . . . . [Here follows an account of Smith's marriage, related below.]

"Smith stated to me that he had given up what he called glass-looking, and that he expected to work hard for a living, and was willing to do so. Soon after this, I was informed they had brought a wonderful book of plates down with them. I was shown a box, in which it is said they were contained, which had, to all appearance, been used as a glass box, of the common-sized window-glass. I was allowed to feel the weight of the box, and they gave me to understand that the book of plates was then in the box, into which, however, I was not allowed to look. I inquired of Joseph Smith, Jr., who was to be the first that would be allowed to see the book of plates? He said it was a young child. After this I became dissatisfied and informed him that if there was anything in my house of that description, which I could not be allowed to see, he must take it away; if he did not, I was determined to see it. After that the plates were said to be hid in the woods.

"About this time Martin Harris made his appearance upon the stage, and Smith began to interpret the characters or hieroglyphics, which he said were engraven upon the plates, while Harris wrote down the interpretation. It was said that Harris wrote down one hundred and sixteen pages, and lost them. Soon after this happened, Martin Harris informed me that he must have a *greater witness*, and said that he had talked with Joseph about it; Joseph informed him that he could not or durst not show him the plates, but that he (Joseph) would go into the woods where the book of plates was, and that after he came back, Harris should follow his track in the snow, and find the book, and examine it for himself. Harris informed me afterward that he followed Smith's directions, and could not find the plates, and was still dissatisfied. The next day after this happened, I went to the house where Joseph Smith, Jr., lived, and where he and Harris were engaged in their translation of the book. Each of them had a written piece of paper which they were comparing, and some of the words were: *My servant seeketh a greater witness, but no greater witness can be given to him.* There was also something said about *Three that were to see the thing*—meaning, I suppose, the book of plates; and that *if the three did not go exactly according to orders, the thing would be taken from them.* I inquired whose words they were, and was informed by Joseph or

Emma (I rather think it was the former) that they were the words of Jesus Christ. I told them then that I considered the whole of it a delusion, and advised them to abandon it.

"The manner in which he pretended to read and interpret, was the same as when he looked for the money-diggers, with the stone in his hat and his hat over his face, while the book of plates was at the same time hid in the woods! After this Martin Harris went away, and Oliver Cowdery came and wrote for Smith, while he interpreted, as above described. This is the same Oliver Cowdery whose name may be found in the Book of Mormon. Cowdery continued a scribe for Smith until the Book of Mormon was completed, as I supposed and understood. Joseph Smith, Jr., resided near me for some time after this, and I had a good opportunity of becoming acquainted with him, and somewhat acquainted with his associates; and I conscientiously believe, from the facts I have detailed, and from many other circumstances which I do not deem it necessary to relate, that the whole Book of Mormon (so-called) is a silly fabrication of falsehood and wickedness, got up for speculation, and with a design to dupe the credulous and unwary, and in order that its fabricators might live upon the spoils of those who swallowed the deception.   ISAAC HALE." *

* For this statement see "Gleanings by the Way," by Rev. John A. Clark, New York, 1842, p. 242. This is one of the most reliable and interesting of the early publications on Mormonism, and is now quite rare. Mr. Clark was rector of St. Andrew's Church, Philadelphia, in 1842, but had previously been a resident of Western New York. Only a portion of his work is devoted to Mormonism, the greater part being given to his travels in various directions.

Smith was a frequent visitor at the Hale homestead, even after the abandonment of the money-digging above described. He found ready acceptance on the part of Emma, the second-born of three daughters, and the only one yet unmarried. When the father was approached by Smith with a request for the hand of his daughter, he answered with a prompt and stern refusal, giving as a reason the fact that Smith was a stranger, and that his methods of earning a living were such as no honest man could approve. Joseph departed, but only to return in secret and accompany the willing young woman across the line into New York State, where they were married at Windsor in February, 1826.

From Palmyra, to which they had proceeded, Emma addressed her father by letter, and, although his anger had been such that he had threatened to shoot

---

The degree of reliance which may be placed upon Mr. Hale's statement can be learned from the following, which precedes it in Mr. Clark's book: "While at Palmyra, I met with a respectable clergyman of the Episcopal Church, who had formerly belonged to the Methodist connection, that was acquainted with Mr. Hale. He represented him to be a distinguished hunter, living near Great Bend, in Pennsylvania. He was professedly a religious man and a very zealous member of the Methodist Church. The letter to which I have referred is accompanied with a statement declaring that Mr. Hale resides in Harmony, Penn. Appended to the letter also is Mr. Hale's affirmation or affidavit of the truth of the statement there made, taken before Charles Damon, Justice of the Peace; and there is also subjoined the certificate of William Thompson and Davis Dimock, Associate Judges of the Court of Common Pleas, in the County of Susquehanna, declaring that they have for many years been personally acquainted with Isaac Hale, of Harmony township, who has attested the foregoing statement, or letter, and that he is a man of excellent moral character, and of undoubted veracity."

his half-vagrant son-in-law on sight, he decided to make the best of a bad bargain, and met the couple on their return to Pennsylvania upon a basis of outward peace. They took possession of a small place near the Hale residence, and Joseph made solemn assertion that he had abandoned his days of idleness forever, and intended to settle down and work for a living. Hale's son was sent to Palmyra after such effects as Joseph and his wife possessed, and, for a while, the future Mormon leader seems to have given his time and physical strength to a manly use, and raised in the minds of his new friends the hope that he intended to make a man of himself at last.

But the poison that had entered his veins was not to be thus lightly driven out. The hoe and the axe became heavy in his unwonted hands, as he dreamed still of the fortune that might come could he but command the publication of the Golden Bible of which he had said so much. For by this time a book had actually taken some sort of shape.* The impromptu lie, of which he had boasted to Peter Ingersol, had been transformed into a fact. Over that book and its origin there hangs yet a mystery which many able men and women have sought to solve, which some have solved to their own satisfaction, but which none have removed altogether from the region of doubt. The box in which the golden plates were claimed to have been hidden came to Pennsylvania with the other household goods, and hints concerning it began to be heard in greater numbers as the scheme, which

---

* See Appendix A.

was soon fully under way, developed. The designs upon the credulity and cupidity of Martin Harris had already been accomplished, and he stood ready to furnish the needed means.*

It was upon September 22, 1827, that Smith claims to have received the plates from the hands of the angel. When the work of transcribing was fully decided upon, Harris for a time wrote as Smith dictated. The latter still insisted that no one could see the plates but himself, which was a convenient method of keeping up his romance as to there being any plates at all. Smith would hang a curtain between Harris and himself, and from behind it dictate the words

* A newspaper writer under date of October 2, 1883, in the *Cincinnati Enquirer*, describes the scene of these events in the following language: "I paid a visit to the old home of Joe Smith. The house stands at the north bank of the Susquehanna, two miles west of the Twin River, and is distant about sixty feet from the New York, Lake Erie & Western Railroad. The house is one story high, and, with its kitchen, is about twenty-four by fourteen feet. At present it is occupied by ex-Sheriff McCune, who was born in the room in which the Book of Mormon was transcribed. Mr. McCune's father bought the house and farm from Joe Smith, and to the former he built a two-story addition. The buildings are very rickety at present, and look as though they would tumble down from rot and age in a few years. They are often visited by tourists from abroad, who generally ask Mr. McCune for a small bit of wood or shingle as a memento of their visit. The money-holes Smith had made in his search for the buried treasure are about half a mile from the house. Though their sides have caved in, they are still visible, and one of them is filled with water; an endless spring having been tapped during the excavations. Not many rods from the house is a country graveyard, in which are interred the remains of one of Joe Smith's children. No slab or headstone marks it, and its precise location is known to only a few of the older people. Many of Smith's wife's kinsfolk still reside in and about this county."

that Martin was to write. He claimed to accomplish his translation by means of the Urim and Thummim, but it is needless to say that they were also hidden from the secretary's view. After a time Harris gave way to Cowdery, who remained with Smith until the task was at an end. The use of the curtain must be regarded only as a dramatic accessory for the purpose of duping Harris; and, as Cowdery was beyond question in the confidence of Smith, it is reasonable to suppose that this mysterious method of work was by no means employed when the accomplices were by themselves.

It was a serious trouble through which Harris passed before he arrived at a decision to bear the expense of publication, and incur all the financial risks of the enterprise. Had he not been spurred on by two powerful incentives, his faith in Mormonism and the belief that he would make money from the sale of the book, he would never have reached that conclusion. His natural caution in the expenditure of money was supplemented by the active opposition of his wife, a woman of sound sense and very positive views as to Smith's character and his designs upon her husband's property.* Doubt has been thrown

* Extract from an affirmation made by Abigail Harris, a relative of Martin's, at Palmyra. November 28, 1883, (Kidder p. 28):

"In the early part of the winter in 1828 I made a visit to Martin Harris's and was joined in company by Joseph Smith, Sr., and his wife. The Gold-Bible business, so called, was the topic of conversation, to which I paid particular attention, that I might learn the truth of the whole matter. They told me that the report that Joseph, Jr., had found golden plates was true, and that he was in Harmony, Pa., translating them. The old lady said, also, that after the book was translated, the plates were to be publicly exhib-

upon the genuineness of Harris's profession of faith, by that answer to his wife's declaration as to the lack of truth in Mormonism, "What if it is a lie! if you will let me alone I will make money out of it." But his whole course in connection with Smith, and many positive acts upon his part, show him to have been a dupe from the beginning to the end.

ited—admittance twenty-five cents. She calculated it would bring in annually an enormous sum of money—that money would then be very plenty, and the book would also sell for a great price, as it was something entirely new. That they had been commanded to obtain all the money they could borrow for present necessity, and to repay with gold. The remainder was to be kept in store for the benefit of their family and children. This and the like conversation detained me till about eleven o'clock. Early the next morning the mystery of the Spirit (being myself one of the order called Friends) was revealed by the following circumstance. The old lady took me into another room, and after closing the door she said, 'Have you four or five dollars in money that you can lend until our business is brought to a close? The Spirit has said you shall receive fourfold.' I told her that when I gave I did it not expecting to receive again; as for money, I had none to lend. I then asked her what her particular want of money was; to which she replied, 'Joseph wants to take the stage and come home from Pennsylvania to see what we are all about.' To which I replied he might look in his stone, and save his time and money. The old lady seemed confused and left the room, and thus ended the visit." Joseph Capron, a neighbor of good character, throws added light on this point. "At length," says he, "Joseph pretended to find the gold plates. This scheme, he believed, would relieve the family from all pecuniary embarrassment. His father told me that when the book was published they would be enabled, from the profits of the work, to carry into successful operation the money-digging business. He gave me no intimation, at that time, that the book was to be of a religious character. . . . . *He declared it to be a speculation*, and, said he, 'When it is completed my family will be placed on a level above the generality of mankind!'" This testimony strengthens the belief that the later developments of Smith's "speculations" were undreamed of in the beginning.

When a number of the pages of manuscript had been prepared, Harris insisted that he should have a chance to prove the truth or falsity of Smith's claims before proceeding further. They were delivered to him, and he showed them to certain neighbors, all of whom told him that he was the victim of a swindle. He also exhibited them to his wife, who proceeded to prompt measures. While Martin slept she confided the paper to the flames. She made no confession as to her action, and thereby placed both Harris and Smith in a dilemma. The former could not account to Smith for the lost property, and naturally fell under suspicion of concealing it for purposes of his own.

A coolness between the two for a time was the result, but as Harris was too essential a part of the scheme to be offended, his story was accepted, and he was again taken into favor. Smith believed that if Harris did not still have the manuscript it must have been purloined by his wife. Should that portion be rewritten from memory, it could not of course be identical with the original draft. Should he print the new version, Mrs. Harris, a determined and energetic foe to his schemes and himself, might produce the old, and prove by comparison the juggling that had taken place. Smith pondered long over this serious problem, but that ingenuity which had never failed him, came to his relief. He boldly announced that the Lord had revealed his displeasure toward Smith for allowing the manuscript to pass into Harris's hands, and in punishment of that act had declared that so much of the golden plates should not again be translated. This left a clear track, and

Smith again hid himself behind the curtain and went to work.*

Doubt still worked its way up from the lower stratum of Harris's business sense, and showed itself

---

* The following appeared as a preface to the first edition of the book, but was subsequently omitted. It proves the clumsy character of the whole scheme:

" To the Reader.

"As many false reports have been circulated respecting the following work, and also many unlawful measures taken by evil designing persons to destroy me, and also the work, I would inform you that I translated, by the gift and power of God, and caused to be written, one hundred and sixteen pages, the which I took from the book of Lehi, which was an account abridged from the plates of Lehi, by the hand of Mormon; which said account, some person or persons have stolen and kept from me, notwithstanding my utmost efforts to recover it again—and being commanded of the Lord that I should not translate the same over again, for Satan had put it into their hearts to tempt the Lord their God, by altering the words; that they did read contrary from that which I translated and caused to be written; and if I should bring forth the same words again, or, in other words, if I should translate the same over again, they would publish that which they had stolen, and Satan would stir up the hearts of this generation, that they might not receive this work, but behold, the Lord said unto me, I will not suffer that Satan shall accomplish his evil design in this thing; therefore thou shalt translate from the plates of Nephi until ye come to that which ye have translated, which ye have retained; and behold, ye shall publish it as the record of Nephi; and thus I will confound those who have altered my words. I will not suffer that they shall destroy my work; yea, I will show unto them that my wisdom is greater than the cunning of the Devil. Wherefore, to be obedient unto the commandments of God, I have, through His grace and mercy accomplished that which He hath commanded me respecting this thing. I would also inform you that the plates of which hath been spoken, were found in the township of Manchester, Ontario County, New York.—THE AUTHOR."

In the later editions Smith is not referred to as "The Author" of the book, but only as translator.

again, to the vexation of Smith. A demand was made upon the latter for a copy of the characters upon the plates, in order that they might be submitted to the examination of learned men. Afraid to refuse, Joseph set himself to work, and evolved from his imagination certain crude and complex characters unlike any alphabet yet seen by man. These were set down upon a paper, with which Harris proceeded to New York City, where he exhibited it to several scientific gentlemen, who pronounced the whole thing a meaningless jumble of marks, that expressed no language of either ancient or modern times.* Yet such was the influence of Smith over him, that on Harris's return home, he was persuaded that the learned men were all in fault, and that once more—to make use of his own version of Scripture—"God had chosen the foolish things of the world to convince the wise."

It was in July, 1828, that the "translation" was suspended because of the prompt action of Mrs. Harris and the writing was not resumed until April 17, 1829. The Mormons claim that after this renewal Smith made use of a dark cave he had dug in a hillside near his home, but the fact doubtless is that the work was carried on in the same manner and at the same place as in the beginning.

The clerical work completed, the next need was a publisher. The negotiations that ensued have been carefully recorded by Mr. Pomeroy Tucker,† who was connected with the printing house at Palmyra where the work was done. As early as January,

---

* See Appendix B.

† "Origin, Rise, and Progress of Mormonism," p. 50.

1829, before the whole of the manuscript was prepared, a call was made at the office of the *Sentinel*, at Palmyra, by Joseph and Hyrum Smith, Oliver Cowdery, and Martin Harris. A few sheets were shown Mr. Egbert B. Grandin, the publisher, and he was asked the price at which he would print three thousand copies. Harris offered himself as security for the payment.

Mr. Grandin hesitated, as he believed that Harris was being used by designing men. As Martin was his friend he quietly took him aside and advised him to that effect. But persuasion was of no avail; and after a number of interviews of the same tenor, and fruitless negotiations with other publishers, the contract was made. Five thousand copies were to be printed for three thousand dollars, Harris giving his bond, and a mortgage on his farm, for that amount. As Mrs. Harris refused to be a party to the transaction, an agreement of separation between herself and husband was arranged. She received her share of the estate, some eighty acres of land and the farm-house; and the two who had lived so long together, became as strangers, and the breach thus made remained through life. The dismemberment of this family was the first-fruit of the new creed that Joe Smith had given to the world.

The book was completed and offered to the public in the early summer of 1830. "In the beginning of the printing," says Mr. Tucker, who read a portion of the proof,* "the Mormons professed to hold their manuscripts as sacred, and insisted upon maintaining

---

* "Origin, Rise, and Progress of Mormonism," p. 53.

THE
BOOK OF MORMON:

AN ACCOUNT WRITTEN BY THE HAND OF MORMON, UPON PLATES TAKEN FROM THE PLATES OF NEPHI.

Wherefore it is an abridgment of the Record of the People of Nephi; and also of the Lamanites; written to the Lamanites, which are a remnant of the House of Israel; and also to Jew and Gentile; written by way of commandment, and also by the spirit of Prophesy and of Revelation. Written, and sealed up, and hid up unto the LORD, that they might not be destroyed; to come forth by the gift and power of GOD unto the interpretation thereof; sealed by the hand of Moroni, and hid up unto the LORD, to come forth in due time by the way of Gentile; the interpretation thereof by the gift of GOD; an abridgment taken from the Book of Ether.

Also, which is a Record of the People of Jared, which were scattered at the time the LORD confounded the language of the people when they were building a tower to get to Heaven; which is to shew unto the remnant of the House of Israel how great things the LORD hath done for their fathers; and that they may know the covenants of the LORD, that they are not cast off forever; and also to the convincing of the Jew and Gentile that JESUS is the CHRIST, the ETERNAL GOD, manifesting Himself unto all nations. And now if there be fault, it be the mistake of men; wherefore condemn not the things of GOD, that ye may be found spotless at the judgment seat of CHRIST.

BY JOSEPH SMITH, JUNIOR,
AUTHOR AND PROPRIETOR.

PALMYRA:
PRINTED BY E. B. GRANDIN, FOR THE AUTHOR.

1830.

[*Title-Page of the Mormon Bible.*]

THE FIRST BOOK OF NEPHI.

HIS REIGN AND MINISTRY.

CHAPTER I.

An account of Lehi and his wife Sariah, and his four Sons, being called, (beginning at the eldest,) Laman, Lemuel, Sam, and Nephi. The Lord warns Lehi to depart out of the land of Jerusalem, because he prophesieth unto the people concerning their iniquity; and they seek to destroy his life. He taketh three days' journey into the wilderness with his family. Nephi taketh his brethren and returns to the land of Jerusalem after the record of the Jews. The account of their sufferings. They take the daughters of Ishmael to wife. They take their families and depart into the wilderness. Their sufferings and afflictions in the wilderness. The course of their travels. They come to the large waters. Nephi's brethren rebelleth against him. He confoundeth them, and buildeth a Ship. They call the place Bountiful. They cross the large waters into the promised land, &c. This is according to the account of Nephi; or, in other words, I Nephi wrote this record.

I, NEPHI, having been born of goodly parents, therefore I was taught somewhat in all the learning of my father; and having seen many afflictions in the course of my days—nevertheless, having been highly favored of the Lord in all my days; yea, having had a great knowledge of the goodness and the mysteries of God, therefore I make a record of my proceedings in my days; yea, I make a record in the language of my father, which consists of the learning of the Jews and the language of the Egyptians. And I know that the record which I make, to be true; and I make it with mine own hand; and I make it according to my knowledge.

For it came to pass, in the commencement of the first year of the reign of Zedekiah, king of Judah, (my father Lehi having dwelt at Jerusalem in all his days;) and in that same year there came many prophets, prophesying unto the people, that they must repent, or the great city Jerusalem must be destroyed

[*Fac-simile Page of Text of the Mormon Bible.*]

constant vigilance for their safety during the progress of the work, each morning carrying to the printing-office the installment required for the day, and withdrawing the same at evening. No alteration from copy in any manner was to be made. These things were 'strictly commanded,' as they said. Mr. John H. Gilbert, as printer, had the chief operative trust of the type-setting and presswork of the job. After the first day's trial he found the manuscript in so very imperfect a condition, especially in regard to grammar, that he became unwilling further to obey the 'command,' and so announced to Smith and his party; when, finally, upon much friendly expostulation, he was given a limited discretion in correcting, which was exercised in the particulars of syntax, orthography, punctuating, capitalizing, paragraphing, etc. Many errors under these heads, nevertheless, escaped correction, as appear in the first edition of the printed book. Very soon, too—after some ten days—the constant vigilance by the Mormons over the manuscripts was relaxed by reason of the confidence they came to repose in the printers."

The great desire of Smith's heart was at last accomplished. He had a new bible as the foundation for the new creed he had formulated and was about to preach to men. With a deep knowledge of the weak side of human nature, he had not declared a gospel in opposition to that of Christendom, nor one that should make war upon it, but, emulating the example of Mother Ann Lee, and the Shakers, declared the Book of Mormon supplemental to Holy Writ, and a later revelation of the same grand truths. In that manner he could win converts without taking them from the strong moorings of the old faith. He could give them range in new pastures without asking them to forsake the church homes they had known and loved so long. One need not repudiate David and John in order to accept Nephi and his brethren. To the other sides of human weakness through which he sought access to their hearts and purses, he added also that of novelty, and the natural desire of men to go out after strange gods.

Smith was now twenty-five years of age, with his natural cunning so sharpened by experience and so encouraged by successful trading on the credulity of his fellows, that he had little difficulty in meeting any emergency that might arise, and shaping it to the desired ends. He had taken the leadership in the small coterie of accomplices and dupes that had gathered about him, and anything he might propose was sure to be seconded by his father and all his brothers. His mastery of men was ever one of his strong points of character, and his facility and adaptability were such that he would have won success as a lawyer or in any minor post of diplomatic responsibility. In later days he would have made his mark in the world of politics.

He had used such opportunities for education as had fallen in his way in the latter years of enlarged ambition, had read such books as could be of special use to him, and made a marked improvement both in the manner and matter of literary composition. Claim what one may as to the aid or suggestions he received from Sidney Rigdon or Oliver Cowdery, Smith owed the greater share of such success as life awarded him, to his own force of character and the Scotch-American shrewdness with which he had been endowed. By this time he had decided upon a definite plan and assumed the risk of its operation, and nothing was to be allowed to stand in the way. How far that purpose then outran the primal desire to live well and in idleness at the expense of others, no one can ever know.

Of the character and purport of this Book of Mormon,* fresh from the press of Grandin, I need say little. The world has already had many descriptions thereof, and the book itself, in this, or later editions, is open to inspection in almost every public library of the land. That it can be of divine origin is proved impossible upon an examination of its errors, crudities, stupid imitations of scriptural language, and its betrayal of ignorance upon many facts of history.

If, as many believe, it is but the unpublished romance of Solomon Spaulding, put to a use of which its author never dreamed, the impress of Smith has been placed

---

* Smith's own definition of the word Mormon, as given in after-years, in *The Times and Seasons*, was as follows: "I may safely say that the word Mormon stands independent of the learning and wisdom of this generation. Before I give a definition, however, to the word, let me say that the Bible in its widest sense, means 'good,' for the Saviour says, according to the Gospel of St. John, 'I am the good shepherd,' and it will not be beyond the common use of terms to say that good is amongst the most important in use and, though known by various names in different languages, still its meaning is the same, and is ever in opposition to bad. We say from the Saxon, *Good;* the Dane, *God;* the Goth, *Goda;* the German, *Gut;* the Dutch, *Goed;* the Latin, *Bonus;* the Greek, *Kalos;* the Hebrew, *Tob* ; the Egyptian, *Mon* ; hence with the addition of *more*, or the contraction, *mor*, we have the word *Mormon*, which means literally, *more good.*" Notwithstanding all this learned parade, scholars have expressed the opinion that the word was derived from the Greek, meaning a spectre, or hideous shape.

upon it with a freedom and to a purpose that has added atrocity to the meanness of the original theft. This first edition consisted of 588 pages, divided into fourteen separate books, of one hundred and fifteen chapters, as follows: The first book of Nephi; the second book of Nephi; the book of Jacob, the brother of Nephi; the book of Enos; the book of Jarom; the book of Omni; the Words of Mormon; the book of Mosiah; the book of Alma; the book of Helaman; the book of Nephi, the son of Nephi, which was the son of Helaman; book of Mormon; book of Ether; the book of Moroni. It would be profitless to undertake a compilation of the long and very tedious narratives found in these several hundreds of pages, but a brief synopsis from the pen of no less a person than Joseph Smith himself, would not be out of place. In "An Original History of the Religious Denominations at present Existing in the United States," by I. Daniel Rupp, Philadelphia, 1844, p. 404, may be found an article on "The Latter-Day Saints," prepared by Smith, in which he speaks as follows of the historical portion of the book:

"In this important and interesting book the history of Ancient America is unfolded, from its first settlement by a colony that came from the Tower of Babel, at the confusion of languages, to the beginning of the fifth century of the Christian Era. We are informed by these records that America in ancient times has been inhabited by two distinct races of people. The first were Jaredites, and came directly from the Tower of Babel. The second race came directly from the city of Jerusalem, about six hundred years before Christ. They were principally Israelites, of the descendants of Joseph. The Jaredites were destroyed about the time that the Israelites came from Jerusalem, who succeeded them in the inheritance of the country.

"The principal nation of the second race fell in battle toward the close of the fourth century. The remnant are the Indians, who now inhabit this country. This book also tells us that our Saviour made His appearance upon this continent after His resurrection; that He planted the gospel here in all its fullness and richness, and power, and blessing; that they had apostles, prophets, pastors, teachers, and evangelists; the same order, the same priesthood, the same ordinances, gifts, powers, and blessing, as was enjoyed on the Eastern continent; that the people were cut off in consequence of their transgressions; that the last of their prophets who existed among them was commanded to write an abridgment of their prophecies, history, etc., and to hide it up in the earth, and that it should come forth and be united with the Bible, for the accomplishment of the purposes of God in the last days. For a more particular account, I would refer to the Book of Mormon, which can be purchased at Nauvoo, or from any of our travelling elders." The manner in which Mormon came to be selected as the one whose name should be attached to a work in which so many eminent ancients had a hand, is thus explained by the Rev. Mr. Clark:[*]

"These records were engraven upon plates, and the plates handed down from one prophet to another, or from one king to another, or from one judge to another

---

[*] "Gleanings by the Way," p. 285.

—the Lord always having raised up some one to receive these plates. When the person in whose hands they had been previously placed was about to die, Mormon, who lived about four hundred years after the coming of Christ, while yet a child, received a command in relation to these sacred deposits.

"The metallic plates which contained the record of all the generations of his fathers, from the flight of Lehi to Jerusalem, to his own time, ultimately came into his hands. From these plates he made an abridged record, which, taken together, in connection with the record of his own times, constitutes the Book of Mormon. Thus we see why the book bears this title. For Mormon was a sort of Ezra who compiled the entire sacred canon contained in this volume. He lived at a very eventful period, when almost all his people had fallen into a fearful apostasy, and he lived to see them all destroyed, except twenty-four persons. Himself, and these sole survivors of his race, were afterward cut off, with a single exception. His son, Moroni, one of the survivors, lived to tell the mournful tale, and deposit the plates under the hill where Jo. Smith found them."

When the books were delivered from the hands of the binder, Martin Harris promptly took possession of them, and proceeded to realize such portion as he might of that evangelization of the world and financial profit, of which he had dreamed. They cost him dearly enough, as he was compelled to sell his portion of the farm in 1831, to meet the bond he gave Grandin.* It had been a part of the agreement

---

* The powers that were invoked to lead Harris into the scheme, were again resorted to in holding him to his contract. A special

with Harris that he alone should have the right of sale; which was made doubly secure to him by a special revelation to Smith, in which was also found an added command that no copy should be sold for less than one dollar and twenty-five cents.

Despite all these commands, and that high mountain of expectation which the Smiths had aided poor Martin to pile up, the enterprise as a source of money-making was a dismal failure from the start. Harris himself went forth as a canvasser, and met more scoffers than purchasers. Ridicule was showered upon him from all sides, and he soon discovered that some other means must be taken to return even a small part of the outlay.

A new revelation was received by Joseph, which allowed his father also to act as salesman, retaining a commission upon each copy sold. He met with a certain share of success, but went forth unmoved by any of the fears that had held Martin to the express stipulation of the revelation. He bartered books for whatever he could get in return, and cut prices with a lofty contempt for that death which Joseph had declared would befall any who should so offend. He would load his books into the old cart that had carried root-beer and ginger-bread in the less ambitious days, and start on a peddling tour through the country lying adjacent to Palmyra; returning home with side-pork, bacon, corn, or such other goods as he could secure from farmers along

revelation was directed to him in March, 1830: "And again I command thee that thou shalt not covet thine own property, but impart it freely to the printing of the Book of Mormon, which contains the truth and the word cf God. *Pay the debt thou hast contracted with the printer. Release thyself from bondage.*"

the route. He made the books for which Harris had so dearly paid, a source of income wherever they could be of avail. When he was preparing for his final removal to Ohio, after Joseph and Hyrum had set their first "stake of Zion" at Kirtland, he fell back upon the new gospel as his base of supplies. "He took," says one narration,* "a basket of bibles in his hand and walked to Palmyra village, ... where sundry unadjusted little scores were ready to confront him. By the then prevailing legal system for the collection of debts, residing as he did over the county line from Palmyra, he made himself liable to suit by warrant and also detention in imprisonment for non-payment. But necessity being his master, he had taken the incautious venture and soon found himself in the constable's custody at the suit of a creditor for a small book account.

"The parties appeared before a Justice of the Peace for Wayne County, by whom the warrant had been issued. After some preliminary parleying by the debtor, he invited and enjoyed a private interview with the creditor in an adjoining room. The debt and costs had now reached the aggregate of $5.63. The embarrassments of the case, after some brief discussion, were found to be of a difficult nature. At last, laying the good-natured claimant under strict confidential injunction, and referring with solemn air to the command by which he was empowered to sell his Mormon work only at the price of $1.25 per copy, the crafty patriarch proposed, nevertheless, on the express condition that his perfidy should not be

* "Origin, Rise, and Progress of Mormonism," p. 62.

exposed, the offer of seven books in full for the demand, being a fraction more than eighty cents apiece. The joke was relished as too good to go unpatronized, and though the books were not regarded as possessing any value,* the claimant, more in a spirit of mischief than otherwise, accepted the compromise willingly."

Smith delivered the books, and then made his exit from a side door, and shook the dust of Palmyra from his feet with such rapidity as his age would permit, lest some other creditor should spy him by the way. He was seen in Palmyra no more, but soon bade farewell to a neighborhood that lost him and his without regret, and that troubled itself concerning him only long enough to formulate the unique certificate of character that has already been quoted in these pages.†

* Time and curiosity which deface and destroy much, will also accomplish much. A copy of this edition of the Book of Mormon cannot now be obtained for twenty times its original price. It has become one of the rare and unique things in American literature.

† "Gleanings by the Way," p. 346: "One thing, however, is distinctly to be noted in the history of this imposture. There are no Mormons in Manchester or Palmyra, the place where this Book of Mormon was pretended to be found. You might as well go down into the crater of Vesuvius and attempt to build an ice-house amid its molten and boiling lava, as to convince any inhabitant in either of these towns, that Joe Smith's pretensions are not the most gross and egregious falsehood. It was indeed a wise stroke of policy, for those who got up this imposture, and who calculated to make their fortune by it, to emigrate to a place where they were wholly unknown."

III.

SIDNEY RIGDON AND THE KIRTLAND HAVEN.

IT will be necessary, before proceeding further in the personal history of Joseph Smith and his earliest coadjutors, to trace the outlines of a remarkable man who gave to Mormonism a powerful impetus, and without whom it might never have been heard of outside of the neighborhood in which it found life.

The occasional visits of an unnamed stranger to the residence of Smith prior to 1830 were noted by the neighbors with comment, and much circumstantial evidence could be produced to prove that this visitor was no other than Sidney Rigdon, who has never been charged with the full measure of his responsibility in this melodrama of religion, as his part has been lost sight of in the overshadowing importance of Joseph Smith, and the strong personality of Brigham Young. He possessed a power as a preacher, and an influence as a teacher equalled by few even in those days of revival excitement. And the education he had acquired by much reading and a constant moving about among men was of a character that made him a valuable ally to the new religion when he at last threw off all show of allegiance to the orthodox creeds and gave his voice and talents to the Mormon faith.

It would not be too much to say that Rigdon was

the intellect of Mormonism in its cradle-days, even as Smith was its bodily force, and Harris its financial foundation. Those who have the most closely studied his connection with the scheme are the most strongly inclined to identify him with those measures that gave it the most tenacious hold on life, and he certainly secured it a welcome in Ohio that few other men could have commanded. Hepworth Dixon says of him in "Spiritual Wives": "He had already changed his religion more than once, as he afterward changed it again more than once. He had been a loud ranter, a hot revivalist; and after his conversion to the Mormon faith he labored in his district among the more exalted members of the most exalted sects. He knew the writings of Mahan, Gates, and Boyle; writings in which love and marriage are considered in relation to gospel liberty and a future life."[*]

His personal appearance has been thus described by an acquaintance: "He was an orator of no inconsiderable abilities. In person he was full medium height; rotund in form; of countenance, while speaking, open and winning, with a little cast of melancholy. His action was graceful, his language copious, fluent in utterance, with articulation clear and musical. Yet he was an enthusiast, and unstable. His personal influence with an audience was very great; but many with talents far inferior surpassed him in judgment and permanent power with the people. . . . . He possessed an imagination at once fertile, glowing, and wild to extravagance, with temperament tinged with sadness and bordering on

---

[*] "Spiritual Wives." By W. H. Dixon, London, 1868, p. 62.

credulity."* In a pen portrait of him in later life, a visitor to Nauvoo makes use of the following language: "Sidney Rigdon, one of the councillors, prophet, seer, and revelator, is 42 years of age, five feet nine and a half inches high, weighing one hundred and sixty-five pounds. His former weight, reduced by sickness produced by the Missouri prosecution, was two hundred and twelve pounds. He is a mighty man in Israel, of varied learning, and extensive and laborious research. There is no divine in the West more learned in Biblical literature and the history of the world than he: an eloquent orator, chaste in his language, and conclusive in his reasoning."†

This is overdrawn somewhat, but points in the direction of truth. He was an eager disputant all through life, and seldom missed an opportunity for theological debate. He seems to have depended upon his eloquence as a preacher and quickness of mental action for success in life, rather than upon any deep force of character or hard work. He was petulant when affairs did not run in a desired groove; naturally full of self-assertion; and his passionate temper too often gained headway against the sober intention of his judgment. He had an ungoverned ambition, and unless full measure of praise was awarded him on the instant, he was disposed to destroy all he had done, and abandon the work he had in hand, whether it was bad or good.

Rigdon was born near the present village of Library, Allegheny County, Pennsylvania, on Febru-

---

* "Early History of the Disciples in the Western Reserve." By A. S. Hayden, Cincinnati, 1876, p. 191.

† In a letter signed "Veritas," published in the *New York Herald*.

ary 19, 1793. An accident which occurred in his early boyhood may have had something to do with his erratic course in after-life, if we adopt the theory of his brother,* Dr. L. Rigdon, of Hamilton, Ohio, who said of him that "when quite a boy, living with his father some fifteen miles south of Pittsburgh, he was thrown from a horse. His foot entangling in a stirrup he was dragged some distance before relieved. In this accident he received such a contusion of the brain as ever afterward seriously affected his character, and in some respects his conduct." Dr. Rigdon was of the opinion that Sidney was a little deranged ever after this mishap. "His mental powers did not seem to be impaired, but the equilibrium of his intellectual exertions seems thereby to have been sadly affected. He still manifested great mental activity and power, but was to an equal degree inclined to run into wild and visionary views on almost every question; hence he was a fit subject for any new movement in the religious world."

Sidney attended the common school of his neighborhood, and was early accounted of promise by those about him. He became a member of the Baptist church when quite young, and possessing marked natural powers of oratory, was encouraged toward the ministry. Even then there was uncertainty concerning his genuineness of faith, and many doubted his conversion, as there was "so much miracle" about it, and "so much parade about his profession" that his pastor was in serious doubt as to how far he should be accepted in good faith; and this same good

* *Baptist Witness*, date of March 1, 1875.

man, David Phillips, became unconsciously prophetic when he expressed the belief that "as long as Sidney lived he would be a curse to the Church of Christ." When, in later days, Harmon Sumner expostulated with Rigdon as to his teaching and said to him, "Brother Rigdon, you never go into a Baptist church without relating your Christian experience," he was met by the cool and characteristic rejoinder, "When I joined the church I knew I could not be admitted without an experience: so I made up one to suit the purpose, but it was all made up, and was of no use, or true."

Some portion of Rigdon's early career was devoted to the printer's trade, but little of detail is known concerning him until 1818 and 1819, when he studied divinity under a minister named Clark, of Beaver County, Pennsylvania. On March 4th, of the year last named, he was received into membership by the Baptist church at Warren, Ohio, and was licensed to preach on April 1st of the same year.

It was at this period of life that he was first brought under the influence of Alexander Campbell, through which he was afterward led to forsake the Baptist church and become a Disciple. Mr. Campbell has himself (in *Millennial Harbinger*, 1848, page 523) described the occasion upon which the two were brought together: "In the summer of 1821, while sitting in my portico after dinner, two gentlemen in the costume of clergymen, as they are technically called, appeared in my yard, advancing to the house. The elder of them, on approaching me, first introduced himself, saying, 'My name, sir, is Adamson Bentley; this is Elder Sidney Rigdon, both of Warren, Ohio.' .... After tea in the evening, we commenced, and prolonged, our discourse till the next morning. .... On parting the next day, Sidney Rigdon, with all apparent candor, said if he had within the last year taught and promulgated from the pulpit one error, he had a thousand.

"At that time he was the great orator of the Mahoning Association, though in authority with the people second always to Adamson Bentley. I found it expedient [did the keen eye already see the fatal flaw in Rigdon?] to caution them not to begin to pull down anything they had built until they had reviewed again and again what they had heard; nor even then rashly and without much consideration. Fearing they might undo their influence with the people, I felt constrained to restrain rather than to urge them on in the work of reformation. .... They went on their way rejoicing, and in the course of a single year prepared the whole association to hear us with earnestness and candor."

Rigdon was married, while residing in Warren, to Phœbe Brooks, a sister to Mrs. Bentley, wife of the minister referred to above. Through the influence of Mr. Campbell* he was chosen to the pastorate of the First Baptist church of Pittsburgh, which comprised a membership of over one hundred, and assumed his new and important duties on January 28, 1822. Some uncertainty exists as to his movements from 1823 to 1826, but at the later date we again find him in Ohio,†

---

* When Thomas and Alexander Campbell renounced Presbyterianism, they joined the Redstone Baptist Association in 1812, and for a number of years worked in harmony with that church.

† He had family connections of some prominence in that State, his cousin, Thomas Rigdon, a Baptist minister, serving for a time in the Ohio Legislature—a position which at that time conferred considerable honor upon its possessor.

the pastor of a small church at Bainbridge, Geauga County. In June of the year last named, he was called to Mentor to preach the funeral sermon of Elder Warner Goodall, pastor of the Baptist church of that village, and acquitted himself in such manner that he was employed as successor of the deceased, beginning the engagement in the fall.

It was at this period that the Disciple Church was making its persistent and courageous fight for recognition and position upon the Western Reserve, and many earnest men under the direct leadership of Thomas and Alexander Campbell, were preaching the new light of the Gospel truth as it had seemed to come to them. The success of their preaching was of the most signal character, and within five years of the commencement of their work, the foundations of many Disciple churches were laid. One congregation that had no fixed connection, but called itself by the general name Christian, listened to a Disciple missionary and surrendered to his teaching as one man. In a Methodist congregation the minister was converted, and we read that the flock "became an easy and willing prey," and that every member accepted the new doctrine and came into the new fold.

In March, 1828, Rigdon paid a visit to Warren, and listened to the preaching of Walter Scott, an eloquent Disciple leader, who had been associated with Rigdon in the Baptist church. The latter was impressed to conviction, and on his return to Mentor commenced to preach the new doctrine with such effect that he soon led his home flock across the line over which he had himself been led. In addition to his Mentor connection, he was also pastor of a small church at Kirtland, some four miles to the south.

During the two succeeding years Rigdon was one of the leading preachers of the Disciple faith upon the Western Reserve, prominent in all the councils of the church, listened to with love and respect, and in close personal fellowship with the great men of that denomination. He preached for a time at Mantua, founded the Disciple church at Perry, and is spoken of as a zealous and hard-working man in almost every chapter of Mr. Hayden's book, and in one place in that able history it is remarked that "among the seniors present were Thomas Campbell and his son Alexander, Adamson Bentley, and Sidney Rigdon, with Walter Scott, to whom most of the young disciples looked with the affection of children to a spiritual father." Rigdon made himself felt with brilliant personality wherever he had a right to be heard, and was happy only when events were in motion. On one occasion, when weary with long discussion upon a proposed measure, he sprang to his feet and thundered out, "You are consuming too much time on this question! One of the old Jerusalem preachers would start out with his hunting-shirt and moccasins, and convert half the world, while you are discussing and settling plans!" A sharp thrust which had its effect, winding up the long debate and producing immediate action.

Just when Mr. Rigdon decided to take part in the Golden-Bible scheme can never be known, but he seemed preparing himself and those about him for its reception some time before its advent in Ohio. He began in 1829 or early in 1830 to preach a common stock of goods and a community of interests, as right and apostolic.* The idea did not gain rapid ground against the New England sense and traditions of the early settlers of the Reserve. In Mentor it was rejected altogether, but a more promising field was found at Kirtland, where results of a practical character were witnessed, when one Isaac Morley threw open the doors of his home and offered welcome to all who would come. The response was immediate from those who believed a living was due them from the world, and we are told that "a number of ignorant and profligate, and others of means" responded, until fully one hundred became members of the communistic society there formed.

Rigdon made a bold and determined effort to engraft the communistic principle upon the Disciple faith, but met with failure. At a notable gathering of the church leaders at Austintown, in 1830, there occurred a passage-at-arms between Alexander Camp-

* The various co-operative movements that occurred in Europe and America at about this period were of a nature to win the attention and attract the desire of a man of Rigdon's mental mould. Success of an unprecedented character had attended the experiments for the bettering of the condition of the working classes, by David Dale, at the New Lanark Mills, Scotland; Charles Fourier was astonishing France by his fascinating and ingenious theory of Communism; Robert Owen was at his work of moulding public sentiment in favor of co-operative societies, and operations under his stimulus had already been commenced at Kendal, Stark County, Ohio, New Harmony, Indiana, and other points; George Rapp was prospering with his Harmony Society at Economy, Pennsylvania; the Separatists had already made the wilderness blossom as a rose in their prosperous community of Zoar; Shaker societies had been successfully founded in several portions of the country; and other trials by which the visions of the dreamers were to become the experiments of practice, were being put to the test in various portions of the land.

bell and himself upon this question, that discomfited Rigdon, and may have had something to do with his easy descent into Mormonism a few months later. In that meeting, Mr. Rigdon made a speech in which he argued that their pretension to follow the apostles in all the New Testament teachings required a community of goods, and that, " as they established this order in the model church at Jerusalem, the church of to-day was required to imitate their example." Mr. Campbell saw immediately the danger of allowing such doctrine from one as prominent as Rigdon to go unchallenged, and he made a vehement speech in opposition. A half-hour's debate ensued between the two, in which Rigdon was put utterly to rout. Chagrined and hurt at the cool reception of his theory, he withdrew from the meeting, and was seen in the Disciple gatherings no more. On his way home to Mentor he passed through Warren, and said bitterly to Mr. Austin, his host, " I have done as much in this reformation as Campbell or Scott, and yet they get all the honor of it."

How Smith and Rigdon were brought together first, no man will ever know. Many believe that Parley Pratt, who was a wandering tin-peddler and a friend of Rigdon's, was the means through which the one was led to the other, and the need that each had for the other made known. Be this as it may, these master-minds of religious invention had been, beyond doubt, brought together, had concocted their scheme, prepared their Mormon Bible from Spaulding's manuscript or other source, and arranged a plan by which they could make a living by imposing upon the credulity of others, for no one who knew the men ever imagined they had a higher object in view. Rigdon at first played his part in the background; yet his occasional business calls from Kirtland and Mentor tallied, as was afterward discovered, with the visits of the mysterious stranger at the Smith residence.

Mr. Z. Rudolph, the father of Mrs. James A. Garfield, recently declared "that during the winter previous to the appearance of the Book of Mormon, Rigdon was in the habit of spending weeks away from his home, going no one knew where; and that he often appeared very preoccupied and would indulge in dreamy, imaginative talks which puzzled those who listened. When the Book of Mormon appeared and Rigdon joined in the advocacy of the new religion, the suspicion was at once aroused that he was one of the framers of the new doctrines and probably was not ignorant of the authorship of the book."[*] That something was stirring in the mind of Sidney long before he made open profession of conversion to the new creed, is established on authority that cannot be disputed. "When I was quite a child," wrote Mrs. Amos Dunlap, of Warren, Ohio, in 1879, "I visited Mr. Rigdon's family. During my visit Mr. Rigdon went to his bedroom and took from his trunk, which he kept locked, certain manuscript. He came out into the other room and seating himself by the fire-place began reading it. His wife at that moment exclaimed, 'You are studying that thing again,' or something to that effect. She then added,

---

[*] From a statement made by R. Patterson, author of "Who Wrote the Book of Mormon?" Philadelphia, 1882; and published in "New Light on Mormonism," by Ellen E. Dickenson, New York, 1885, p. 252.

'I mean to burn that paper.' He said, 'No indeed you won't. This will be a great thing some day.' When he was reading this he was so thoroughly occupied that he seemed entirely unconscious of anything else around him." We have the following significant statement from Mr. D. Atwater, who sat under Rigdon's preaching in the Mantua church:* " For a few months before his professed conversion to Mormonism it was noticed that his wild, extravagant propensities had been more marked. That he knew before of the coming of the Book of Mormon is to me certain from what he said during the first of his visits at my father's, some years before. He gave a wonderful description of the mounds and other antiquities found in some parts of America, and said that they must have been made by the aborigines. He said there was a book to be published containing an acount of those things. He spoke of these in his eloquent, enthusiastic style, as being a thing most extraordinary."

The foundation of the Mormon Church organization was laid and its machinery set in motion by Smith and his followers in the same year that saw the publication of their book. With that ease he ever possessed for making the circumstances of the case fit into his purpose, Joseph announced that the ministry had been already prepared in Cowdery and himself, to whom formal ordination had come on May 15, 1829, by the hands of no less a personage than John the Baptist. " He commanded us," proceeds his narration, " to go and be baptized, and gave us directions that I should baptize Oliver Cowdery

* " History of the Disciples on the Western Reserve," p. 239.

and afterwards that he should baptize me." In this message John assured Joseph that he was acting under the direction of the Disciples Peter, James, and John.

In accordance with this command, if we may believe Smith, Cowdery and himself went into the water* together and administered the sacred rite unto each other; the one laying his hands upon the head of the other and pronouncing solemn words of ordination. And "as they came out of the water they experienced great and glorious blessings, and the Holy Ghost fell upon Oliver, and he prophesied, and then Joseph stood up and he prophesied." In this story, that Smith no doubt fabricated entirely for the occasion, one can see only a clumsy imitation of that grand scene by the Jordan, where Jesus came from Galilee to be baptized of John. In that very resemblance Smith discerned a new hold upon the credulity of those who believed that mysterious things were at hand, and that that which had been done in the days of the prophets or the apostles was about to be repeated in their own.

On Tuesday, April 6, 1830, the Mormon Church was organized in the house of Peter Whitmer,† in

---

* This baptism is said by Smith to have occurred at Harmony, Susquehanna County, Pennsylvania.

† The six members of this new church were Joseph Smith, Sr., Hyrum Smith, Joseph Smith, Jr., Samuel Smith, Oliver Cowdery, and Joseph Knight. The Whitmers had no small part in the beginnings of Mormonism, and were apparently honest in their professions of belief. Peter was a "Pennsylvania Dutchman," in the colloquial language of the day—a plain, honest, simple-minded man. His sons John, Christian, Jacob, and Peter, Jr., were among the famous "eight witnesses," while his son David was one of the famous "three." Hiram Paige, also one of the eight, was an itinerant root-doctor, who had married a daughter of Peter, Sr. When

Fayette, Seneca County, New York—an event which, according to the ingenuity of Orson Pratt, was afterward figured out as happening exactly eighteen hundred years, to a day, from the resurrection of Christ.

Those who were placed upon the roll of church membership entered into a covenant to serve the Lord, and partook of the sacrament. On the Sabbath following, Cowdery preached the first public sermon of Mormondom, dwelling upon the new dispensation and the principles of the gospel as they had been newly revealed to Joseph. Events moved forward rapidly. In June the first convention of the church was held in Fayette, at which thirty members were present. From this date forward Smith threw off all reserve, and claimed in public everywhere full possession of the powers and responsibilities that he held to through all his after-life. Angels constantly visited him and ministered unto him; the will of the Lord was ever present to him in special revelations; men were called, ordained, and sent hither and thither at command; and he became, in the language of a Mormon hymn, "the mouthpiece of God." And

it became noised abroad that the honest old German was being led dupe by Smith, his pastor, Rev. Diedrich Viliers, of the German Reformed Church, called upon him to remonstrate against his folly. The only reply he could gain from the old farmer was, " Jesus Christ, yesterday, to-day, and forever." All the property he possessed was finally turned over to the use of the church. David Whitmer claimed to have been converted by a miracle. He was laden with sap, and on his way from the woods sat down to rest. After much thinking upon the wonderful things that had been recently told him, he suddenly knelt in prayer, and asked God, in case Mormonism was true, to make his load lighter in token thereof. He then shouldered his burden, and found it one no longer: the buckets weighing no more than a feather. All doubt was forever gone.

whatsoever he uttered was carried to the ear of his believer with the awful weight of meaning that could have been laid upon a message sent by angel messengers from the great white throne itself. Men who wonder at the obedience and unquestioning loyalty of the dupes of Mormonism in these early days, should ponder well this fact before they ridicule and condemn.

During the winter preceding the advent of the book, Rigdon had absented himself from his communistic community at Kirtland for several weeks, explaining to no one his whereabouts, and carrying himself with a mysterious manner on his return. That he was with Smith during this absence, and engaged in the promotion of their scheme, there can be little doubt. In his preaching after this absence he seemed to be paving the way for some new change in the spiritual life of his community; and much in his course that was not then understood became as clear as noontide in the light of after-events. He prepared the ground with great care, so that the transplanted tree, when it was brought into their midst, would take sure root. He declared to his people that he did not possess the full comfort of his religion as he desired, and stood in the attitude of one seeking new light. He so shaped the thought of those who looked up to him as a spiritual guide, that they were watching night and morning for the coming of a sign, and were prepared for any new trend of belief to which their ignorant credulity should be directed. Always fervent, and by nature a powerful actor, Rigdon played upon their souls with such power and to such purpose as he willed, and carried them a long way toward the new creed, before they had knowledge of its existence.

The deft hand of Parley Pratt was not wanting in these manipulations of many things toward a common end, nor was his part one of minor importance. A tin-peddler who at times ascended the pulpit, he represented a combination of business shrewdness and theological investigation that made him a powerful factor in this scheme that had for its foundation faith and the making of money. Such pen pictures of his character as have been preserved show him to have been of baser instincts, and one to whom the later adjuncts of Mormonism made powerful appeal. Mrs. B. G. Ferris, wife of the Secretary for Utah, in one of her letters from that remote point,* writes under date of February, 1853: "The man (Pratt) has a very even flow of language, and converses with great ease." She describes him as of burly figure, with a bland manner, and a readiness to borrow money that was not duplicated when it came time to pay. He was at that date in the possession of five wives.

That Pratt had acquaintance with Smith before the two had anything of common in public, there can be no doubt; although Pratt himself suggests, rather than declares, to the contrary. His own account of his conversion to Mormonism is given in the following words: † "I took a journey to the State of New York, partly on a visit, ... and partly for the purpose of administering the word. This journey was undertaken in August, 1830. I had no sooner reached Ontario County, than I came in contact with the Book of Mormon, which had then been published

* "The Mormons at Home." By Mrs. B. G. Ferris, New York, 1856, p. 169.

† "Mormonism and the Mormons," p. 67.

about six months, and had gathered about fifty disciples, which were all that then constituted the Church of Latter-Day Saints. [That name was not adopted until some years after.] I was greatly prejudiced against the book, but, remembering the caution of Paul—'Prove all things, and hold fast to that which is good'—I sat down to read it, and, after carefully comparing it with the other Scriptures, and praying to God, He gave me knowledge of its truth by the power of the Holy Ghost; and what was I that I should withstand God?

"I accordingly obeyed the ordinances, and was commissioned by revelation and the laying on of hands to preach the fullness of the Gospel. Then, after finishing my visit to Columbia County, I returned to the brethren in Ontario County, where, for the first time, I saw Mr. Joseph Smith, Jr., who had just returned from Pennsylvania to his father's house in Manchester. About the 15th of October I took my journey in company with Elder O. Cowdery and Peter Whitmer to Ohio. We called on Elder S. Rigdon, and then, for the first time, his eyes beheld the Book of Mormon. I myself had the happiness to present it to him in person. He was much surprised, and it was with much persuasion and argument that he was prevailed upon to read it."

This apparently candid statement does not suggest the deeper current of quiet arrangement that lay beneath it. The fact is, that a few months of earnest propagation of the new gospel in and about Palmyra, Manchester, Fayette, and the vicinity, convinced Smith and his accomplices that the seed they had sown was fallen upon barren ground, and that a more fertile field must be laid under cultivation. Smith and others went forth to preach, but with meagre results; and it is recorded that Joseph's personal efforts were so little appreciated, that, instead of converts, he won much advice touching an immediate abandonment of the field.

When all the arrangements for the migration westward were completed, the first open movement in that direction was made.

In the latter part of October, 1830, four men—Oliver Cowdery, Parley Pratt, Ziba Peterson, and Peter Whitmer, Jr.*—were sent forth on an ostensible mission to the Indians of the far West: a people for whose salvation Smith declared the new revelation had been largely made.

En route they made it convenient to call at Kirtland, where Pratt already had acquaintance. They boldly went among the members of Rigdon's Disciple communistic congregation, exhibiting the Book of Mormon and preaching its new plan of salvation. To the narrow life and hedged-in hearts and intellect of the people to whom their appeal was made, the sensation was like the sparkle and exhilaration of new wine, and the whole community opened mouth and stood waiting, as men perpetually athirst.†

* When Whitmer and his associates arrived in Ohio, they were greeted with this welcome from the Painesville *Telegraph:* "But the more important part of the mission was to inform the brethren that the boundaries of the Promised Land, made known to Smith from God—the township of Kirtland, a few miles west of this, is the eastern line, and the Pacific Ocean the western line; if the north and south lines have been described, we have not learned them."

† There were many at that time who believed the millennium was at hand, and in 1830 there were those who were convinced it had dawned, and that, to again quote from Mr. Hayden ("History of the Disciples in the Western Reserve," p. 183), "The long-expected

Rigdon played his part with consummate skill, and to the complete success of the programme. Although he no doubt had a hand in the making of the book, he received it with apparent amazement, and as one to whom it was all a matter of surprise.

Two of the missionaries sent into Kirtland spent the night of their arrival at Rigdon's house. All that passed in their interview has been kept a secret by those whom it most concerned. On the morning following, as the family of Judge Clapp, a neighbor, sat at their breakfast, Rigdon came in, laboring under apparent excitement. Hardly waiting for the usual salutations, he burst forth with the information, " Two men came to my house last night on a curious mission."

When all looked up, and some one voiced the general desire to hear, he proceeded to relate in an impressive and dramatic manner how the Book of Mormon had been found, and how wonder after wonder of a supernatural character had befallen one Joseph Smith, a country boy of Northern New York. The story was told with such an air of wonder and belief that all who heard were amazed, while one to whom the fallacy of much of it was suggested, cried out in contempt, " It is all a lie."

There were many, however, more ready to surren-
day of gospel glory would very soon be ushered in. . . . . These glowing expectations formed the staple of many sermons. They were the continued and exhaustless topic of conversation. They animated the hope and inspired the zeal to a high degree of the converts and many of the advocates of the gospel. Millennial hymns were learned and sung with a joyful fervor and hope surpassing the conception of worldly and carnal professors." It was amid a people full of these expectations, and with hearts fired with these things, that Mormonism was brought, and there is small wonder that it found a welcome.

der to the strangers and their book. Rigdon was soon openly confronted with their claims, and compelled to meet them in such manner as he should deem best. He promised to read the book, and carried a copy to his home. He returned, and strongly condemned a portion of its doctrines; and the debate between himself on the one hand, and Pratt and Cowdery on the other, was carried on with earnestness and vehemence. It seemed to be a part of Rigdon's plan to make such fight that when he did surrender, the triumph of the cause that had defeated him, would be all the more complete.

Many openly sided with Rigdon, while others accepted the doctrine and the book. In a few days a Mormon society was formed, and Cowdery rebaptized its members to the number of seventeen. Rigdon denied the right to do this, and declared that they were proceeding contrary to the Scriptures.

When they called upon him at his residence on the day following this important move, he told them they had acted "without precedent," and demanded proof of the divine authority of their mission. Each of the four in response related his experience. They had "obtained faith by praying for a sign, and an angel was shown unto them."

Rigdon responded by proving from Scripture the possibility of their being deceived, as Satan had power to transform himself into an angel of light.

"But," responded Cowdery, "do you think if I should go to my Heavenly Father, with all sincerity, and pray to Him, in the name of Jesus Christ, that He would not show me an angel; that He would suffer Satan to deceive me?"

"If the Heavenly Father," was Rigdon's reply, "has ever promised to show you an angel, to confirm anything, He would not suffer you to be deceived, 'for,' says John, 'this is the confidence we have with Him, if we ask things according to His will He hearkens to us.' But if you should ask the Heavenly Father to show you an angel when He has never promised you such a thing—if the devil had never had an opportunity of deceiving you before, you give him one now." Rigdon was finally prevailed upon to promise that he would also ask God for a sign, but would not then further commit himself in the direction of Mormonism.

This discussion, and others of the same tenor, were carried on in the presence of the gaping populace, and each point made by the visitors had its weight and effect in preparing the way for many future conversions. The excitement was at a fever heat, and was by no means lessened when Rigdon appeared after a seclusion of a couple of days and announced his complete surrender. With an apparent earnestness of manner, and with such eloquent words as he could so surely command, he declared that he had asked for a sign, and had received a revelation from heaven that Mormonism was true. He said that he had prayed for the sign, and explained the response that was vouchsafed him, in the following language: "To my astonishment, I saw the different orders of professing Christians passing before my eyes, with their hearts exposed to view, and they were as corrupt as corruption itself. That society to which I belonged also passed before my eyes, and to my astonishment it was as corrupt as the others. Last of all that little man, who brought me the Book of Mormon, passed before me with his heart open, and it was as pure as an angel; and this was a testimony from God that the Book of Mormon was a divine revelation."

Imagination can well measure the effect of this surrender upon Rigdon's simple followers. The last stay upon which their doubt hung gave way, and they went into the new fold almost en masse. Rigdon and his wife were publicly baptized by Cowdery on the Sabbath following. He seemed to be altered in demeanor to such an extent that his wife said, "The religion must be of divine origin, else it could not have produced so wonderful an effect."

The results of this surrender far outran the changes of temper and feeling in one man. New life was given to the struggling and uncertain Mormon Church by the accession within a short period of over one hundred members; and a house of refuge was provided in its days of weakness and need. The Prophet, as Smith was now called, was in honor among his new disciples, who had not known him as he was known at home; and when Rigdon made his preparation for a formal pilgrimage to Manchester, he carried with him many messages of affection and respect. He was absent two months, and had not been long at the home of the Prophet before he was accepted in full fellowship, and honored by Smith with all the means at his command. He became the first regular minister of the Mormon Church. He was announced to speak in Palmyra soon after his arrival in New York, and Martin Harris attempted to secure the use of a church building, but met with failure. Harris's good name and evident sincerity of purpose finally obtained for him access to a public hall.

At the designated hour a small but well-behaved audience assembled. Rigdon introduced himself as the messenger of God, and declared that he was under command from on high to preach the new revelation. In his opening prayer he gave fervent thanks for the new gospel that had been given to man. His text was chosen from the Mormon Book; and in opening he declared that "the Book of Mormon and the Bible were one in inspiration and importance." With the one held aloft in his right hand and the other in his left, he suddenly brought them together with force, and pronounced them the revealed word of God. His sermon was preached with unusual earnestness and eloquence, yet it so far failed of its intended effect that it not only won no converts, but caused Harris to be refused the use of the hall for the future. The first Mormon sermon in Palmyra was also the last.

It was not possible for Rigdon to remain altogether in the background when perseverance and assertion would carry him toward the front, and ere long Smith found it necessary to unburden himself of a revelation that gave his partner a recognized position of spiritual authority second only to his own. In December he addressed to his followers a lengthy document in which Rigdon was favored with special mention; and of which the following constitutes the opening clause:

"A commandment to Joseph and Sidney, December 7, 1830: saying, Listen to the voice of the Lord your God even Alpha and Omega, the beginning and the end, whose course is one eternal round; the same to-day as yesterday and forever. I am Jesus Christ, the Son of God, who was crucified for the sins of the world, even as many as will believe on my name, that they may become the sons of God, even one in me, as I am in the Father, as the Father is one in me, that we may be one. Behold, verily, verily, I say unto my servant Sidney, I have looked upon thee and thy works; I have heard thy prayers, and prepared thee for a greater work—thou art blessed, for thou shalt do great things. Behold, thou wast sent forth, even as John, to prepare the way before me and before Elijah which should come, and thou knewest it not; thou didst baptize by water unto repentance, but they received not the Holy Ghost; but now I give unto thee a commandment, that thou shalt baptize by water, and they shall receive the Holy Ghost by the laying on of hands, even as the apostles of old."

This special indorsement of Rigdon was not without its purpose. It gave him authority among those who had accepted Mormonism, and aided him in his preparations for Smith's removal to Kirtland.

A step was taken toward that removal, when John Whitmer was detailed to take charge of the new church at Kirtland. He was one of the four Whitmers of those eight witnesses who made declaration that they had in reality seen the plates of gold from which the Book of Mormon had been translated. He carried to Kirtland an autographic letter from Rigdon to the waiting brethren, which said: "I send you this letter by John Whitmer. Receive him, for he is a brother greatly beloved, and an apostle of this church. With him we send all the revelations we have received; for the Lord has declared unto us that you pray unto him that Joseph Smith and myself go speedily unto you; but at present it is not expedient for him to send us. He has required of us, therefore, to send unto you our beloved brother John, and with him the revelations which he has given unto us, by which you will see the reason why we cannot come at this time."

"The Lord has made known unto us," continues the writer, desiring to make what points he may against those upon whose credulity he is at work, "some of his great things which he has laid up for them that love him, among which the fact (a glory of wonders it is) that you are living on the land of promise and that *there* (at Kirtland) is the place of gathering, and from that place to the Pacific Ocean, God has declared to himself, not only in time but through eternity, and he has given it to us and our children, not only while time lasts, but we shall have it again in eternity, as you will see by one of the commandments received day before yesterday. Therefore, be it known to you, brethren, that you are dwelling on your eternal inheritance; for which cease not to give ceaseless glory, praise, and thanksgiving to the God of Heaven."

Bearing such astonishing news, how could John Whitmer fail of welcome?

Smith had by this time commenced a new translation of the Old Testament, in which he was assisted by Rigdon. In December this work was temporarily suspended by the revelation to which reference is made in the above. Kirtland was declared to be the Promised Land for Mormonism, and Smith was told to remove himself and church to that favored spot, where the way had been already prepared. These orders indeed came at an opportune time, for the fact had been already demonstrated that there was no place for him among his old neighbors in Western New York.

Rigdon returned to Kirtland, to make ready for the Prophet and the church. The story of his conversion had spread far and wide, and as he was known all through Northeastern Ohio and Northwestern Pennsylvania as a man of brilliant although erratic powers, and had preached from many of the most prominent Baptist and Disciple pulpits in his wanderings to and fro, his adhesion to the new faith gave it an advertisement that few other things could have as effectually accomplished. The almost passionate attention which the mass of the people were then giving to spiritual phenomena, and the expectations of many that the days for the fulfilment of Scriptural prophecy were at hand, gave the stories and rumors that were afloat a meaning and power that to-day would be beyond their possible reach.

Many eyes were therefore turned with expectation or scepticism toward Kirtland. Upon Rigdon's return he found the fame of his doings and the knowledge of Smith had preceded him. Many came to question him, and to learn the truth from his own lips. While to those who questioned in a sincere desire for knowledge, he was gentle and willing to reply, he was met by much which was only curiosity or a veiled purpose of placing him in a corner for the confusion of himself and the condemnation of the new doctrine.

Two of his callers, friends of former days, who had sat under his preaching at Mentor, were among the first to engage him after his return. They asked him the reason for his new hope, and why he had renounced the Disciple for the Mormon, as he had renounced the Baptist for the Disciple. He declined to be questioned, saying that he was weary from his long journey from New York.

They continued their solicitation, and he his refusal. At last one of the two said: "Mr. Rigdon, you have no more evidence to confirm the Book of Mormon than there is to the Koran of Mohammed." With that his patience came to an end, and springing to his feet he said with anger, "Sir, you have insulted me in my own house. I command silence. If people come to see us and cannot treat us with civility they may walk out of the door as soon as they please."

An apology was made by the offender, whereupon Rigdon explained the reason of his deep feeling. He had been "trampled upon and insulted by old and young" since his conversion, and he had stood about all that one man's patience would bear. A few days later Mr. Rigdon was in dispute with a Methodist Elder, when a caller approached the former and asked him for a candid reason for the faith that was within him.

His answer was given with patience, and an evident desire to justify the course of himself and followers. To quote the language of a listener,* he "commenced a long detail of his researches after the character of Joseph Smith—he declared that even his enemies had nothing to say against his character. He had brought a transcript from the dockets of two magistrates, where Smith had been tried as a disturber of the peace, which testified that he was honor-

* "M. S. C.," who tells the story in the Painesville *Telegraph* of February 1, 1831.

ably acquitted. But this was no evidence to us that the Book of Mormon was divine.

"He then spoke of the supernatural gifts with which he said Smith was endowed; he said he could translate the Scriptures from any language in which they were now extant, and could lay his finger upon every interpolation in the sacred writings; adding that he had proven him in all these things. But my friend, knowing that Mr. Rigdon had no knowledge of any language but his own vernacular tongue, asked him how he knew these things, to which Mr. Rigdon made no direct reply. . . . . We then asked Mr. Rigdon what object we could have in receiving the Book of Mormon —whether it enjoined a single virtue that the Bible did not, or whether it mentioned or prohibited a single additional vice, or whether it exhibited a new attribute of Deity. He said it did not. 'The Book of Mormon,' said he, 'is to form and govern the Millennial church; the *old* revelation was never calculated for that, nor would it accomplish that object; and without receiving the Book of Mormon there is no salvation for any one unto whose hands it shall come.' He said faith in the Book of Mormon was only to be obtained by asking the Lord concerning it. To this, Scriptural objections were made. He then said: 'If we have not familiarity enough with our Creator to ask of Him a sign, we were no Christians'; and that if God would not condescend to His creatures in this way, He was no better than Juggernaut."*

* With all deference to the honesty of the narrator, one would like to have seen Mr. Rigdon's account of this contest He was hardly the man to let an argument go altogether against him, whether right or wrong in his premises.

IV.

THE LIFE OF THE TRANSPLANTED TREE.

SMITH and his family made their final departure for Kirtland in January, 1831. They were accompanied by others who had accepted the Mormon faith. The gospel of the golden plates was preached by the wayside as they went, to such as would consent to hear. Some converts were thus made. Their destination was not reached until February, and the new-comers were welcomed with earnest zeal by their disciples, and with great curiosity by the surrounding unbelievers.* The full machinery of the church and its attendant commune was set in operation as rapidly as circumstances would admit; some of the developments that followed each other in rapid succession had no doubt been planned from the beginning, while others grew from the suggestions of experience. Revelation followed revelation, according to the hu-

---

* The Painesville *Telegraph* of March 15, 1831, states that Martin Harris arrived from the East on the Saturday previous, and immediately planted himself in "the bar-room of the Painesville tavern," and commenced to expound and explain the Mormon Bible in a loud and aggressive manner. All who offered a denial of any sort, to any of his statements, were denounced as infidels. The hotel-keeper finally asked him to vacate the premises, and as he obeyed he declared that all who accepted Mormonism and believed, would see Christ in fifteen years, and all who did not would be damned, The manner in which this incident is related gives some idea of the spirit in which Mormonism was received by the mass.

mor of Joseph, or the needs of the cause.* With a shrewdness suggestive of the money-digging exploits of earlier days, the Prophet had already made it impossible for any of his followers to aspire to communications from on high.

In a revelation uttered in September, 1830, for the benefit of Oliver Cowdery, that point had been disposed of in the following words: "Behold, I say unto thee, Oliver, that it shall be given unto thee that thou shalt be heard by the church in all things whatsoever thou shalt teach them by the Comforter, concerning the revelations and commandments which I have given. But behold, verily, verily, I say unto thee, *no one shall be appointed to receive commandments and revelations in this church excepting my servant Joseph Smith, Jr.*, for he receiveth them even as Moses, and thou shalt be obedient unto the things which I shall give unto him, even as Aaron, to declare faithfully the commandments and the revelations, with power and authority unto the church."

At a subsequent point in this remarkably transparent document it is ordered of Oliver that he shall not "command him who is at thy head, and at the head of the church; for I have given him the keys of the mysteries and the revelations which are sealed, until I shall appoint unto them another in his stead." Others seem to have attempted something in the

---

* Of the revelations thought worthy of record in the official history of the Mormon Church, fourteen were given in 1829; twenty in 1830; thirty-seven in 1831; thirteen in 1832; and thirteen in 1833. In addition to these, the Prophet had frequent celestial orders upon minor things, that were not thought of sufficient importance to place upon the record.

line of prophecy, and Joseph found it necessary to limit the power, for in this same document Oliver is ordered to "take thy brother Hirum Page between him and thee alone, and tell him that those things which he hath written from that stone are not of me, and that Satan deceiveth him, for behold, these things have not been appointed unto him, neither shall anything be appointed to any of this church."

A communication was addressed about the same time to Emma Smith, the wife of Joseph, which made her support one of the material charges upon the church, and instructing her to act as the Prophet's scribe. Therein it was declared to her that "thy time shall be given to writing and to learning much; and thou needst not fear, *for thy husband shall support thee from the church.*"

These commands had been given before the migration to Kirtland. Among those received first after that transfer was one commanding the Mormons to build Smith a house, which was obeyed. Then came another ordering all the faithful except Rigdon and Smith to go forth and preach the Mormon gospel. In a short time still another directed John Whitmer to write the annals of the church, for the benefit of posterity.

These things were not occurring at Kirtland without determined and aggressive opposition. As the ministers of the orthodox churches saw their members drawn under an influence that could do only harm materially and spiritually, they made vehement protests, and at times put Mormonism upon such defense as became a struggle for life itself. While the several denominations joined in this onset, the brunt of the battle naturally fell upon the Disciples, because of Rigdon's former high standing in their church. From the moment that his defection became known, Alexander Campbell threw himself into the breach with all the vehemence and energy of his nature, to thwart Rigdon's purpose, and to prevent his leading any astray. He published an exposé of the Book of Mormon, showing its many absurdities, and laying bare the pretensions of those by whom it was brought into the world. In June he proceeded to Ohio, and spent twenty-two days in combating the new creed.

Under date of February 4, 1831, the venerable Thomas Campbell wrote to Rigdon, his old friend and fellow-laborer. His letter* was full of sadness over the fall of one whom he had esteemed, and contained a challenge for a public debate as to the truth or falsity of Mormonism, at any time or place Mr. Rigdon might select. Therein he said: "It may seem strange that instead of a confidential and friendly visit, after so long an absence, I should thus address by letter one whom for many years I have considered not only as a courteous and benevolent friend, but as a beloved brother and fellow-laborer in the Gospel; but alas, how changed, how fallen!" When the epistle was received, Rigdon read until he came to a passage wherein Mormonism was characterized as "infernal," when he arose in anger, and threw the letter into the fire. He made no answer, and the challenge was never accepted.

Despite this opposition from many sources, the new religion grew. The love of the marvellous to

* "Early History of the Disciples in the Western Reserve," p. 217.

which men are heir, the preaching of the many missionaries sent hither and thither, and the personal efforts of Rigdon and Smith, had their natural results, and by May numerous additions had been made to the little church. Converts came from all directions, many of them from New York and the New England States. Some fifty families had come from the vicinity of Smith's old home. The lines along which the founders of the creed had done their work were found to be those most nearly allied to human superstition and fear, and each successful venture gave new encouragement for another trial in the same direction.

The preaching of Rigdon in these early missionary days was marked by an unwonted power and fervor, whether from an ambitious desire to make a success of the strange cause he had espoused, or because his heart had in reality been touched by some new ray of spiritual light. In illustration of this point, the following from the pen of the late John Barr, of Cleveland—an authority upon matters of Western Reserve history—will be found of exceeding interest. Said he:* "In 1830 I was deputy sheriff, and being at Willoughby on official business determined to go to Mayfield, which is seven or eight miles up the Chagrin River, and hear Cowdery and Rigdon on the revelations of Mormonism. Varnem J. Card, the lawyer, and myself started early Sunday morning on horseback. We found the roads crowded with people going in the same direction.

"Services in the church were opened by Cowdery, with prayer and singing, in which he thanked God

---

* "The Early Days of Mormonism." By Frederick G. Mather, *Lippincott's Magazine*, 1880, p. 206.

fervently for the new revelation. He related the manner of finding the golden plates of Nephi. He was followed by Rigdon, a famous Baptist preacher, well known throughout the eastern part of the Western Reserve, and also in Western Pennsylvania. His voice and manner were always imposing. He was regarded as an eloquent man at all times, and now he seemed fully aroused. He said he had not been satisfied in his religious yearnings until now. At night he had often been unable to sleep, walking and praying for more light and comfort in his religion. While in the midst of this agony, he heard of the revelation of Joe Smith, which brother Cowdery had explained. Under this his soul suddenly found peace. It filled all his aspirations.

"At the close of a long harangue in this earnest manner, during which every one present was silent, though very much affected, he inquired whether any one desired to come forward and be immersed. Only one man arose. This was an aged dead-beat by the name of Cahoon, who occasionally joined the Shakers, and lived on the country generally.

"The place selected for immersion was in a clear pool in the river above the bridge, around which was a beautiful rise of ground on the west side for the audience. On the east bank was a sharp bluff and some stumps, where Mr. Card and myself stationed ourselves. The time of baptism was fixed at two P.M. Long before this hour the spot was surrounded by as many people as could have a clear view. Rigdon went into the pool, which, at the deepest, was about four feet, and after a suitable address with prayer, Cahoon came forward and was immersed. Standing in the water Rigdon gave one of his most powerful exhortations. The assembly became greatly affected. As he proceeded he called for the converts to step forward. They came through the crowd in rapid succession to the number of thirty and were immersed, with no intermission of the discourse on the part of Rigdon.

"Mr. Card was apparently the most radical, stoical of men—of a clear, unexcitable temperament, with unorthodox and vague religious ideas. While the exciting scene was transpiring below us in the valley and in the pool, the faces of the crowd expressing the most intense emotion, Mr. Card suddenly seized my arm and said, 'Take me away.' Taking his arm I saw his face was so pale that he seemed to be about to faint. His frame trembled as we walked away and mounted our horses. We rode a mile toward Willoughby before a word was said. Rising the hill out of the valley he seemed to recover and said: 'Mr. Barr, if you had not been there I certainly should have gone into the water.' He said the impulse was irresistible."

When Cowdery and his friends had performed the work assigned them in Kirtland, they proceeded westward in obedience to Smith's command that they should convert the Indian tribes and bring them to a belief in the Mormon creed. Upon reaching the frontier, they were stopped from further progress by the officers of the general government, under the law preventing the white man from entering the Indian reservations for trading or other purposes. As winter was well upon them, they turned aside and located at Independence, Missouri, where they obtained sufficient employment to enable them to live, and preach Mormonism as occasion offered. In the spring of 1831, one of their number returned to Kirtland, where he rendered such report as led Smith to look upon the frontier as the proper place for the founding and permanent location of the great church, and perhaps temporal kingdom, of which he had come to dream. He had already been made aware that Ohio was too near civilization for an easy or safe fulfillment of his plans.

Early in June there was a formal meeting of all the believers in Mormonism at Kirtland. In the call thereto an intimation was given that a revelation of vital interest to the church was to be promulgated, and the believers assembled in expectant hope and half-fear. Smith solemnly made known the decree of which he was the messenger. All the leading men and elders were commanded to forsake whatever they had in hand and proceed forthwith to Missouri, which God had chosen as the promised land. Each was designated by name, and there was no room for refusal or excuse. They were to go by twos, each twain choosing a separate road, and all preaching by the way. Only two weeks' preparation for the long journey and exile were given.

On June 19th, Smith, in company with several of his disciples, set out upon the route he had chosen, others taking the roads assigned them. He passed through Cincinnati, Louisville, and St. Louis, and from the latter city onward on foot to Independence, which he reached in the middle of July.

Upon reaching his destination he ordered the purchase of a tract of land, upon which the foundations of his new city of Zion should be laid. The work was put under way in a manner that proved Smith a man of action as well as of words. The Rev. Ezra Booth, a Methodist preacher of Mantua, who had been converted in the previous May, and who was at that time still under the influence of Mormonism, but afterward broke his bonds and warned men against it with all the power there was within him, has given us this description of the events that there transpired, in a series of letters to Rev. Ira Eddy, his presiding elder: "The laying of the foundation of Zion was attended with considerable parade, and an ostentatious display of talents, both by Rigdon and Cowdery. The place being designated as the site where the city was to commence, on the day appointed we repaired to the spot, not only as spectators, but each one to act the part assigned him in the great work of laying the foundation of the 'glorious city of the new Jerusalem.'

"Rigdon consecrated the ground by an address, in the first place, to the God whom the Mormons professed to worship, and then making some remarks respecting the extraordinary purpose for which we were assembled, prepared the way for administering the oath of allegiance to those who were to receive their 'everlasting inheritance' in that city. He laid them under the most solemn obligations to constantly obey all the commandments of Smith. He enjoined it upon them to express a great degree of gratitude for the free donation, and then, as the Lord's vicegerent, he gratuitously bestowed upon them that for which they had paid an exorbitant price in money.

"These preliminaries being ended, a shrub oak, about ten inches in diameter at the butt, the best that could be obtained near at hand, was prostrated, trimmed, and cut off at a suitable length; and twelve men, answering to the twelve apostles, by means of hand-spikes conveyed it to the place. Cowdery craved the privilege of laying the corner-stone. He selected a small rough stone, the best he could find, carried it in one hand to the spot, removed the surface of the earth to prepare a place for its reception, and then displayed his oratorical powers in delivering an address suited to the important occasion. The stone being placed, one end of the shrub oak stick was laid upon it; and there was laid down the first stone and stick, which are to form an essential part of the splendid city of Zion."

Wonderful stories were told by Smith and his immediate accomplices as to the greatness that should befall this city chosen of God, and built under His command, as was Jerusalem of old, and of the marvellous things that should be witnessed in its streets. It should, in future time, exceed all that the world had ever seen. Its streets would be paved with gold —"all who escaped the general destruction, which was soon to take place, would there assemble with all their wealth; the ten lost tribes of Israel had been discovered in their retreat, in the vicinity of the North Pole, where they had for ages been secluded by immense barriers of ice, and became vastly rich; the ice in a few years was to be melted away, when those tribes, with St. John and some of the Nephites, which the Book of Mormon had immortalized, would be seen making their appearance in the new city, loaded with immense quantities of gold and silver."

Under the quickening effects of this generous promise of help and riches, the poor dupes dug and delved and carried as Smith ordered, and counted pain and isolation and exile as nothing in comparison with the spiritual and temporal rewards that were to be.

The day after the foundation of the city was thus formally marked, the ground upon which the temple was to stand was consecrated. Smith reserved to himself the honor of laying the corner-stone. Mr. Booth, whose testimony was placed on record almost immediately after the occurrence of the events he describes, wrote as follows: " Should the inhabitants of Independence feel a desire to visit this place, destined at some future time to become celebrated, they will have only to walk one-half of a mile out of the town, to a rise of ground, a short distance south of the road. They will be able to ascertain the spot by the means of a sapling, distinguished from the others by the bark being broken off on the north and on the east side. On the south side of the sapling will be found the letter T, which stands for temple; and on the east side Zom, for Zomas, which Smith says is the original word for Zion. Near the foot of the sapling they will find a small stone covered over with bushes, which were cut for that purpose. This is the corner-stone of the temple. They can there have the privilege of beholding the mighty work accomplished by about thirty men, who left their homes, travelled one thousand miles, most of them on foot, and expended more than one thousand dollars in cash."

There was so much of ridiculous failure connected

with this attempt to build a city and erect a temple out of nothing, that some of the less credulous among Smith's followers began to question the divinity of his mission and the correctness of his claims. Turmoils and dissensions broke out, in the midst of which Smith found it convenient to be delivered of a revelation commanding himself and a majority of his followers to return to Ohio. A portion of the company set out to sail down the Missouri River in a canoe, which Smith determined to manage according to his own idea. The result was an overturn and a ducking, which was the culminating point of the storms already gathering, which broke in open rupture among the leading spirits of the campaign, and open charges of cowardice in the hour of danger were made against both Rigdon and Smith. An encampment was made upon the river bank, and after the dripping and disheartened little party had dried their clothing and effects, and partaken of such refreshment as the situation would allow, the better judgment of those most concerned resumed its sway, and an attempt was made to patch up a peace.

Sharp words and many recriminations ensued, before the desired end was reached. Cowdery, Rigdon, and even Smith himself, were roundly censured for things they had done since the departure from Kirtland.

Joseph showed symptoms of a recourse at last to his old weapon of a special revelation, with which to beat down rebellion and opposition, but when a grim "None of your threats!" issued from one of the opposing faction, he withheld his purpose, and depended only upon his diplomacy and such human arguments as he could command. A reconciliation was not finally effected until toward daybreak, and even then there were doubts not set at rest, and grudges and heart-burnings left unsatisfied, that made themselves felt in the rebellions and secessions of later days. Smith had already discovered that he held in leash many discordant elements, and that the role of "prophet, seer, revealer, and translator," which titles he had now assumed, was one of worry, perplexity, and even personal danger.

In the morning Smith showed a strong dislike to further journeying upon the dangerous river, and to silence the opposition of those who still desired to proceed by canoe, he gave utterance to a commandment from on high, laying an awful curse upon the waters, and forbidding the faithful to navigate them. The name of the stream was changed to "The river of destruction," and Joseph and his band proceeded forward on foot.

It was decided, when the nearest town was reached, that Smith, Rigdon, and Cowdery should proceed rapidly forward by stage, while the rest of the weary, homesick, and discouraged band should reach Kirtland on foot, preaching as they went. "The method by which Joseph and company designed to proceed home," writes Mr. Booth, "it was discovered would be very expensive. 'The Lord don't care how much money it takes to get us home,' said Sidney. Not satisfied with the money they received from the bishop, they used their best endeavors to exact money from others, who had but little compared with what they had; telling them, in substance, 'You can beg your passage on foot, but as we are to travel in the stage, we must have money.'

"The expense of these three men was one hundred dollars more than three of our company expended while on our journey home; and for the sake of truth and honesty let these men never again open their mouths to insult the common sense of mankind, by contending for equality and the community of goods in society, until there is a thorough alteration in their method of proceeding. It seems, however, they had drained their pockets when they arrived at Cincinnati, for there they were under the necessity of pawning their trunk, in order to continue their journey home.

"Here they violated the commandment by not preaching; and when an inquiry was made respecting the cause of that neglect, at one time they said they could get no house to preach in; at another time they stated that they could have had the court-house had they stayed a day or two longer, but the Lord made it known to them that they should go on; and other similar excuses, involving like contradictions."

While in Missouri, under date of "Zion, August 1st, 1831," Smith was delivered of a new revelation which was sent forth to the Mormons East and West as the will of the Lord concerning the purchase of land in Missouri, and the building up of Zion. After explaining to the Elders and their followers why they had been brought so far from home—"that you might be obedient, and that your hearts might be prepared to bear testimony of the things which are to come, and also that you might be honored of laying the foundation, and bearing record of the land upon which the Zion of God shall stand,"—he proceeds to restrengthen the faith of Martin Harris, so that he might devote yet more of his money to the Mormon cause, in the following warning words: "It is wisdom in me that my servant Martin Harris should be an example unto the church, in laying his monies before the bishop of the church; .... and let him repent of his sins, for he seeketh the praise of the world."

In that remarkable document it was further ordered that "it is wisdom also, that there should be lan's purchased in Independence for the place of the storehouse, and also for the house of printing"; that Rigdon should "write a description of Zion, and a statement of the will of God, as it shall be made known by the Spirit unto him, and an epistle and a subscription unto all the churches to obtain moneys to put into the hands of the bishop, to purchase lands for an inheritance for the children of God."

Smith's desire at this time was to secure enough money to carry forward his ambitious purposes, as without that he could do nothing.

Upon his return to Kirtland, on August 27th, Smith found sufficient work in holding his followers to their faith, in meeting the sharp assaults of the many and strong enemies who had sprung up on all sides, in translating an "inspired" edition of the Bible, in looking after the commercial and mercantile ventures he had attempted, and in seeking for converts wherever they were to be found. In an attempt to set a stake of Zion in Hiram, a small village half a dozen miles to the south, famous now as the seat of the college over which James A. Garfield presided, the Mormon leader met with such fierce hostility, which at last culminated in physical attack and personal indignity, that he was more than ever persuaded there was sufficient room for Mormonism and himself only in the far West. He opened a general store in Hiram, which he was commanded to continue in operation for five years, in order to make money for the upbuilding of Zion, and it was as a clerk in that store that he first knew Orson Pratt, who was converted to Mormonism, and became a leader in the church.

The history of the attempted conversion of this sedate little village upon the hill, is one of failure and of many mishaps. Rev. Ezra Booth, the Methodist minister whom we have already quoted, had given his adhesion to the Mormon faith, and was filled with zeal for the warning of others. He attended service on Sabbath in May, 1831, and listened to an address by Symonds Ryder—an Elder in the Disciple church, and a strong man, with an ancestry running back to the *Mayflower*. Upon its conclusion, he asked permission to speak. It was granted, whereupon he explained "in strong, clear language of impassioned enthusiasm, the ground of his new faith, and the inspiring hopes which it gave him."

A deep impression was made upon the minds of all who heard. Mr. Ryder was so much wrought upon that he did not dare deny, while he was as yet unable to accept and believe. In a stern determination to discover the truth at a point as near the fountain-head as it was possible to attain, he went direct to Kirtland, and talked with Smith, Rigdon, and others. He hesitated as to his course until in June, when he saw in a public journal a description of the destruction of Pekin, China, which a Mormon

girl had announced by prophecy six weeks before.
This appeal to the superstitious part of his nature
was the final weight in the balance, and he threw the
whole power of his influence upon the side of Mormonism. His surrender caused an excitement almost
equal to that which followed the fall of Rigdon.

A saving clause, however, was inserted in his acceptance, that would leave him free to desert the
new as speedily as he had abandoned the old, in case
it should prove to be a snare. A pledge was given
by Booth and himself to each other, that they would
often compare notes out of their experience, and be
of mutual aid in discerning the false from the true.

Ryder was speedily fastened by those bonds of
self-interest and ambition which Smith had so well
learned to lay upon men. He was made an Elder of
the Mormon Church; but as his name was wrongly
spelled in his official commission, doubt as to the
Mormon truth found in that fact a slight resting-
place; and he was still in this uncertain mood when
he again met Booth, upon the return of the latter
from the fiasco at Zion. Each then gave to the
other such information as led to the complete overthrow of all belief in the new creed, in the minds of
both. The effort made by these two men to defeat
the purpose of Smith and Rigdon was of a determined and effective kind, and bore abundant fruit.
They made public acknowledgment of error, and were
taken again into full fellowship with the churches to
which they had before given their faith.

Smith had personally appeared at Hiram early in
the winter of 1831, and many eloquent sermons were
preached by Sidney Rigdon and others, in a school-

house to the south of the town. "Such was the apparent piety, sincerity, and humility of the speakers," wrote Mr. Ryder to a friend, "that many of the hearers were greatly affected, and thought it impossible that such preachers should lie in wait to deceive. During the next spring and summer several converts were made, and their success seemed to indicate an immediate triumph in Hiram." This movement toward the evangelization of the town came to a sudden end, when Ryder and Booth joined forces in opposition; and the feelings of distrust and hate that were engendered in this conflict of moral forces culminated in an open attack upon Rigdon and Smith, on the night of the 25th of March, 1832. If we accept the declaration of Mr. Ryder, the foray was by "citizens of Shalersville, Garrettsville, and Hiram," who "proceeded to headquarters in the darkness of night, and took Smith and Rigdon from their beds, and tarred and feathered them both and let them go." And if we accept the evidence of Smith, Ryder himself was numbered among his assailants.

Smith had been holding a series of meetings, at which great excitement was manifest, and some conversions made. On the night of the attack he was domiciled with his wife and family in the house of John Johnson, a worthy man, who had been brought fully under the Prophet's influence. Joseph and his wife had been up with a sick child, and when she told him to take some rest he lay down upon a trundle-bed and soon fell asleep. He was suddenly awakened by her scream of "murder!" and almost instantly found himself going out of the door in the hands of several stalwart men, some having him by the hair, some by the throat, and others by the legs. He made a desperate struggle, as he was forced out, to extricate himself, but only cleared one leg, with which he made a kick at one man and knocked him off the doorstep. They again gained control of him, and declared they would kill him if he did not be still, which quieted him.

"As they passed around the house with me," said Smith, in an after-description of the occurrence,* "the fellow I kicked came to me and thrust his hand into my face all covered with blood (for I hit him on the nose), and with an exulting, hoarse laugh muttered, 'Gee.! Gee! I'll fix you.' Then they seized my throat and held on till I lost my breath. After I came to, as they passed along with me about thirty rods from the house, I saw Elder Rigdon stretched out on the ground whither they had dragged him by the heels. I supposed he was dead."

Smith began to plead with them, saying, "You will have mercy and spare my life." At this point a number of people came from several directions. He was carried some thirty rods further, when a man cried out, "Ain't you going to kill him? Ain't you going to kill him?" While several held him, others went to one side and held a council, the conclusion of which was shown by subsequent events.

One man was heard to cry, "Symonds, Symonds, where is the tar bucket?"

"I do not know," came the answer, "it's where Eli left it."

They ran back and brought the bucket, when one

* "History of the Mormons." By Samuel M. Smucker, New York, p. 78.

exclaimed, "Let's tar up his mouth." And the suggestion was carried into effect.

Accounts differ at this point. Those who had a hand in it declared that Smith was stripped naked, coated with tar, and covered with feathers from head to foot. Smith's account is that he was only "covered with the feathers in places." When the mob left him he found his way as rapidly as he might to Johnson's house, and when he appeared at the door covered with tar and feathers, his wife thought it was blood, and fainted.

About this time a number of Mormon sisters had reached the house and were collected in Mrs. Smith's room. Joseph discreetly called for a blanket. Some one threw one to him, and closed the door. He wrapped it around him and went in. The night was spent in scrubbing and removing the tar, and in washing and cleaning his body, so that by morning he was able once more to don his clothes. It was the Sabbath, and nothing daunted he led service as usual, and in the afternoon baptized three people.

Rigdon was even more harshly treated than Smith. He was dragged by his heels over the frozen ground, and then furnished with a coat of feathers taken from the pillows in the room in which he had been found asleep. He was delirious for some time, and in consequence a small difficulty arose between Smith and himself. Smith afterward declared that Rigdon was innocent in all that was said or done, but Joseph's mother publicly charged that Sidney "contrived to be out of his mind, in order to mislead the saints into the belief that the goods of the kingdom had been taken from the church and must not be restored, as he said, until they had built him a new house. This gave rise to great scandal, which Joseph, however, succeeded in silencing."

Rigdon repented and was forgiven, and declared that in punishment of his fault the devil had three times thrown him out of bed in one night.

Partly that this episode might be forgotten, and partly that the affairs of Zion might receive due attention, Smith again visited Missouri in April, where in a general council of the church he was proclaimed president of the high-priests. During that visit he was very busy both in spiritual and temporal things, ordering the printing of three thousand copies of the "Book of Doctrines and Covenants," and a selection of hymns made by his wife Emma to be published. He then returned to Kirtland, where many fresh labors and not a few new troubles awaited him.

During this mission effort at Hiram and before its failure had become apparent, affairs had not been idle at Kirtland, where Smith and Rigdon spent most of their time, and which was their official headquarters. The zeal of the missionaries at various points had been prolific of results, and almost every day saw an accession of new members to the little community. Many came from a distance, and among them were families of character and wealth. Smith was treated with the consideration due one to whom the mantle of Elijah and the rod of Aaron had fallen in the direct line of prophetic heirship, and was loved by many and feared by all. One who was present during these scenes declares that "Kirtland presented the appearance of a modern religious Mecca. Like Eastern pilgrims, they came full of zeal for their new religion. They came in rude vehicles, on horseback, on foot. They came almost any way, filling, on their arrival, every house, shop, and barn to the utmost capacity."

While the "common stock" principle may not have been entirely adopted, a course so akin thereto was pursued that the results were the same. The plan which the ingenuity of the leaders pointed out as the safest and most effective, can be best understood by a quotation of the revelation through which it was imposed upon the church: "If thou lovest me, thou shalt serve me and keep my commandments; and behold, thou shalt consecrate all thy properties, that which thou hast, unto me, with a covenant and a deed which cannot be broken;* and they shall be laid before the bishop of thy church, and two of the elders such as he shall appoint and set apart for that purpose.

"And it shall come to pass, that the bishop of my church, after that he has received the properties of my church, that it cannot be taken from the church, he shall appoint every man a steward over his own property, or that which he has received, inasmuch as shall be sufficient for himself and family;

---

* With a worldly wisdom that did not leave all to love and faith, Smith was careful that these papers of transfer were so made that they would hold good under the laws of Ohio. John Hyde says in relation to this question of the support of the church: "Smith, in the beginning of the church, attempted to establish communism, each giving their all to the bishop, and only drawing out of the office sufficient to live upon. This, however, was not more practicable for Smith than for Fourier or Cabet, and it was silently permitted to glide into the payment of tithing. In 1854, however, Brigham attempted to revive the old law in an improved shape."

and the residue shall be kept to administer to him who has not, that every man may receive accordingly as he stands in need; and the residue shall be kept in my storehouse, to administer to the poor and needy, as shall be appointed by the elders of the church, and bishop; and for the purpose of purchasing land, and the building up of the New Jerusalem, which is hereafter to be revealed; that my covenant people be gathered in one, in the day that I shall come to my temple; and this I do for the salvation of my people. And it shall come to pass, that he that sinneth and repenteth not, shall be cast out, and shall not receive again that which he has consecrated unto me; for it shall come to pass, that which I spoke by the mouth of my prophet shall be fulfilled, for I will consecrate the riches of the Gentiles unto my people, which are of the house of Israel."

V.

MIRACLES, AND THE GIFT OF TONGUES.

THE desire to make the best possible financial use of the enlarging opportunities that chance and circumstances had thrown into their hands, led the Mormon leaders to establish a bank, through which the final overthrow of their power at Kirtland was largely brought about. An application was made to the Ohio Legislature for a charter, but the request was refused. As the enterprise had been announced and commanded in a special revelation, which declared that this bank would ultimately "swallow up all other banks," nothing remained except to go forward as a private institution and take the chances of success. A nominal capital of four million dollars, based upon a large amount of real estate of not much value and by no means paid for, was announced, and the doors of the institution opened. Through much labor, begging, and borrowing, an actual capital of five thousand dollars was finally raised, and upon the strength of this, paper money, or rather mere printed promissory notes, to the amount of from fifty to one hundred thousand dollars, were set afloat.

This bank, of course, had no bonds or other securities anywhere upon deposit, and depended solely for its strength and credit upon the financial responsibility and honesty of its managers. These were sufficient for the Mormons, who accepted the paper notes without suspicion, and soon came to look upon them as the safest and best medium of commercial transactions, the more especially as many of them were looking daily for an overturn and destruction of all things outside of Mormonism.

Their example was an encouragement to the people elsewhere in Northeastern Ohio, and it was not long before the paper was in general circulation. A Pittsburg banker thus described the situation: "As this man (Smith) professes to be a prophet of the Lord, having daily communion with angels, ... no one supposed that they would leave things to a fraudulent issue of bank paper. Those who saw the notes supposed the bank to be simply a savings institution in which the Saints could deposit their earnings, while they would be invested so as to pay interest and that the notes represented actual money in bank, or the paper of good men." Smith announced that the bank was not established for the making of money for the use of its managers, but that all profits were to be devoted to the propagation of the faith, and the building up of the City of the Saints in Missouri.

The narration of events transpiring in the West will be deferred for the present, and the history of Kirtland continued until the close.

During the summer of 1832 Smith was very busy, making sure of that which he had already established, and laying plans for greater gains and achievements in the future. He continued the translation of the Scriptures, established a School of the Prophets, and attended to the publication of *The Evening and*

Morning Star. Everything was made tributary to his cause, and even the cholera, which had made its appearance in America and was doing its fatal work in a number of the larger cities, was cited as a warning to the world to turn from the error of its ways and accept the new prophet and his creed. Step after step was taken along the road of fraud and delusion to which he had become so thoroughly committed, and in which his success had already exceeded his wildest dreams. When firm in one position, he advanced to another. Having visible proof that his power for divine things was accepted, he added a new phase of belief on January 22, 1833, when the "Gift of tongues" was made manifest. It was of a nature to appeal with personal force to the most ignorant and insignificant of his followers, as it allowed any one of them to claim connection direct with the power on high, and to deliver themselves of any jargon of nonsense to which their imagination might be moved, or their ingenuity be able to compass.

The manner in which this "gift" was displayed was original and unique. A meeting would be called, and previous thereto the announcement made that some one would be moved to "speak with tongues" before dismissal. Each believer who attended carried with him the solemn possibility of being the chosen mouthpiece of the Most High, and was in a mood to accept and obey any emotional impulse by which he might be moved. Rigdon or Smith would be in attendance, and call upon some one to arise and deliver the message with which he was charged, saying, "Father A, if you will rise in the name of Jesus Christ, you can speak in tongues."

The old gentleman would stand up in a startled, half-scared mood, and perhaps say, "My faith fails me, I have not faith enough."

"Oh, yes, you have," from the leader; "speak in the name of Jesus Christ, make some sound without further thought, and God will make it a language."

The old gentleman would therefore mutter any unintelligible sounds that came to his aid, and no matter what he said, it would be called a tongue. Others would follow in the same strain, some talking, some singing, and others furnishing a mixture of the two. The rule given to believers was as follows: "Arise upon your feet, speak or make some sound, continue to make sounds of some kind, and the Lord will make a tongue or language of it." The interpretation of what was said was to be given in the same way. After the nonsense had been voiced, some other brother was to arise and translate it, and whatever he happened to utter on the spur of the moment, was to be regarded as the true exposition of that which had been previously heard.

The description of one of these meetings will suffice for all, and convey to the reader of modern days some idea of the manner in which Joe Smith controlled and directed the flock that had intrusted itself to his care. The account has been furnished by an eye-witness,* who was at that time a believer in Mormonism, but afterward forsook it. The gathering was held in a small upper room, and some fifteen elders and high-priests were present.

Exhortations, something after the style of the

---

* "Mormonism and the Mormons," p. 88.

backwoods camp-meeting, were delivered by several of the elders, when the Prophet himself arose. With much seeming earnestness he warned his hearers to be zealous, and to remain faithful to their duties, saying, "It is our privilege to see God face to face—yes, I will prophesy unto you, in the name of the Lord, that the day will come when no man will be permitted to preach unless he has seen the Lord. People will ask each teacher, 'Have you seen the face of the Lord?' and if he say 'Nay,' they will say, 'Away with this fellow, for we will have a man to teach us that has seen the face of the Lord.'"

After a few moments of solemn pause the Prophet resumed: "The Lord is willing we should see his glory to-day, and all that will exercise faith, shall see the Lord of glory."

There was a moment of longing expectancy among those who had laid their simple faith at the feet of Joseph, and who bore patiently in their hearts the hope that at last the long wish and desire was to be granted, and that their souls would be rested and sustained by one glance from the Most High. All sat silent in their seats, with eyes bent upon the floor.

Then Joseph turned to Rigdon, and in a voice full of solemn earnestness, asked, "Sidney, have you seen the Lord?"

Then came the slow-spoken answer: "I saw the image of a man pass before my face, whose locks were white, and whose countenance was exceedingly fair, even surpassing all beauty that I ever beheld."

"I knew you had seen a vision, Sidney, but would have seen more, were it not for unbelief."

With penitent air Rigdon confessed that his faith

was indeed weak that day; while others away down upon the back seats were sad in heart because even that much of Heaven's blessing had been denied them.

Hyrum Smith described a vision like that granted unto Rigdon, which Joseph pronounced to have been the appearance of the Son of Man himself.

Then one of the leaders, R. Cahoon, fell upon his knees, holding his hands heavenward. In ten minutes he arose, and declared that he "had seen the temple of Zion, filled with disciples, while the top was covered with the glory of the Lord, in the form of a cloud." Others who essayed to follow his experience declared they could see nothing, and were duly rebuked because of weakness of faith.

Joseph next passed about the room, and laid his hand upon the head of each one present, uttering a series of unmeaning sounds which to the ear of the narrator ran something like this: "*Ah man oh son oh man ah ne commene en holle goste en esac milkea, Jeremiah, Ezekiel, Nephi, Lehi, St. John,*" etc.

Sacrament was administered, after which there was more speaking in tongues, which at times elicited applause. The narrator was himself finally called upon to give an exhibition of his faith, and was told to speak or sing as suited him best. Feeling no divine supply of words, he set, to the tune of "Bruce's Address," a combination of such sounds as came to him first—a performance, he remarks, that "astonished all present." The whole day was given up to the services of this character, accompanied with fasting.

This attempt to engraft upon Mormonism a weak imitation of the wonders that befell the disciples of Jesus of Nazareth upon the day of Pentecost, was probably of more injury than aid to the cause, as it opened the road to ridicule and exposure, which was made of good use by the Gentile world. One apostate from the church at Nauvoo, in later days, dates the first growth of doubt in his mind from attendance upon a meeting where this ceremony was being performed. Having thorough acquaintance with the Choctaw language he suddenly arose and delivered a long address in that tongue and was followed by a brother Mormon, who gravely translated it into an account of the glories of the great temple then in course of construction. Lieutenant Gunnison* relates the story of a boy who had become so famous in the interpretation of these strange addresses that he was called upon by the elders when any very difficult case presented itself. On one occasion when a woman arose suddenly in the meeting and called out, "O mela, meli, melee," the lad was requested to reduce the exclamation to English. He promptly gave the translation, "O my leg, my thigh, my knee," and even when the angry and disgusted elders had him before the council, he persisted that he had given the right translation. As the woman herself did not know what she had been aiming at, they were compelled to give him an admonition, and let him go.

Eliza R. Snow,† the Mormon poetess who afterward

---

* "History of the Mormons." By J. W. Gunnison, Philadelphia, 1852; in Lovell's late edition, on p. 74.

† The following, from the *Salt Lake Herald* of December 8, 1887, records the end of the long and eventful life of this earnest believer in Mormonism: "Eliza R. Snow Smith died in the Lion House a few minutes past one o'clock Monday morning, ... being at the time of her death eighty-three years old. . . . . She had been closely

won some sort of fame by her doleful muse, and who had been lured from her home in Mantua by the eloquence of Rigdon in the early Mormon days, was supposed to be unusually favored in the gift of tongues, and often in the days of early wanderings would rush into the room of some woman and cry, "Sister, I want to bless you." She would then lay her hands upon the head of the other, and pour forth a stream of jargon in unlimited length.

All through the earlier days of his career, Smith made a persistent endeavor to repeat the mysteries and even the miracles of Bible times, and many stories might be related of his attempts. When he met with failure, as he usually did, he found some cause in the depth of his ingenuity, and dismissed the matter with as few words as possible. When through happy accident, legerdemain, or the unconscious nervous co-operation of his subject, he was able to accomplish that which was out of the usual line, he gave credit to divine power, and saw that the fact was duly heralded to the world.

The case of Newell Knight has been often cited in support of Smith's claims, and is dwelt upon at length in his autobiography. It was in the early days of Mormonism, and Smith was exciting attention by his performances in his old home in the East.

Knight had been greatly exercised over his spirit-

identified with the church in its early history, and was with the leaders during the troublous scenes in Missouri and other places, and in 1847 came to Salt Lake. . . . . Before and since that time her life has been prominently before the public, and to enlarge upon her kindly qualities, her literary abilities, or her worth as a woman, would be simply to repeat facts that nearly every one is cognizant of."

ual condition, and often went into the forest to pray for enlightenment. He became mentally and physically sick, and while in this pliable and receptive condition, his wife sent for Smith. The world has Joseph's own story * concerning what next happened: "I went, and found him suffering very much in his mind, and his body acted upon in a very strange manner, his visage and limbs distorted and twisted in every shape and appearance possible to imagine, and finally he was caught up off the floor of the apartment and tossed about most fearfully.

"His situation was soon made known to the neighbors and relatives, and in a short time as many as eight or nine grown persons had got together to witness the scene. After he had thus suffered for a time, I succeeded in getting hold of him by the hand, when almost immediately he spoke to me, and with very great earnestness required of me that I should cast the devil out of him, saying that he knew that he was in him, and that he also knew I could cast him out. I replied, 'If you know that I can, it shall be done,' and then almost unconsciously I rebuked the devil and commanded him in the name of Jesus Christ to depart from him, when immediately Newell spoke out and said that he saw the devil leave him, and vanish from his sight. This was the first miracle that was done in this church." Newell was "overwhelmed with the good spirit and joyous beyond expression," and was lifted up by invisible power from the floor to the roof, until "the beams would allow him to go no further."

He afterward declared that when the devil departed

* "Rocky Mountain Saints," p. 33.

from him, he bore the form of a black cat and ran into the bush.

Before Smith left Palmyra, one Green, who had joined the Mormon Church and deeded it his property to aid in the removal to Kirtland, was suddenly called out of life. His widow refused to sanction the contract until prayers had been offered for the return of his soul to its tenement of clay. As the petitions met no response, she still refused to yield her possessions, but failed to retain them. Several reputable people who resided in Minerva declared that Smith set a day for the village to sink, but afterward repented of his curse and withdrew it.

Upon another occasion, while still in New York, he made announcement that in the twilight of a certain evening he would walk upon the water. The unbelieving boys of the village kept close watch, and saw one of his adherents construct a bridge of boards just beneath the surface of the pond. When the accomplice had gone, the urchins removed the outer plank; and when the time of exhibition came and Smith went down, he swam ashore, and said to his followers, "Woe unto ye of little faith! Your faith would not hold me up!"*

Upon one occasion when John Morse, an aged convert to Mormonism, had been called to his last account, Smith was asked by his weeping and believing friends to recall him to life. The Prophet looked upon the body long and steadily, and then remarked that he should let him rest—he would not return him to his suffering, as he was so old that he would soon

---

* I confess to no good authority for this anecdote; but it is characteristic, and may be true.

die again! "This," it has been said, "was something like Brigham's refusal to restore a lost leg to one of his Mormons, on the ground that if he did it the man would be obliged to walk on three legs all through eternity"—his new one, and the two original legs that would be raised with him in the resurrection day.*

The chief claim for the possession of miraculous power put forward by Smith, and the one most often and effectually quoted by the Mormon missionaries in the days in which it occurred, is the remarkable cure of Mrs. Johnson, of Hiram. The case is well authenticated; and those who seek to explain it away will be compelled to base themselves upon mesmeric influence or the unconscious nervous co-operation of the lady affected, rather than in cunning upon the part of Smith. It seems to have been simply a case where his audacity was rewarded with an accident of fortune it by no means deserved.

When Ezra Booth and Symonds Ryder were investigating Mormonism, and the latter had not yet fully committed himself thereto, they determined to put Smith's claims to a crucial test. Their neighbor, Mrs. Johnson, had been unable to use her right arm for six years, because of a stroke of paralysis. Accompanied by this lady, her husband, and a physician, the two orthodox ministers set out for Kirtland, and made a call upon Smith. Nothing was said to him concern-

* Smith's reputation as a Prophet, which had spread through all the land, brought him many annoyances that had their grotesque side. In November, 1835, another "Prophet," named Matthias, from the East, called upon him, but was not made as welcome as he expected. He soon departed, declaring that Smith was a false prophet, and possessed of a devil; which exactly tallied with a description of himself, as already given by Smith.

ing the main purpose of their visit, but a discussion was opened as to the truth of the new doctrine that had created such turmoil in their midst. Smith held his own with unusual eloquence. In the course of the conversation Ryder asked him if it was true that he pretended to the performance of miracles.

"*I* cannot work miracles," was the response, "but I believe that God, working through me, can do so."

At a signal from one of the party, Mrs. Johnson stood before him. Said Mr. Ryder, "Here is Mrs. Johnson with a lame arm; has God given any power to men now upon earth to cure her?"

Smith must have felt that it was the moment to try the soul of any man not grounded in a perfect knowledge as to the power at his command, but to the eyes of those present he betrayed no fear. A calm assurance upheld him. Moving backward a few steps he looked intently into the eyes of the lady, as if to get her under his mental control.

Then he moved to her side, and taking hold of her palsied hand, said in a deep and solemn tone, "Woman, in the name of the Lord Jesus Christ, I command thee to be whole!" With no further word or look, he abruptly turned, and left the room. The hand that he had lifted did not fall. The lady attempted to move it, and found that it was once more under her control. Upon her return home she discovered that she could use it equally with the other, and thus it remained until her death, fifteen years later.*

* From a sermon preached in Hiram, O., on August 3, 1870, by B. A. Hinsdale, then President of Hiram College, after a narration of the above circumstance: "The company were awe-stricken at

Fanatic zeal, credulity, and imposition seemed to be in the very air; and even yet the visitor who crosses the narrow Chagrin and stands before the old temple, can find men and women to whom many strange things seemed real, and who remember the vagaries of hundreds whose simple faith was worthy of a nobler shrine. In the days immediately following the advent of the four apostles from Palmyra and the conversion of Rigdon, the excitement and the expectation of marvellous spiritual gifts grew to so intense a pitch that Smith, upon his arrival, was compelled to resort to repressive measures of the most rigid character.

If we may accept without hesitation the testimony of Mr. Eber D. Howe,* the scenes among the new converts were of a character hardly surpassed by the devotees of Oriental lands. "They pretended," says he, "that the power of miracles was about to be given to all those who embraced the new

the infinite presumption of the man, and the calm assurance with which he spoke. The sudden mental and moral shock—I know not how better to explain the well-attested fact—electrified the rheumatic arm. Mrs. Johnson at once lifted it up with ease, and on her return home the next day she was able to do her washing without difficulty or pain."

* Mr. Howe was the descendant of a well-known New England family, and was born in Clifton Park, New York, on June 9, 1798, and died at Painesville, Ohio, on November 10, 1885. He founded the Painesville *Telegraph* in 1822. When the Mormons made their appearance in Ohio in 1830, Mr. Howe chronicled all their movements, and in 1834 published a book, entitled "Mormonism Unveiled," which caused wrath and confusion among the Saints, and opened the eyes of the people to the proceedings at Kirtland. The volume has now been out of print for over forty years. For above account, see page 104.

faith, and commenced communicating the Holy Spirit by laying their hands upon the heads of the converts, which operation at first produced an instantaneous prostration of body and mind. Many would fall upon the floor, where they would lay for a long time apparently lifeless. They thus continued these enthusiastic exhibitions for several weeks. The fits usually came on during or after their prayer-meetings, which were held nearly every evening. The young men and women were more particularly subject to this delirium. They would exhibit all the apish actions imaginable, making the most ridiculous grimaces, creeping upon their hands and feet, rolling upon the frozen ground, go through with all the Indian modes of warfare, such as knocking down, scalping, ripping open, and tearing out the bowels.

"At other times they would run through the fields, get upon stumps, preach to imaginary congregations, enter the water and perform all the ceremony of baptizing, etc. Many would have fits of speaking all the different Indian dialects, which none could understand. Again, at the dead hour of night, the young men might be seen running over the fields and hills in pursuit, as they said, of the balls of fire, lights, etc., which they saw moving through the atmosphere. . . . . Three of them pretended to have received commissions to preach, from the skies. . . . . One of the young men referred to freely acknowledged some months afterward that he knew not what he did for two or three weeks."

These half-insane vagaries caused such adverse commotion in the neighborhood, that Smith saw he must put his foot squarely down upon them if he hoped his scheme would succeed, and it soon became known that no one must pretend to have communications with the upper powers but himself.

The men who had been sent into the Gentile world to warn it against the wrath to come, did not hesitate to work when possible upon the superstitious fears of their hearers. Many who listened made haste to escape the threatened wrath, and sold their possessions for such price as they could command, and hurrying to Kirtland, cast their lot in with the Mormon Church. It was preached through Western New York that the State would be sunk within two years, and that only such places as were designated as Stakes of Zion would escape. Even Martin Harris began to prophesy, and the following samples of his new art have been preserved to the world:

"Within four years from September, 1832, there will not be one wicked person left in the United States; that the righteous will be gathered to Zion (Missouri), and that there will be no President over these United States after that time." Second: "I do hereby assert and declare that within four years from the date hereof, every sectarian and religious denomination in the United States shall be broken down, and every Christian shall be gathered unto the Mormonites, and the rest of the human race shall perish. If these things do not take place, I will hereby consent to have my hands separated from my body."

With these prophecies, and one attempt at a miracle, Martin seems to have remained content. While marching westward as a member of Smith's famous army of relief, he discovered in the road a black snake, some five feet in length. Declaring that power had been given him to "take up serpents" unharmed, he took off his shoes and stockings and offered his toes to the mouth of the serpent. As the reptile made no effort to harm him, he made boast of his success, and was looked upon by his associates as favored above most men. Not content with this much of victory, he repeated the experiment with the next serpent of the same variety, a few rods further on. The snake promptly bit him in the leg, drawing blood, and making an ugly but not dangerous wound.

The subjoined prophecy, issued by Smith in 1832, may be taken as an illustration of the many random expressions to which he gave utterance in the early days, but which afterward confronted him because of their non-fulfillment: "Let the bishop go into the City of New York, and also to the City of Albany, and also to the City of Boston, and warn the people of these cities, with the sound of the Gospel, with a loud voice, of the desolation and the dread affliction which awaits them, if they do reject this thing; for if they do reject these things, the hour of their judgment is nigh, and their houses shall be left unto them desolate."

Oliver Cowdery at one time essayed the role of a miraculous healer, but the results of his experiment were not of a character to encourage him to further efforts. He was called to the relief of a young woman who had been confined to her bed for two years. He prayed over her, laid hands upon her, and in the name of Jesus bade her arise and walk. There was no movement upon her part. On the day following he persuaded her to leave her bed at the repetition of the command, and make the attempt. She had hardly taken two steps when she fell in a fainting fit, and being removed to her couch, remained there. In explanation of his failure the disciple followed the course of the Prophet when in close quarters, and explained it all to the satisfaction of Mormondom—he first denied the trial, and upon being confronted with witnesses, explained that if he did order her to walk, it was only as a joke.

A Painesville man was in the last stages of consumption. Cowdery declared he could cure him, while the more vehement Rigdon made declaration that he would get well—"as sure as there was a God in heaven!" The man soon afterward died. The declaration of Rigdon in this case was equalled by that made by him at another time, when he stated that an angel had appeared to him and commanded him to visit Queen Victoria, and "hurl her from her throne" if she should refuse to embrace Mormonism. There is no evidence of any attempt upon his part to carry out these instructions.

Some of the Saints believed they had no need of physicians or medicines, as all diseases could be cured by the laying on of hands. One poor young dupe, named Doty, who was but twenty years of age, was made a martyr to his belief. He had deluded himself into the idea that he was to live a thousand years, and when laid low with fever refused all medical aid, saying he would be about in a few days. Several of the Mormon elders called upon him, and encouraged him in his delusion by telling him that he was improving, when even they could see that he was dying, and soon left him to his fate. Smith came once, and sat for a time with his hands upon the head of the poor boy, and then went away. When Doty at last realized his condition, his delusion fell away from him like a rotten garment, and he lost all faith in the Mormon creed. Said he to one of his callers, "What a wonderful mistake I have made! You may profit by my experience, but for me it is too late!"

The hand of an elder was badly twisted out of shape as the result of an accident, and the Prophet was asked to straighten it. Taking the injured member in his hand, he said: "Brother Murdock, in the name of the Lord I command you to straighten your hand," at the same time using all his muscular strength to open the other palm. The result was an utter failure. The command was repeated in a still louder voice, but the hand remained set, and Smith was compelled to abandon the attempt.

Another elder was lame. Smith told him to arise and be whole. The man had sufficient faith for the attempt, but when he endeavored to walk he hobbled as badly as ever, and continued to for the remainder of his life. The child of a Mormon was taken sick. The father was anxious to procure a physician, but the elders persuaded him to the contrary, and declared the little one would recover. They laid hands upon it, and repeated many mummeries over it, and ordered it to improve; but it rapidly sank, and was soon no more. Rigdon told the parents it would be raised again, and he and Smith actually prepared to make the attempt. The father was even yet full of faith, but when he saw all Mormondom stand helpless as the beloved form was laid away in the tomb, the shadows passed from his vision, and he turned his back upon Mormonism forever.

Smith made his power felt in every movement, and at every turn of public affairs. He was unburdened of revelations almost daily, ofttimes concerning the most trivial things. When he uttered his fiat, that decision must be regarded as the word of the Lord, and end all controversy. For instance, two elders who had been splitting theological hairs equal to the abstruse absurdities of the Middle Ages, approached him with a request that he would decide this question: Will a bucket of water grow heavier when a live fish is placed in it? He promptly decided in the negative, adding the conclusion, "I know by the spirit that it will be no heavier." * He claimed to have constant access to the inhabitants of the upper world, seeing them with his spiritual rather than his natural vision, and with his eyes shut or open. He was once heard to describe an angel as a "tall, slim, well-built,

---

* John Hyde, the Mormon apostate, has related an instance which may be quoted in connection with the above. He says: "One very striking illustration of this mental abnegation occurred in the late Doctor Richards' office in 1854. Mr. Thomas Bullock, Mr. Leo Hawkins, and some others were talking to Kimball about the resurrection. The Mormons believe in a literal physical resurrection, and were desirous to learn 'whether, when the body came forth from the grave, it would leave a visible hole in the ground?' 'No,' said Kimball, 'not at all, the atoms would be reunited, and they won't leave no hole.' He proceeded to explain his reasons for this opinion, and presently Brigham came in, when this important question was referred to him, for his prophetic decision.

"'Why, yes, certainly it will,' was his verdict. 'Christ is the pattern, you know; and He had to have the stone rolled away from the sepulchre, and that left the hole visible, for did not the soldiers see it?'

"'Brother Brigham!' immediately cried Kimball, '*that is just my opinion!*'"—"Mormonism: Its Leaders and Designs," by John Hyde, Jr., formerly a Mormon Elder. New York, 1857, page 126.

handsome man, with a bright pillar upon his head"; and the devil came once in the same form, except that the pillar upon his head was coal black. The shooting stars of November, 1833, were declared by him to be signs of the second coming of Christ, and he returned thanks for their appearance.

Never free from the influence of the old money-digging days, Smith would at times encourage his followers by wonderful tales of hidden riches in New York State, which the Mormons would be able to discover and appropriate, as soon as they became sufficiently pure.

VI.

KIRTLAND STAKE OF ZION, AND BRIGHAM YOUNG.

ON February 15, 1833, Smith announced that his translation of the New Testament was complete, but that he had been commanded to seal it up, and so keep it until they should arrive at Zion. Three days later, when the high-priests were assembled in the school of the Prophets, Joseph laid hands on Rigdon and Frederick Williams, and ordained them councillors of the presidency; and these two, with the Prophet, constituted the government of the high-priests. On the 23d of this same month, at a meeting of these governing powers, it was decided to purchase all the land at Kirtland that their resources could command, and build a branch of Zion.

The building of a grand temple at Kirtland, in which the power and prosperity of the Mormon Church were to be shown, was among the earliest desires of Smith, and he made use of every means and power at his command for the accomplishment of that end. Its construction was made the subject of a special revelation, received upon May 6th. Besides the tithes that were to be paid into the treasury as a building fund, each Mormon was compelled to give one-seventh of his time in labor. It was at first ordered that it should be of brick; but as some difficulty was experienced on this point, a change was made to rough stone, plastered over, painted blue, and marked to imitate regular courses in masonry. The first stone was laid on July 24th. Joseph Bump, of Silver Creek, N. Y., was appointed master builder, and each night was handed a special revelation concerning the work of the following day. The structure as finally decided upon was sixty by eighty feet in size, and one hundred and twenty feet from its base to the top of the spire. The work of construction was pushed forward as rapidly as circumstances and means would permit, but two years elapsed before its completion.

The growth of the church was rapid during these days, and while many were still coming to Kirtland, or joining the settlement in the West, zealous and hard-working missionaries were preaching the new faith in all corners of the land. Their success was such, that within three years after the arrival of Smith in Ohio, Mormon societies had been organized in nearly all of the Eastern and Middle States. Smith found occupation for every moment of his time, and his powers seemed to enlarge with the demands upon them. We see him returning from still another visit to the West, to take up with renewed vigor the internal administration of the church. He delivers a message defining the orders of Melchisedek and Aaron; orders the twelve apostles forth to new missionary efforts; collects money for the building of the temple; and at a meeting of the council it is declared that these and like labors shall have some recognition, and it is therefore ordered that he shall not only have his expenses paid, but a salary of ten dollars per week —a like sum being voted him for the payment of his private secretary.

An episode that possessed a grotesque side, and proved something concerning the ignorance and credulity of the Mormon rank and file, had its beginning in July of this year, when one Michael H. Chandler, who was travelling through America exhibiting a collection of curiosities, of which several Egyptian mummies were a part, made a halt at Kirtland. His goods were for sale, and as Smith had evinced a desire to possess these ancient strangers from the land made famous by Joseph and his brethren, his wish was gratified by the church, and the purchase made.

Upon the bodies were discovered papyri, which Joseph had no sooner seen than he proceeded to read the writings thereon with ease. The "genial showman," who probably knew as much ancient Egyptian as Smith himself, and no more, recognized in the Mormon leader a kindred spirit, and unhesitatingly endorsed his translation of the scroll, in the following somewhat remarkable certificate :

"This is to make known to all who may be desirous concerning the knowledge of Mr. Jos. Smith, Jr., in deciphering the ancient Egyptian Hieroglyphic characters in my possession, which I have in many cities shown to the most learned, and from all the information that I could ever learn or meet with, I find that of Joseph Smith, Jr., to correspond in the most minute matters.

"MICHAEL H. CHANDLER,
"*Traveling with, and proprietor of, Egyptian Mummies.*"

If Joseph's information was correct, a bargain of rare character had indeed been made in this purchase.

Assisted by W. W. Phelps and Oliver Cowdery as secretaries, he immediately set himself to work upon the translation, and " much to our joy," he writes, " we found that one of these rolls contained the writings of Abraham; another the writings of Joseph. Truly we could see that the Lord is beginning to reveal the abundance of truth."

The fact that Smith's translations were altogether different in language and meaning, from those afterward made by an eminent European scholar, does not seem to have disturbed the Mormons in the least. A gentleman who called at the temple, accompanied by a couple of ladies, soon after the mummies were received, tells me that he was compelled to pay the Patriarch, to which title the elder Joseph Smith was ordained in December, 1833, a half-dollar for a sight of these precious relics. A dingy scroll hung on the wall. "That," said their aged guide, " is the handwriting of Abraham." Near by was a picture, in which a ladder was represented leaning against a wall. " This is Jacob's ladder," was his explanation. " But I thought," said one of the ladies, " that his ladder was much longer than that—reaching clear to Heaven "—at which the Patriarch was greatly offended, and marched the party out of the temple.

These ancient additions to the curious things already found in Kirtland, gave the enemies of the surrounding country and neighboring towns further food for ridicule and contempt. The half-jocular and good-natured spirit with which the new religion and its Prophet had been at first received, gave place to anger and fear, as the demands and boasts of the Saints as to their intentions, and final victory over all non-believers, grew more loud and frequent. Many visitors came to Kirtland, and the prying curiosity of some of these, and the open criticisms of others, added fuel to the growing flame; and it needs no close investigation to see the wisdom of the Mormon leaders, as they laid their plans and carried forward their purpose, of an early migration to a less settled portion of the country.

The world has hardly dealt justly by the Mormons in its treatment of this portion of their early history. It is difficult now, after the lapse of half a century, to enter into the home life and personal experiences of the members of this little community, so strangely set apart from the current course of the world, alien from the homes and churches to which they had formerly belonged, and counted as foes by the people located round about them. The impressions and incidents, few at best, placed upon record by such as did look in upon them, were mainly printed with some purpose against them, or insensibly colored by the prejudices of those through whom the narration came. One visitor, who doubtless met with a hospitality not altogether requited in his free expressions of opinion after his departure, has left in the *Ohio Atlas* (March 16, 1836) a letter which may be profitably quoted in this connection:

"I have been to Kirtland, and witnessed the operations of that most deluded set of visionaries that our land, or any other enlightened, has ever witnessed. You would naturally suppose that the Mormons were the most ignorant, degraded, and stupid set of beings on the earth. This is true of some of them; but there are not wanting men of sagacity and information and some men of strong powers of mind. From what I saw I should suppose that they were generally real believers in the doctrines of their Prophet. They are quite polite and affable to strangers. . . . . I was introduced to the Immortal Prophet, Joe Smith, and his renowned coadjutor, Sidney Rigdon, and a host of inferior satellites, and could scarcely suppress a laugh during the formality of making acquaintance and shaking hands with the exalted dignitaries, high-priests, etc., of Mormonism. I have no doubt that Joe Smith's character is an equal compound of the impostor and fanatic, and that Rigdon has but a small spice of the latter, with an extraordinary portion of the former; while the mass of the disciples are men of perverted intellect and disordered piety, with no sound principles of religion, with minds unbalanced and unfurnished, but active and devout, inclined to the mystical and dreary, and ready to believe any extraordinary announcement as a revelation from God.

"None of them appeared to be within reach of argument on the subject of religion. They profess to have the gift of tongues; and one individual, after becoming very much excited in conversation, offered to give me a specimen; but I shuddered at the proposal to exhibit such blasphemy and mockery of a miraculous gift, and he desisted. The Mormons have increased with astonishing rapidity. They say, and they are probably not far from the truth, that their numbers in the United States amount to forty-five thousand."

Another visitor,[*] who made his call at about the

[*] Interview with Col. W. H. Leffingwell, in St. Louis *Republican*.

same date, paid his respects to Rigdon, whom he seems to have known, and then asked to see the Prophet, of whom he had heard so much.

Mr. Rigdon replied, " It is our dinner-time. You cannot see him now, as he is up the street, marking goods"—forty wagon-loads of merchandise having been received from the East the previous day.

The caller was afterward introduced to Smith, and his narration continues: "Smith had a round face, and his hair was cut short down on his forehead. The color of his hair was between a deep brown and a dark red. He sent a young man with us into the temple, which was but newly finished. We entered the portico, when the young man, our guide, said, 'Take off your hats.' I replied, 'Our hats are already off, sir. We have a long way to drive, and want you to hurry up, sir.' We were then conducted into the interior of the temple. A broad aisle ran through the middle of the temple with a cross aisle in the centre, above which a curtain hung dividing the temple into two parts, Sidney Rigdon occupying, we were told, the eastern portion, and Joe Smith the western portion, which included the grand altar. The arrangements seemed to be thus made in consequence of the still incomplete state of the temple. By mounting on one another's shoulders we were enabled to pull ourselves up through the hole into the attic, where we were shown several mummies, including that of Joseph and other patriarchs mentioned in the Bible. After visiting the temple we were invited into the tent, where we were provided with a good dinner."

Smith had his troubles to meet, and cares to carry, from within as well as from without. The fanatical character of his followers made his burdens all the more annoying. There was a grotesque, if not a comical side, to these troubles. Elder George A. Smith, a cousin of the Prophet, delivered a now forgotten sermon at the Salt Lake Tabernacle in 1855,* in which he solemnly related a few of the annoyances Joseph was compelled to meet. Speaking of a certain class of converts, he said: "In a few weeks some of them apostatized; the trials were too great, the troubles too severe. I know persons who apostatized because they supposed they had reasons; for instance, a certain family, after having travelled a long journey, arrived at Kirtland, and the Prophet asked them to stop with him until they could find a place. Sister Emma (Joseph's wife), in the meantime, asked the old lady if she would have a cup of tea to refresh her after the fatigue of the journey, or a cup of coffee. The whole family apostatized because they were invited to take a cup of tea or coffee after the word of wisdom was given. Another family, about the same time, apostatized because Joseph Smith came down out of the translating-room, where he had been translating by the gift of the power of God, and commenced playing with his little children. Some such trials as these, you know, had to be encountered. I recollect a gentleman that came from Canada, and who had been a Methodist, and had always been in the habit of praying to a god who had no ears, and as a matter of course had to shout and halloo pretty loud to make him hear.

"Father Johnson asked him to pray in their fam-

* *Cleveland Herald* of July 18, 1855, copied from the *Deseret News*.

ily worship in the evening, and he got on such a high key, and hallooed so loud, that he alarmed the whole village. Among others Joseph came running out, saying, 'What is the matter? I thought by the noise that the heavens and the earth were coming together'; and to the man, that 'he ought not to give way to such an enthusiastic spirit, and bray so much like a jackass.' Because Joseph said that, the poor man put back to Canada, and apostatized; he thought he would not pray to a god who did not want to be screamed at with all one's might. Four hundred and sixteen elders, priests, teachers, and deacons met in Kirtland temple on the evening of its dedication. I can see faces here that were in that assembly. The Lord poured His Spirit upon us, and gave us some little idea of the law of anointing, and conferred upon us some blessings. He taught us how to shout hosanna; gave Joseph the keys of the gathering together of Israel, and revealed to us—what? Why, the fact of it was, he dare not yet trust us with the first keys of the priesthood. He told us to wash ourselves, and *that* almost made the women mad, and they said, as they were not admitted into the temple while this washing was being performed, that some mischief was going on, and some of them were right huffy about it."

An accession to the little colony that meant far more to Mormonism than any for a moment dreamed, came in November of this year, when Joseph Smith and Brigham Young were for the first time brought face to face. The new-comer was one who by no means gave promise of the personal strength and leadership he developed in later days. He came of a family of average character and ability. His grandfather was in belief a New England Methodist, and his father performed patriotic service in the Revolutionary war, removing in 1804 from Vermont to Sherburne, Chenango County, New York. Brigham was the ninth of a family of eleven children, and was born at Whitingham, Windham County, Vermont, on June 1, 1801. No detailed account has been left by himself or his family of his early days, which were spent upon a farm until he was old enough to care for himself, when he learned the painting and glazing trade. In 1832, in his thirty-first year, he was brought under the influence of Mormonism, and was either converted thereto, or was moved to announce a conversion. He gave his allegiance to the church under the ministration of Samuel H. Smith, the Prophet's brother, and was baptized by Eleazer Miller. It may be remarked in passing that all of his father's family became Mormons eventually, following Brigham to Nauvoo, and onward to Salt Lake.

Young proceeded directly to Kirtland upon his admission to the church, and almost immediately became the close friend and companion of Smith. He was the counsellor needed by the latter, and no doubt his influence was often exerted for the prevention of mistakes which the erratic Rigdon would have led Joseph to commit. Young was ordained an elder, and commenced preaching. His native ability and deep knowledge of character, added to an intense earnestness, and a zeal that did not lead him to overlook the practical side of things, gave him a leadership almost from the first. His advancement was rapid and certain. On February 14, 1835, he was ordained one of the newly-organized quorum of the twelve apostles. When Thomas P. Marsh apostatized in 1836, Young was chosen to succeed him as president of the twelve.

It has been claimed by some that when Joseph first beheld Young, he prophesied the time would come when Brigham should preside over the church; while others have been heard to relate that some time before his death Smith made the remark: "If Brigham Young ever becomes president of the church, he will lead it to hell." It certainly cannot be shown that Young ever made an attempt to supplant Smith in any respect, but stood firmly by him, upholding his authority, and never challenging his right to do as he pleased—possessed, possibly, by the very legitimate ambition of gaining the succession if Joseph should fall by the way. He supplied many points of strength where Smith was lacking, aiding in the executive department even as Rigdon performed the brilliant work of the pulpit. "As an official or political leader," it has been said, "he was far superior to Smith, while as a religious leader he was much his inferior. He was a good speaker, using oratory, however, as a means to accomplish certain ends. His manner in the pulpit was impressive and authoritative, his illustrations apt, his sentences to the point, and often sarcastic. His lack of education passed unnoticed in the ignorance which surrounded him." Of his personal appearance in mature years, a keen observer (Hepworth Dixon, in "New America,") has said: "A large head, broad, fair face, with blue eyes, light brown hair, good nose, and merry mouth."

Young's first wife was Marion Works, to whom he

was married in 1824. She died eight years later, leaving two children. His second wife was found in Kirtland. He was married on March 31, 1834, to Mary Ann Angel, whose parents lived a mile and a half from the Mormon village. Kirtland was at that time a part of Geauga County, and in the old and time-worn records of the Probate Court at Chardon, may still be seen his application for a marriage license, as well as the license itself, as follows:

"THE STATE OF OHIO, Geauga County, *ss.*: Personally appeared Brigham Young and made application for a marriage license for himself and Mary Ann Angel, of the township of Kirtland, in said County, and made solemn oath that he, the said Brigham Young, is of the age of twenty-one years, and the said Mary Ann Angel* is of the age of eighteen years. That they are both single, and no nearer of kin than first cousins. That he knows of no legal impediment against their being joined in marriage.

"Sworn and subscribed this tenth day of February, 1834, before me, Ralph Cowles, Deputy Clerk."

Following the above is this:

"Be it remembered that on the thirty-first day of

---

* Hepworth Dixon, in speaking in after-years of his visit to Salt Lake City, says of this wife: "The queen of all is the first wife, Mary Ann Angel, an aged lady, whose five children, three sons and two daughters, are now grown up. She lives in a white cottage, the first house ever built in Salt Lake Valley." When Young was sued for divorce and alimony by Ann Eliza, the nineteenth, he paid a Geauga County attorney fifty dollars for furnishing him with an official copy of the above certificate, and with it coolly proceeded to show that, as he was already married to Mary Ann, he could not legally be the husband of Ann Eliza.

March, in the year of our Lord, 1834, Brigham Young and Mary Ann Angel, of the County of Geauga, were legally joined in marriage by competent authority, in conformity with the provisions of the statute of the State of Ohio, in such cases made and provided, and a certificate of the said marriage signed by Sidney Rigdon, the minister who solemnized same, has been filed in the office of the Clerk of Common Pleas of the said County of Geauga, this third day of April, A.D. 1834. A. D. AIKEN, Clerk."

The signature of Young appears to the above application, and, according to his own spelling, stands "Brickham," and the "Young" commences with a small y.

No very definite or fixed form of government for the Mormon Church had as yet been adopted, affairs, spiritual and ecclesiastical, being largely left to the Prophet and his immediate advisers. The time had now arrived when even Smith could see that something more adhesive and restrictive than his personal authority was needed, to control and hold in check the many and diverse elements now composing the Mormon Church. In accordance with that conclusion the leading men of the church were commanded to assemble at Kirtland, on February 17, 1834. The meeting was held in the house of the Prophet, and its result was the organization of "The High Council of the Church of Christ." This body was to consist of twelve high-priests, and one or three presidents, as the case might require. As we are told by the Mormon record, "the High Council was appointed by revelation, for the purpose of settling important difficulties which might arise in the church, which could not be settled by the church or the Bishops' Council to the satisfaction of the parties."

As early as March of 1832, Smith had been acknowledged President of the High-Priests, while one year later the Quorum of three High-Priests, consisting of Joseph Smith, Jr., Sidney Rigdon, and Frederick G. Williams, was organized as a presidency of the church. These three were chosen also to be presidents of the new High Council, while the Council itself consisted of Joseph Smith, Sr., John Smith, Joseph Coe, John Johnson, Martin Harris, John S. Carter, Jared Carter, Oliver Cowdery, Samuel H. Smith, Orson Hyde, Sylvester Smith, and Luke Johnson, all High-Priests. As the first President of the Council and also of the church, Smith saw no abridgment of his power, nor any portion of it delegated to other hands. He had simply added the force of organization to the authority already held by a supposed commission from on high.

On May 3d, at a conference of the elders, the name of "The Church of Jesus Christ of Latter-Day Saints" was formally chosen. The remaining important ecclesiastical measures adopted at Kirtland may be summarized in a few words. On February 14, 1835, a quorum of twelve Apostles* was organized,

---

* The first twelve Apostles were as follows, selected in the order named: Lyman E. Johnson, Brigham Young, Heber C. Kimball, Orson Hyde, David W. Patten, Luke Johnson, William E. McLellin, John F. Boynton, Orson Pratt, William Smith, Thomas B. Marsh, and Parley P. Pratt. As constituted at Nauvoo, at a later date, when changes were made by death or defection, the twelve were named as follows, the added designation of each being be-

among whom were Brigham Young and Heber C. Kimball, then two of the coming men of the church. Seven days later the first meeting of the twelve apostles was held; and on February 28th, the organization of the Quorum of Seventies began. At a general assembly of the church, on August 17th, the "Book of Doctrines and Covenants" was accepted as a rule of faith and practice, including Rigdon's "Lectures on Faith." On January 4, 1836, a Hebrew professorship was established; and on June 12, 1837, the first foreign mission was established, Heber C. Kimball, Orson Hyde, and four others being sent to convert England.

That dissensions and backslidings should occur in a community or congregation drawn together as had been the Kirtland "Stake of Zion," and bound by the ties in which its members were held, follows almost as a matter of natural law. The attacks from without had become more frequent and determined, and any discontented or aggrieved Mormon found no lack of sympathizers and advisers in the communities surrounding the little village. Among those who had given their adhesion to Mormonism when it was first preached in Ohio, was "Doctor" D. P. Hurlburt, a man of fine address and excellent personal appearance. Many believed that he had become a Mormon simply

---

stowed upon them by the poetic W. W. Phelps: Brigham Young, *the Lion of the Lord;* Parley P. Pratt, *the Archer of Paradise;* Orson Hyde, *the Olive Branch of Israel;* Willard Richards, *the Keeper of the Rolls;* John Taylor, *the Champion of Right;* William Smith, *the Patriarchal Jacob's Staff;* Wilford Woodruff, *the Banner of the Gospel;* George A. Smith, *the Entablature of Truth;* Orson Pratt, *the Gauge of Philosophy;* John E. Page, *the Sun Dial;* and Lyman Wight, *the Wild Ram of the Mountains.*

in the hope of pecuniary gain through some channel that might be opened by opportunity, or that his undoubted natural shrewdness should open.

Be that as it may, he soon forsook the doctrines and church he had so readily espoused, and became one of the most active enemies of Smith and the Mormon cause. Joining hands with Eber D. Howe and others who were engaged in an exposure of the Mormon scheme, he became a thorn in the side of his old enemies, and hurt them whenever and wherever he could. He was among the first, if not the first, to couple the Book of Mormon with the unpublished romance of Solomon Spaulding, and made a strong effort to establish a logical connection between the two.

Naturally, a personal enmity arose between the Prophet and himself. Charges and counter-charges soon ran into threats of personal violence, and a point was finally reached when Smith found it necessary, or at least expedient, to seek the aid of the Gentile courts. Going before a Justice of the Peace, in April, 1834, he made complaint that Hurlburt had made such threats that he was in fear of his life. The defendant was arrested, ordered to give bonds to keep the peace, and cited to appear before the Court of Common Pleas. The case was heard in Chardon* a few days later. The fact that Hurlburt had himself been a Mormon elder, and had been baptized by Smith, made the occasion one of rare interest to the surrounding country.

The house was filled with spectators, among them

---

* Kirtland was then in Geauga County, the County of Lake being created on March 6, 1840, out of portions of Geauga and Cuyahoga.

many Mormons who were outspoken in their championship of their leader. It was shown in the trial that Hurlburt had been excommunicated from the church for alleged misconduct, and in revenge had denounced Smith as a false prophet, and made threats against him. Many witnesses made oath to the latter charge; and when Hurlburt's lawyer asked one of them why he did not tell Smith of his danger, the response was that he did not think it necessary, as he could not believe the man lived who could do physical harm to the person of Joseph Smith. This abundant faith did not seem to possess the one most concerned, as Smith went upon the witness-stand and swore that he was in daily bodily fear of an attack from his late convert. The court was possessed of no special love for Smith and his friends, but as a matter of public justice and peace, ordered Hurlburt to find security in the sum of two hundred dollars to keep the peace for six months.*

During the remainder of his life in Kirtland, Smith had occasion to make many weary and vexatious journeys to Chardon, and hardly a term of court was held that did not see him or some of his followers moving down over the hills of Geauga to make answer to some charge evolved from the ingenuity, or through the unrequited wrongs, of some individual who held no love for the Mormons or their creed.

These journeyings to and fro were not all because of troubles from without. The natural heart of man was also present in Kirtland, and its promptings were

---

* Hurlburt never returned to the Mormon fold. He spent the closing years of his life in Gibsonburgh, Ohio, where he died in 1882.

not always those of peace. In June, 1835, we find an indictment pending against Smith himself, on complaint of a brother Mormon, who occupied, in addition, the close relation of brother-in-law. The charge was that of assault and battery upon the person of Calvin W. Stoddard. The case was set for hearing on the twenty-fourth of the month above named, and Smith was bound over to the Court of Common Pleas, and upon the final hearing, the Prophet, his mother, and other members of the family appeared in force. The assault was not denied, but the plea of self-defense advanced in justification.

It was developed by the testimony that the two had fallen into dispute concerning the water in a certain lot. As the contention waxed warmer and still more warm, the wrath of Stoddard gained the better of his loyalty and discretion, and he shouted out so that the curious and waiting neighborhood could hear: "I don't fear you, nor no other man!"

As Smith made no pretension to physical prowess, he received this challenge in silence, but as Stoddard added the declaration that he was but a false prophet at best, and emphasized it with an oath, patience gave way, and he felled his defamer to the earth, and while he was down gave him a lesson not soon forgotten. When questioned in court, Smith stated that Stoddard had asked his pardon, which had been freely granted. A case of self-defense was made out and Smith acquitted; although it was noticed that Stoddard's allegations upon the first hearing were far more vehement and pointed than upon the last. Family and church influence had no doubt been brought to bear for the healing of the feud.*

The first formal attempt on the part of the opponents of Mormonism to bring the machinery of the law to bear upon any of its leaders, occurred in June of the same year, when such statements were made before the grand jury of Geauga County, as led it to return a bill of indictment on the sixteenth against Sidney Rigdon. Quoting the language of that ancient document direct from the record, we are told that "Sidney Rigdon, of Kirtland, on the fourth of September, 1834, attempted to solemnize the marriage contract between Orson Hyde and Miranda N. Johnson," when not legally authorized to perform such service. Reuben Hitchcock, afterward one of Ohio's most eminent jurists, was prosecuting attorney, and after the jury had been sworn, in the October term of the court, decided to *nolle* the case; doubtless concluding that as Rigdon had for years been a regular minister in the Baptist and Disciple churches, his right in the premises was hardly to be questioned.

A brief season of renewed comfort and hope was

---

* Upon the conclusion of the suit, Smith made his way into print through the following card:

KIRTLAND, *June*, 1835.

EDITOR " PAINESVILLE TELEGRAPH ":

In a late number of your paper the fact was noticed of my being bound over to Common Pleas Court to keep the peace, for an assault upon the person of my brother-in-law. Since my honorable acquittal before said court last week, there being no evidence to prove the same, I believe you will do me the justice to make the last as public as the former, and oblige,

Your obedient servant,
JOSEPH SMITH, Jr.

granted the Saints in the early days of 1836, when their first temple was completed and ready for dedication. The work had been prosecuted in the face of many difficulties and discouragements, and when the last stone was laid and the last curtain hung, the burden upon the souls of the devout was lifted, as they hoped that their willing obedience and severe toil in the completion of this house of worship would bring a season of fruitful revival, and place upon them and theirs the blessings so long promised and so long deferred.

The structure had cost them nearly forty thousand dollars—a sum of no small magnitude considering their resources and the scale of prices of those days. Devoid of architectural beauty, it was still imposing, and not without a dignity of the rigid and angular sort. Making use of a description of the temple penned a short time after its erection,* we obtain the following:

"In front, over the large window, is a tablet, bearing the inscription:

'House of the Lord
Built by the Church
of the Latter-Day Saints.
A.D. 1834.'

"The first and second stories are divided into two grand rooms for public worship. The attic is partitioned off into about a dozen small apartments. The lower grand room is fitted up with seats as an ordinary church, with canvas curtains hanging from the ceiling, which, on the occasion of prayer-meetings,

* "Ohio Historical Collections," p. 282.

are let down to the top of the slips, dividing the room into several different apartments, for the use of the separate collections of worshippers. At each end of the room is a set of pulpits, four in number, rising behind each other. Each pulpit is calculated for three persons, so that when they are full, twelve persons occupy each set, or twenty-four persons the two sets. These pulpits were for the officers of the priesthood. The set at the farther end of the room are for the Melchisedek priesthood, or those who minister in spiritual concerns. The set opposite, near the entrance of the room, are for the Aaronic priesthood, whose duty it is to simply attend to temporal affairs of the society. These pulpits all bear initials, signifying the rank of the occupants."

The temple was dedicated on March 27th. That occasion may be regarded as the culminating point of Mormon success and influence in Ohio. The leaders used every means within their power to raise it above the level of temporal things, and to impress upon it an apparent stamp of special divine acceptance and favor. The ceremonies of dedication and consecration were conducted with a mysterious solemnity intended to impress believers and mark itself with effect upon spectators from the outer world. The various quorums of the church officially recognized Smith as their Prophet and Seer; and if Joseph's word is to be taken as conclusive, there were august visitors in attendance—Moses, Elias, and Elisha appearing unto him, and surrendering into his possession the Keys of the Priesthood, which conferred upon him great power in spiritual and material things. He also saw angels, which came down and held converse with him, but were seen not by the dull eyes of those about him.

Brigham Young, not to be too far behind Joseph in the manifestations of spiritual power, was favored with an eloquent outburst of tongues, and made an address which neither he nor any one else could understand, but which some brother made an effort to translate. A pillar of fire was seen above the temple, and supernatural sounds heard in the air. Many who had heretofore been content to remain in the background, arose and gave utterance to prophecy. The brethren shut themselves in the temple, and washed and anointed themselves. This exaltation of spirit, and the excitement of which it was a part, continued several days. On the evening of March 29th the ceremony of washing feet was performed, each Saint humbling himself in the service of another. Hundreds, we are told in the Mormon records, remained in the building all night, "glorifying God and prophesying." At daybreak they partook of the sacramental bread and wine.

The excitement continued until March 31st. During this time all business of a secular character was suspended. Many spectators were drawn from the neighboring towns and farms. No such season had been witnessed at Kirtland even in the early days of spiritual riot, and none was possible in the times of gloom and trouble that were even now closing in from every side.

VII.

ENEMIES WITHOUT AND WITHIN.

THE problems that Mormonism was now set to solve were no longer confined to the polemic challenges of Thomas Campbell and an allied orthodoxy, nor to the newspaper attacks of Hurlburt and Howe. Nor were they all resultant from envyings and dislikes among the Saints themselves,—of which there never was a lack, and which increased in noise and turmoil as the storm of financial difficulty gathered about the head of Smith and his immediate associates in the government of the church. It was from this last-named source that the overthrow finally came. Bad management; a haste for riches that outran the resources of capital at command; a bank that, in defiance of law, issued a worthless scrip that was hardly meant to be redeemed; over-confidence that was the natural result of placing an almost autocratic power in untrained hands, and numerous speculations based upon an optimistic view of the future, combined to a ruinous conclusion, which the financial panic of 1837 precipitated.

Looked at from the dispassionate ground of a business view alone, one can hardly criticise the Mormon leaders for many of the ventures into which they were led. It was a time when the canals of New York and Ohio, the waters of Lake Erie and the Ohio River, and the highways between the East and the great unsettled West, were filled with people bent upon the founding of new homes in the new lands, and lured by a future that, however bright it might have seemed, has been far outrun by the magnificent developments of the half-century past. Cities were springing up as if by magic. Settlements were made to-day where the forest had stood untenanted and unbroken but yesterday. Farms were marked out in lands that were on the far frontier a year before. With any advantage in natural gift or commercial creation, one spot seemed equal to the rest in a hope for the future, and those whose interests were staked upon it felt justified in calling the attention of the world to their possessions, and in offering to others a part of the harvest they hoped to reap.

Kirtland lay upon one of the roadways the hand of the pioneer had cut through the forests of Northern Ohio, while the waters of Lake Erie could be seen from her temple roof. The nucleus of a large town seemed to have been formed in the settlement of so many strangers about the temple, and the limits to which it might yet grow could only be defined by the future. Those who had seen that which had already been done, had a reason for their hope of yet greater things in times to come. As there was a material and financial side to Mormonism,—a thing needless to note in the presence of such men as Brigham Young and Parley P. Pratt,—it was but natural that advantage should be taken of the chances offered from day to day. Speculation in land was indulged in. All through 1836 and 1837, as shown by the books of the County Recorder at Chardon, sales in abundance were made by the Smiths and other leading Mormons. The multiplicity of these transactions in realty on the part of the two Josephs and their kin, suggests a curious change from the money-digging and root-beer selling Palmyra days of only a half-dozen years before.

In fact, a great city was laid out, of which the temple was to be the centre, and around which the Saints were to live in happiness and content until the

KIRTLAND CITY.

millennium should dawn and the whole earth be delivered into their hands. All that remains of that Utopian dream to-day is a finely-executed plat upon the county books, forgotten of men and scarcely seen by the eyes of this generation.*

* The history of Kirtland City as told in the record, is brief, and of official terseness. The plat is the handiwork of Willard W

The building of Kirtland City was interrupted by the financial and personal difficulties that rapidly gathered about the Prophet and the church. In his autobiography Smith speaks of his troubles in the following words: "At this time the spirit of speculation in lands and property of all kinds, which was so prevalent throughout the whole nation, was taking deep root in the church; as the fruits of this spirit, evil surmisings, fault-finding, disunion, dissension, and apostasy followed in quick succession, and it seemed as though all the powers of earth and hell were combining their influence in an especial manner to overthrow the church at once, and make a final end. . . . . The enemy abroad and apostates in our midst united in their schemes; flour and provisions were turned toward other markets; and many became disaffected toward me, as though I were the sole cause of those very evils I was most strenuously striving against, and which were actually brought upon us by the brethren not giving heed to my coun-

---

Beals, surveyor of Geauga County. Proceedings attested by F. G. Williams, a Mormon Justice of the Peace. Among those by whom the allotment was made were Emma Smith, the Prophet's wife; Eliza R. Snow, the Mormon poetess; Reynolds Cahoon, Hyrum Smith, Oliver Cowdery, Heber C. Kimball, Joseph Smith, Sr., Joseph Smith, Jr., and Sidney Rigdon. The plat was made in April, 1837, and recorded May 24th. There were to be thirty-two streets, all laid at right angles, and each four rods wide. There were two hundred and twenty-five blocks, each containing twenty lots of equal size. In the naming of the streets the new dispensation, which stood sponsor, had an advantage over the old, twenty-nine being allotted to the Mormons, while the disciples of Holy Writ were forced to be content with three; or were even Peter, John, and Luke numbered among the Whitmers and others of the Mormon flock?

sel. No quorum in the church was entirely exempt from the influence of those false spirits who were striving against me for the mastery; even some of the Twelve were so far lost to their high and responsible calling, as to begin to take sides, secretly, with the enemy."

An occurrence that had its culmination in the early days of this year, did not allay the feeling of enmity and distrust already prevalent in the outer world. Grandison Newell, a prominent farmer of Kirtland township, who lived a mile and a half from the village, had for a long time been an avowed enemy of Smith and the Mormons, and lost no chance to make his dislike apparent in his acts. A young man who had been a member of the Mormon Church, but had departed from and denounced it, gave Newell such information as led him, on April 13, 1837, to lodge a complaint before Justice Flint, of Painesville, charging Smith with conspiring to take his life. Giving form and substance to the grave rumors that had been for a long time afloat as to the dangers to be apprehended from the Mormon Church, this charge caused the wildest excitement. The hearing was awaited with the deepest interest. It occurred on June 3d. The young man above referred to—whose name appears in none of the records—made oath that Smith had directed himself and a fellow Mormon named Davis, to take Newell's life, declaring him to be an avowed enemy to the true faith, who ought to be put out of the way, and that on two occasions they had gone to the complainant's residence at night, with a purpose of carrying out their instructions, but had not found him at home.

This evidence made a sensation, and the Mormons used every means in their power to break its effect. Rigdon, Cowdery, Hyde, and other prominent members of their church were placed upon the stand, and made as good a case for Smith as the circumstances would admit.* The court appears to have believed there was some foundation for the charge, as Smith was placed under bonds of five hundred dollars to keep the peace, and appear at the next term of court. Rigdon, L. W. Denton, and Orson Hyde were accepted as bail. On the final hearing, Smith was discharged, the evidence not being considered sufficient to make good the charge.

The business troubles that accumulated with such rapidity during the year of which we write, made their influence felt with malign dexterity at almost every point. An illustrative incident can be related. One Samuel Brown, a shrewd money-lender of Kirtland, had reason to believe that a financial crash would naturally follow in the wake of wild speculation, and as he had loaned three thousand dollars to the Mormons, determined on a plan by which to make himself secure. Going to Smith, he declared that he was in sudden need of money for a short time, but would re-loan it to Smith, and with it a much larger sum. The Prophet greedily swallowed

---

* In this trial, Gen. J. H. Payne, of Painesville, appeared for Newell, and in a quizzical way asked each of the Mormon witnesses if he believed Joe Smith to be a true prophet. The answer upon each occasion was an emphatic "Yes." When Rigdon was reached with the same inquiry, he sat back in his chair and coolly responded: "Well, I guess he is as much of a Prophet as you are, General, or Eber D. Howe"—the latter's book against Mormonism having already appeared.

the bait, and by much effort secured the three thousand dollars, which he gave Brown. In a few weeks he again called on Brown, and suggested that he would like to borrow the promised larger sum. Brown laughed in his face, and dismissed the Prophet with the remark: "Now that I have got my money safe, do you suppose that I am so big a fool as to throw it away?"

Other creditors were possessed of a like fear, and attempt after attempt was made to force collections. As many persuasions and appeals had failed, a resort to the courts of law was the natural result. A promissory note for several thousand dollars, given on January 2d, to the Bank of Geauga, at Painesville, was the starting-point of many troubles, and the first point of attack. In default of its payment, Joseph Smith, Jr., Newell K. Whitney, and Sidney Rigdon were brought into court and compelled to give bonds for eight thousand dollars. The case never came to trial, but was settled out of court. The members of the mercantile firm of Rigdon, Smith & Cowdery, which had done a large business of late years, and purchased East and West, wherever credit could be obtained, were called to the bar of county justice at about the same time, to answer to one Hezekiah Kelley, as indorsers of paper issued by the firm of R. Cahoon, J. Carter & Co.—Hyrum Smith being the company. Judgment to the full extent of the claim was allowed.

Other suits of a like character were heard at the same term of court, and in each the award was to the plaintiff. Such indeed became their need of money in a time of financial stringency, that in

July we find Sidney Rigdon, Joseph Smith, Oliver Cowdery, Hyrum Smith, Reynolds Cahoon, and Jared Carter—members of the two firms mentioned above—joining in a promissory note of forty-five hundred dollars to Mead, Stafford & Co., wholesale merchants of New York, for which they gave as security nothing less than a mortgage upon the interest they severally and jointly held in the temple—described in the instrument as "The Stone Temple, called also the Chapel House." The conveyance covered the land upon which the building stood, all furniture "used in or about said house," and "all ancient curiosities, writings, paintings, and sculpture therein,"* all claims held by them against the temple, and in particular one of sixteen thousand dollars due for advances at the time of its erection.

Even this assignment did not prevent the stream of claims from pouring steadily in. Some were settled out of court, while others went to trial. Nor did their troubles end here. A proceeding which must have caused both Smith and Rigdon great uneasiness, and promised worse disaster than all the suits for debt yet entered, was commenced against them during this year of culminating ruin. It was an action for the unlawful assumption of banking powers, without the charter rights the law required.

As has been already related, the so-called bank that was established, in the face of a refusal of the Ohio Legislature to grant a charter for the same, had issued an unlimited number of bills, and performed all the

---

* With an unwillingness, perhaps, to make merchandise of the bearers of the rolls of Abraham, the mummies in the temple were named as exempt from the provisions of this deed.

functions incident to a bank. As the law then stood in Ohio, informers in certain cases were granted a portion of the fines imposed. The penalty incurred in unlawful banking was of this character, and accordingly, one Samuel D. Rounds decided to enrich himself, harass the Mormons, and vindicate the law by one bold stroke. In the March term of court, he caused the arrest of Rigdon and Smith, and demanded from each, in the name of himself and the State, " a penalty of one thousand dollars, incurred by acting on the fourth day of January, 1837, as an officer of a bank not incorporated by the law of this State, denominated 'The Kirtland Safety Society Anti-Banking Company,' contrary to the statute in such case made and provided." The offenders were brought into court, and once more compelled to call upon their friends and partners for bail, which was furnished.

The case was called in the June term of court, when a desperate effort was made to clear them by a demurrer, which was overruled, and a continuance granted. In October they were tried by a jury, adjudged guilty as charged, and ordered to pay the fine. Their defense was based upon the claim that they had acted for an association instead of a bank, and that the bills they had issued were individual notes in effect and not money. Upon that ground an appeal was taken, and measures set on foot to carry the matter to a higher court; but before a decision could be reached, the bank was a thing of the past, its notes no longer money in law or in fact, and its president and cashier safe in the Mormon fold of the far West.

Specimens of these bills were introduced in evidence in the above cases, and becoming a part of the record can be found neatly wafered in an ancient volume of the Geauga Criminal Records. They are almost as fresh and crisp as when first issued. Even a casual examination will show upon their face an attempt at evasion. The bill as originally issued bore, in large, bold letters, the inscription: "The Kirtland Safety Society Bank will pay on demand to W. Parrish or bearer, three dollars." As danger under the law began to threaten, an addition was stamped upon the engraved bill, in very small letters, so that the anti-banking clause would be inserted, in this form:

Anti-BANK-ing Co.

At first glance one would not see the added words because of their diminutive size. The evasion was of no use, however, when placed to the crucial test of the law. The personal signatures of Smith and Rigdon appeared upon each bill.

While the bank was one of the main avenues through which these tribulations came, it was by no means without its uses in the days when doubt and suspicion had not filtered into the public mind. Its notes were taken by every one, and by many were regarded as preferable to the "wildcat" currency with which the West was flooded. Free use of this confidence was made in the fitting out of emigrant trains to the West, in the purchase of horses, wagons, farming and mechanical tools, and other needed supplies. More than one keen Yankee farmer and trader, who had sold his wares at the full market price, had occasion ere long to regret that the suspicion he had at-

FAC-SIMILE OF MORMON MONEY.

tached to the Mormon's religion and patriotism, had not been extended to his printed notes as well.

The printing-press was, indeed, kept so busy, that the genuine banks of neighboring cities became suspicious, and began to investigate the solidity of the foundation upon which so great a business was done. A practical test was decided upon by the Pittsburg bankers, who sent one of their number, Mr. Jones, to Kirtland upon a tour of investigation. Loading a hand-satchel with the "Safety Society" notes, he took the stage to Ohio, and made an early morning call upon Rigdon and Smith.

He questioned them in a general way as to the prosperity of Mormonism spiritually and materially, and received such glowing responses as only these two adepts in the art of impressing men, could give. The conversation was then adroitly turned by the visitor to the bank, and its solidity and usefulness extolled by its president and cashier.

Mr. Jones expressed his pleasure thereat, and confessed to a personal interest of no small extent. Producing his bundle of notes, he asked for their immediate redemption in coin.

The response of president Rigdon was prompt and to the point. He declined to exchange, politely suggesting that the paper had been put forth as "a circulating medium for the accommodation of the people," and that he would be thwarting that purpose to call any of it in. In short, he dishonored the express promise of the note, and Mr. Jones carried home a bundle of bills that had no value beyond that of the paper of which they were composed.

The long-foreshadowed end could not be long delayed. Early in November, 1837, the bank formally suspended payment, and its doors were closed. The knell of Mormonism in Ohio was sounded; and even had peace and harmony reigned inside the church, the feeling of the outer world was such that continuance in Kirtland would have been impossible. Thousands held the worthless promises to pay, and the feeling everywhere was that of anger, distrust, and hatred. It was, indeed, time that the Prophet was going, since prestige, business success, and the last remnant of public confidence had already gone.

Smith made such defense of his course as the circumstances would admit. He declared that the bank itself was victim rather than offender, and charged a defalcation of twenty-five thousand dollars upon Warren Parrish, a clerk of the institution, who had left Kirtland some time before. Be this as it may, the defense was not accepted by the world, and the blame was laid upon those to whom, beyond all question, it belonged. The failure was denounced by many of the Mormons themselves, and served to open still wider the breach already existing in the church. One Boynton, an elder, met Smith, and publicly upbraided him for his course, telling him that, as the bank had been established "by the will of God," he did not see how it could fail, no matter what men might do against it.

Smith's response was characteristic. He threw all the blame upon those who had been associated with him in its management, and declared that the blessings had been promised only on the condition that the bank should be conducted on business principles.

The majority of those who held an unshaken and

devout belief in the divine commission of Smith, had already departed to the new field of labor in the West, while among those who remained, were many who were his enemies, secretly or openly, as their fear or policy might suggest. Although the acknowledged prophet, seer, and revelator of the church, and chosen its president by a unanimous vote, his authority was often questioned by rebellious acts, while opposing claims were even set up against it. Almost daily renunciations of the church on the part of the disgusted or dissatisfied, were occurring, while excommunications followed as a matter of course. Men high in the councils of the church to-day, might find themselves outcast and given over to the buffetings of Satan on the morrow. A girl, almost a mere child, began suddenly to utter prophecies, and deliver herself of spiritual revelations in opposition to the commands of Smith, and even his prompt and emphatic denunciation of her works as those of the devil, hardly saved her from a following that would have caused division and contentions in the church.

The final blow at the authority of the Prophet came when a faction calling themselves " Reformers," sought to take control into their own hands, and opposed him and his in every quarter and at every point. The closing months of 1837 were filled with contentions, and as Saint warred against Saint, and prophecy was uttered in refutation of other prophecy, the Gentile world stood not aloof, but used all means within command to fan the enmity into still more open war, and cause the breach to widen so that it might be put forever beyond repair.

Smith, Rigdon, and Young stood side by side in

these tempestuous times, and gave blow for blow, and shot their shafts into the opposing ranks with such power and to such effect as still lay within their command. The magic of such belief as was still held in Smith's prophetic mission, was used to frighten and dismay the opposition. Thunderbolts of anathema were hurled at the rebellious, and many were no doubt held to the church by no loftier emotion than a servile and superstitious fear.

I have received from the mouth of a witness yet living[*] an account of the final public appearance of Smith and Rigdon in the temple which their influence and energy had done so much to create. It was in December, on a Sabbath directly preceding their wild flight by night. Schism, apostasy, secret enmity, malice, and even outspoken opposition confronted them in the church, while debt, revenge, arrest, prosecution, and punishment threatened from the world without. The faithful, many upon whom dependence could be placed at all times, were already far away in the West, while here were left the hostile few. A demand had been made by the Prophet that condemnation and excommunication should be pronounced upon several in revolt, and it became apparent ere long that the votes by which the behest was to be obeyed, were not forthcoming.

Such natural power as Smith held for the control of men, answered to the demand now made upon it. He came into the gathering with a resolution and courage that the situation seemed to demand, and carried himself as one who felt that his soul and be-

---

[*] L. E. Miller, an aged resident of Painesville, O.

ing had found themselves set firmly on the rock, while all else was but the shifting of sand or the swaying of reeds in the summer wind. The deep experiences of nearly a decade of spiritual and material command, had given power and play to every faculty, and carried him far outward from the uncouth and flimsy experiences and assertions of the early days. The natural grain of greatness, which no honest and watchful man could deny as a part of his endowment, had seen much smoothing and polishing in his constant contact with the world; and he was no longer the ungainly boy who looked into the white stone for lost money or straying flocks, but the clear-sighted and ambitious man, who aspired to a place with Mohammed as the founder of a vast religious empire. There could be no show of weakness on his part now that was not fraught with danger, and he played his game with boldness and courage clear on to its tragic end.

Rigdon had been sick, and was aided to his seat by the steadying arms of friends. The debate was long and stormy. Three hours of the Sabbath passed away, and no decision had been reached. Rigdon's address was not soon forgotten by those who heard it. Physical weakness was upon him, but the pathos of his plea and the power of his denunciation swayed the feelings and shook the judgment of his hearers as never in the old days of peace, and when he had finished and was led out, a perfect silence reigned in the temple until its door had closed upon him forever.

Smith made a resolute and determined battle; false reports had been circulated, he declared, and those by whom the offense had come must repent and acknowledge their sin, or be cut off from fellowship in this world, and from honor and power in that to come. He made his demand as head of the church, for the sake of the church, and he would abate not one jot therefrom.

The accused plead their case, and many who had done faithful and obedient service for Joseph in the past, spoke boldly in opposition to the Prophet's will. As the contest grew to a white heat, one of those who had fallen under the Prophet's displeasure gave him the lie to his face, and fire from heaven did not consume him, nor the earth open to receive him.

At last Joseph, impatient with opposition, and tired with the long turmoil of argument, suggested that a vote upon excommunication should be taken, and further pleas for the victims heard at a later date. "Yes," shouted one of the latter, who was immediately upon his feet, "you would cut a man's head off and hear him afterward!"

Lyman Cowdery, a Mormon lawyer, suggested a postponement of the whole matter for a few days, and was sustained by vote.

Further proceedings had little interest for Smith. There came to his ears one day a rumor that Grandison Newell, his old enemy, was on his way to Chardon for a warrant for Rigdon and himself on a charge of fraud in connection with the late bank.* With no heart for further contests in the arena of public justice, he made hurried and secret arrangements for

---

* The rumor had no foundation in fact, although there were many who desired such arrests made. Newell used to relate the story with great gusto, and tell at length how he "run the Mormons out of the country."

flight. Young had gone some weeks before. Fleet and stout horses were secured, and late in the evening of the 12th of January, 1838, Smith and Rigdon bade their few devoted friends farewell, and galloped over the frozen roads and through the snow toward the West. There was much outcry, but no legal action when they were gone, and in due season they were welcomed as heroes and hailed as martyrs by that portion of the Mormon world to which their coming was a blessing and surprise.

As one may suppose, Smith's version of this unfortunate episode in his life and of misfortune to the church, varied from that furnished by his opponents, the more especially as he was compelled to justify himself and companion before the main body of the church. "A new year," he writes,* " dawned upon the church at Kirtland in all the bitterness of the spirit of apostate mobocracy, which continued to rage and grow hotter and hotter, until Elder Rigdon and myself were obliged to flee from its deadly influence, as did the apostles and prophets of old, and as Jesus said, 'When they persecute you in one city, flee ye to another.' And on the evening of the 12th of January, about ten o'clock, we left Kirtland on horseback, to escape mob violence, which was about to burst upon us under the color of legal process, to cover their hellish designs and save themselves from the just judgment of the law. The weather was extremely cold, and we were obliged to secrete ourselves sometimes to elude the grasp of our pursuers, who continued their

---

* From *The Evening and Morning Star*, the organ of the Mormon Church.

race more than two hundred miles from Kirtland, armed with pistols, etc., seeking our lives."

It is perhaps needless to say that the conclusion of the above quotation must be charged to Smith's imagination, which was compelled to aid him out of the dilemma in which he had been placed. Before leaving Kirtland, Smith had said to his enemies, "You will see me again, whatever happens. God has promised me that nothing shall prevail against me, and that my life is safe for five years to come."

The sheriff was now an almost daily visitor at Kirtland. The dream of a great city was gone, and those who had the most at stake thought only of how they might save something from the wreck. The foreclosure of mortgages followed each other in quick succession. On January 14th the printing-office of the church, containing many books and a large amount of paper, was disposed of at sheriff's sale, the purchaser being one of the Reformers or seceders from Smith. During the night the building and contents, and a small Methodist chapel standing near, were burned to the ground, and stories were put afloat that Mormons of the old school had become incendiaries, in the hope that the blaze would extend to the temple, which they did not wish to see left in the hands of their enemies.*

Referring once more to the records of Geauga County, we find the last transfer of property by

---

* Extract from the *Cleveland Herald and Gazette* of January 25, 1838: "The Mormon Society of Kirtland is breaking up. Smith and Rigdon, after prophesying the destruction of the town, left in the night. The Reformers are in possession of the temple, and have excluded the Smith and Rigdon party."

Smith occurring in July, 1838, after he had been in the West some months. The deed was made in Caldwell County, Mo. Rigdon had not hesitated to secure safety from creditors by placing his property out of his hands before the final crash, and in April, 1837, had joined with his wife in deeding an acre of land in Kirtland to their daughter Nancy. Only one sale on the part of Brigham Young can be found on the books of the county—that of a plat valued at six hundred dollars, disposed of in July, 1837, to Solomon Angel, no doubt the father-in-law of the grantor.

Before closing the Kirtland chapter of Mormonism, the testimony of Dr. Storm Rosa, one of the then leading physicians of Ohio, upon a number of points touching which he had personal knowledge, can be profitably introduced. It appears in the form of a letter to the Rev. John Hall, rector of St. Peter's church, of Ashtabula, Ohio, under date of Painesville, Ohio, June 3, 1841,* from which the following is extracted:

"I think the history of Mormonism as published by E. D. Howe, a copy of which can be obtained in our place, contains all the material truths connected with the rise and progress of that miserable deception. There are occasionally new doctrines introduced and incorporated with their faith, such as being baptized for the dead. This is a common custom here. When a member is satisfied that his father, mother, or brother, or any other friend is in hell, he steps forward and offers himself to the church in baptism for that individual, and when properly baptized, the tormented individual will in-

---

* "Gleanings by the Way," p. 315.

stantaneously emerge from his misery into perfect happiness. There are many such follies which the simple-hearted are ready and willing to believe. There is no permanent separation in the society. There were a few seceders a few years since, some of whom left them entirely, and became infidels, and others held to the original purity of the doctrines, as they termed it. As to Martin Harris, of late I have heard but little of him. My acquaintance with him induces me to believe him a monomaniac; he is a man of great loquacity and very unmeaning, ready at all times to dispute the ground of his doctrines with any one. He was one of the seceders, and for a time threatened the Mormons with exposure, as I have been informed. [It will be remembered that Dr. Rosa penned this letter some time after Smith had commenced his operations in the West.] But where he is now I cannot say.

"Joe Smith is regarded as an inspired man by all the Mormons. Sidney Rigdon is at the western settlement. He embraced the Mormon religion in the latter part of October, 1830 (see page 102 of the book as published by E. D. Howe, above referred to). In the early part of the year, either in May or June, I was in company with Sidney Rigdon, and rode with him on horseback a few miles. Our conversation was principally upon the subject of religion, as he was at that time a very popular preacher of the denomination calling themselves Disciples, or Campbellites. He remarked to me that it was time for a new religion to spring up; that mankind were all rife and ready for it. I thought he alluded to the Campbellite doctrine; he said it would not be long before something would make its appearance; he also said that he thought of leaving for Pennsylvania, and should be absent for some months. I asked him, how long?—he said it would depend upon circumstances. I began to think a little strange of his remarks, as he was a minister of the gospel. I left Ohio that fall, and went to the State of New York, to visit my friends, who lived in Waterloo, not far from the mine of Golden Bibles.

"In November I was informed that my old neighbor, E. Partridge, and the Rev. Sidney Rigdon were in Waterloo, and that they both had become the dupes of Joe Smith's necromancies; it then occurred to me that Rigdon's new religion had made its appearance, and when I became informed of the Spaulding manuscript I was confirmed in the opinion that Rigdon was at least accessory, if not the principal in getting up this farce. Any information that I can give shall be done cheerfully.

"Respectfully, your obedient servant,

"S. Rosa."

VIII.

THE ARMY OF ZION.

THE story of Joseph Smith's first visit to Missouri, and the founding of Zion, has been already told. His second trip Westward was made in April, 1832, the month following his severe personal experiences at Hiram. Between one and two thousand Mormons had by that time gathered at Zion, and forebodings of the troubles that afterward befell them, were found in the dislike and suspicion of the non-Mormon settlers about them.

The emphatic announcements made some time before by the Prophet, that his people were soon to possess all that land to the exclusion or destruction of such as did not believe, had not added to the welcome of the new community, while the continued accessions to the Mormon population by emigration from the East, had turned to fear that which in another case would have been scorn or contempt. The Mormons had pursued a policy hardly in accord with the ideal of a chosen race, but perhaps natural to an ignorant community that lived in the belief that it alone found favor in the sight of God. They assumed a superiority of manner and conduct that did not accord with their professions, and lent color to some of the grave but often groundless charges which enemies set afloat against them. There was much to confront Smith, and cause him anxiety on this visit, not only from the Gentiles, but through the mistakes of judgment or waywardness of purpose on the part of many under his spiritual care. But he met it all with an even countenance and a dexterity of management that showed no trace of anxiety or alarm. He transacted such business as came to hand, and on May 1st presided at a grand council of the church, where many matters of moment were transacted. Five days later he set out upon his journey home. In June, in pursuit of arrangements made while he was present, the publication of *The Evening and Morning Star* was commenced at Independence, under the direction of W. W. Phelps, formerly a printer at Canandaigua, New York, and reputed author of all Smith's political letters and speeches.

Early in 1833, the difficulties that had for a long time disturbed the relations between the Mormons and their neighbors, began to take the form of open hostilities, and muttered threats were changed to actual attacks by voice, by pen, and finally by physical force. A meeting of Missourians was held in April, which some three hundred attended, and at which an emphatic resolution was adopted ordering the Mormons to leave the country. Defiant replies to this autocratic demand were made by the Mormon press. A counter response came from the Missourians, in a series of meetings of a character similar to that described above, where a decision to exclude, by force if necessary, was on each occasion reached.* Finally,

---

* The publication of an article in the Mormon organ, in June, 1833, entitled "Free People of Color," probably had something to do with this sudden anger of a community in which the strongest pro-slavery principles prevailed.

a general meeting of the citizens of Jackson County was held, on July 20th, at which between four and five hundred made their appearance. An address had been prepared, and was read and adopted unanimously. After a statement of causes leading to this conclusion, the following specific demands were made:

"That no Mormon shall, in future, move and settle in this country.

"That those now here, who shall give a definite pledge of their intention, within a reasonable time, to remove out of the country, shall be allowed to remain unmolested until they have sufficient time to sell their property and close their business without any material sacrifice.

"That the editor of the *Star* be required forthwith to close his office, and discontinue the business of printing in this country; and, as to all other stores and shops belonging to the sect, their owners must, in every case, comply with the terms of the second article of this declaration, and upon failure, prompt and efficient measures will be taken to close the same.

"That the Mormon leaders here are required to use their influence in preventing any further emigration of their distant brethren to this country, and to counsel and advise their brethren here to comply with the above requisitions.

"That those who fail to comply with these requisitions, be referred to those of their brethren who have the gifts of divination and of unknown tongues, to inform them of the lot that awaits them."

The meeting adjourned for two hours, while a committee of twelve resolute and well-armed men presented this unwarranted and impudent demand to the Mormon leaders, among whom were Bishop Partridge, and Mr. Phelps, the editor of the *Star*. Naturally, they were not prepared to quietly submit, nor did they feel strong enough to answer with defiance, and threaten blow for blow. They asked for delay, which the committee promptly refused. When report was made to the meeting upon its reassembling, it was determined that active measures should be commenced at once.

The building in which the *Star* was published was razed to the ground, while Bishop Partridge and a fellow-Mormon were caught, stripped of their clothing, and treated to a coat of tar and feathers. The mob then announced three days for reflection on the part of the Mormons, in which they must decide as to their future course. When the adjourned meeting was held on July 23d, and the demand repeated, the Saints had no alternative but to submit. An agreement was made and signed, that one-half the Mormons should depart by January 1, 1834, and the rest by the first of the following April. The offending newspaper was to be discontinued, and no new members should be allowed to join the society in Zion during the nine months of truce.

Advice was sought of the Prophet and rulers of the church at Kirtland, while an appeal for protection was made to the Governor of Missouri. The response of the latter was plain and direct. He declared that the attack upon them had been made without reason or justice, and advised them to remain where they were. Word to the same effect came from Kirtland. Believing that an agreement wrung from them by physical force was not binding morally, as it certainly was not in law, the Mormons felt it no wrong to refuse to carry out its provisions, and announced their purpose to that effect.

The Missourians were as good as their word. On October 31st, an attack was made upon the Mormons by a body of armed men, several houses were destroyed, and a fight ensued in which two Missourians were killed. For the sake of appearances the authorities called out the militia, but as the troops were enemies of the Saints almost to a man, the latter saw no other alternative but to go, and made hurried preparations to leave the State. They crossed the Missouri River in November, with great loss of property and no small degree of suffering, the majority finding a temporary resting-place in Clay County, some going to Van Buren, and others to other parts of the State.

While Smith made little haste to take a personal part in these difficulties and dangers, he was by no means idle, nor forgetful to turn the troubles of his followers to such good to himself and his creed as they might be made to yield. He could write better than fight, and such consolation as he could give the persecuted Saints by revelation was forthcoming. He was first unburdened of a message that he should retain Henry Clay for the legal defense of Mormon rights, and next issued a command of a character that caused no small degree of excitement in the church, and was virtually a declaration of war against their persecutors. He promised the Saints a final and eternal possession of the Zion from which they had been expelled, and did not fail to tell them that they had been stricken because of their sins—"Verily I say unto you, concerning your brethren who have been afflicted, and persecuted, and cast out from the land of your inheritance—I the Lord hath suffered the affliction to come upon them, wherewith they have been afflicted, in consequence of their transgressions; yet I will own them, and they shall be mine in that day when I shall come to make up my jewels."

The command to Joseph himself, in this revelation, was direct, personal, and as full of war as some of the Hebraic commands of old : "Therefore get ye straightway unto my land ; break down the walls of mine enemies ; throw down their tower and scatter their watchmen ; and inasmuch as they gather together against you, avenge me of mine enemies, that by and by I may come with the residue of my house and possess the land."*

* From an address delivered by the Apostle Wilford Woodruff, at the celebration of the entrance of the pioneers into Great Salt Lake Valley, on the thirty-third anniversary of that event, July 24, 1880; in the pamphlet publication, "The Utah Pioneers," Salt Lake City, 1880, p. 17: "In 1833 the Saints of God were driven out of Jackson County, Missouri, by a lawless mob, into Clay County. Some were massacred, some whipped with hickory goads, and others were tarred and feathered. Their houses were burned, and their property was destroyed, and they were driven, penniless and destitute, across the river. . . . . Parley P. Pratt, who, with his family, was now destitute of all earthly means of support, and Lyman Wight, with his wife lying beside a log in the woods, with a babe three days old, and without food, raiment, or shelter, volunteered to go to visit the Prophet of God. . . . . When Elders Pratt and Wight arrived in Kirtland, they told their tale of woe to the Prophet Joseph, who asked the Lord what he should do. The Lord told him to go to and gather up the strength of the Lord's house, the young men and middle-aged, and go up and redeem Zion. It

Mormondom was immediately placed upon a war footing. Men and money were asked for, and Joseph announced that he intended to head the army of rescue and relief in person, and lead it against the offending Missourians. This bold stand gave hope and courage to his followers. He set forth and preached the new crusade to the Mormon churches. The High-Priests and Elders took up the war-cry and repeated it everywhere. Mormons old and young responded, some through a high and genuine devotion to their faith, others because they did not dare refuse, and still others from a love of excitement and adventure. The army was rendezvoused in Kirtland in May, 1834, and numbered one hundred and thirty men, which increased to two hundred and five by accessions on the way. Among its members were Brigham Young, Heber C. Kimball, George A. Smith, Orson Hyde, Orson and Parley P. Pratt, and many other leading officers of the church.*

The rank and file, taken collectively, were hardly of a character to strike terror to any brave or organized foe, but the army looked upon itself as invincible, and certain to carry the day of battle in triumph.

was the will of God that they should gather up five hundred men, but they were not to go with less than one hundred. . . . . I have not time to repeat the history of that journey here to-day, but the counsel and the word of the Lord, through the Prophet of the Lord, and its fulfillment, with our joys and our sorrows in connection with those scenes and events, are engraven upon our hearts as with an iron pen upon a rock, and the history thereof will live through all time and in eternity."

* The particulars of this march are taken from the account of "An Eye-Witness, one of the Sharp-Shooters" of the Army of Zion, given in " Mormonism and the Mormons," pp. 111 to 116.

The men were a motley lot, if we may take the word of some who saw them pass by, and of others who were among their numbers. Some who had offered themselves were rejected because they could not furnish weapons and show themselves in the possession of five dollars. Their arms were of a mixed character. Some had rifles, some pistols, and others old muskets. A few had swords that had been bequeathed by Revolutionary grandsires, while others wore huge butcher-knives. Many weapons were borrowed, others secured on credit and never paid for, while a few had been manufactured to order in the Mormon blacksmith-shop.

The army left Kirtland on Monday, May 5th. Before its departure Joseph delivered a lengthy speech full of fire and wrath for his enemies, and glory and honor for his friends, and ending with the expectation that his own bones would be left to bleach upon the field of battle. The line of march was taken in the direction of Summit County, and on the second night an encampment was made at New Portage, forty miles from Kirtland and just below Akron. Here they were joined by more men. Smith organized them into bands of fourteen each, and assigned to each a captain, baggage-wagon, and a tent.

Smith was so far true to his old self that he looked carefully after the matter of finances. Before they left New Portage he said to his men, "I have this to propose: That you shall appoint a treasurer to take charge of whatever money you may have with you, and to pay it out as our general necessities may require."

They agreed. Smith was, of course, named as

treasurer, and elected. He pocketed the cash, and ordered the army to move on. Their flag was of white, with the word "Peace" upon it in letters of red.

Smith made his men behave themselves on the line of march, and molest no one of the country through which they travelled. They tramped by day and camped at night. There were twenty baggage-wagons in all, carrying food, clothing, and goods for the use of the destitute brethren in the West. Each of the bands above mentioned had its own cook, two firemen, two tent-makers, two watermen, one commissary, and two wagoners. At night there was a blast on the trumpet, at which sound, worship was held in every tent. In the morning this order of exercises was repeated. They crossed Ohio and Indiana, and the first halting-place of which special mention is made, was at Salt Creek, Illinois, where Lyman Wight and the Prophet's brother, Hyrum Smith, joined them, with a reinforcement of twenty men.

Those who have discerned the true character of Smith, need hardly be told that he made the most of each occasion and incident found by the way, and of every possible turn and feature of the campaign. While the majority tramped through mud and sand, he had four fine horses for his special use. He carried an elegant brace of pistols that had been purchased on credit, a rifle, and a sword four feet in length, in the use of which he became quite expert. He had the usual number of revelations. In speaking of his army, he afterward said: "Their enemies were continually breathing threats of violence; the Saints did not fear, neither did they hesitate to prosecute their journey, for God was with them, and His angels were before them, and the faith of the little band was unwavering. We knew that the angels were our companions, for we saw them." On reaching the borders of Illinois, a large mound or tumulus was discovered, and Smith ordered it to be opened. A foot from the top the bones of a human skeleton were discovered, and taken out and laid upon a board.

The chance here given to make an impression was not overlooked. The Prophet gathered his men about him, and made a speech. "He was," said Joseph, pointing to the bones, "a Lamanite, a large, thick-set man, and a man of God. He was a warrior and chieftain under the great prophet Omandagus, who was known from the hill Cumorah, to the Rocky Mountains. His name was Selph. He was killed in battle by the arrow found among his ribs, during the last great struggle of the Lamanites and Nephites."

One cannot but admire the wonderful power of Smith in meeting each event as it came, and in fitting the circumstances of any extraordinary occurrence to his own purpose. Nothing was so unexpected that it could take advantage of him; no truth so mighty that it could unhorse him or put his imagination to shame.

At Salt Creek the army remained in camp three days. The men were drilled in the use of the gun and sword. Their arms were inspected and put in repair. Lyman Wight was made second in command, with the title of "Fighting General." Smith and Wight each had an "Armor-Bearer," who was expected to be in constant attendance on his chief. Two companies of rangers or sharpshooters were organized, who were to act as scouts or flankers when they should arrive upon the field of battle. Hyrum Smith was given charge of the battle-flag, which he kept constantly unfurled.

The march toward Missouri was resumed, and at the end of several days a halt was taken, and the soldiers ordered to go through a sham battle, in order to learn more fully the art of war before engaging the enemy. Four divisions were formed, and assigned to positions. The battle opened on true scientific principles, but as the men came to close quarters they began to do their work on a personal plan, and each fought as was the bent of his mind and his previous training. Some got behind trees, and fought Indian fashion. Some ran away. Some dropped their guns, and went back to the natural fist. Some noses were tapped, and one or two men wounded, while a number of guns and swords were broken. Smith warmly complimented his men on their courage and skill, and everybody was full of happiness and pride.

The Mississippi was reached, and here some of the enemy came in sight. They were certain people of Missouri who wanted no more Mormonism over there. But Smith determined to push ahead. As the river was a mile and a half wide, and the army possessed of one ferryboat, it took two days to get everybody across. Once over, the army was placed on a war footing; scouts on horseback kept a lookout several miles in advance. Smith, who knew how to take care of himself as well as any man alive, dressed in disguise, changing his disguises frequently, riding a great deal of the time in the baggage-wagons, and, as one of the men has since said, "looking as though he expected every moment to be his last." One night they approached a large prairie, on which could be seen no sign of a habitation. Smith insisted that they must move on, or the enemy would attack them where they were. Wight refused to enter the prairie, as the men were tired, and no water or wood could be found for miles ahead. "Well," said Smith, "if we can cook nothing, I will show the men how to eat raw pork."

"I will not go ahead," said Wight.

"We must go on," said Hyrum Smith, the standard-bearer. "I know by the spirit that it is dangerous to remain here."

"But I will not go on," said Wight. "This is the place where we should remain."

Finally Joseph fell back on his weapon of last resort. He had a revelation, and exclaimed: "Thus saith the Lord God, march on!" And on they marched.

They tramped for fifteen miles, which brought them near the middle of the prairie, and encamped beside a muddy pool. Here the squabble broke out afresh, and Smith became especially arrogant. He declared: "I know exactly when to pray, when to sing, and when to laugh, by the Spirit of God."

Wight and his supporters retorted, and before morning broke there was serious danger of mutiny in the camp.

Smith, as another safeguard to his person, kept an ugly bulldog that was especially cross at night, and had attempted to bite a number of people. One of the captains, who was also high-priest, said to Smith: "If that dog ever attempts to bite me, I will shoot him on the instant."

"If you continue in that spirit," was the retort, "and do not repent, the dog will yet eat your flesh off your bones, and you will not have power to resist." * Whether or not the man repented, the fulfillment of the prophecy was made impossible a few nights later, when a sentinel to whom the dog was too attentive, ended its career forever.

On June 3d the Prophet, who may have had information not open to his followers, of a new danger ahead, mounted a wagon, and calling his men about him, declared that he would deliver a prophecy. After an exhortation to faithfulness and humility, he said that the Lord had revealed to him the coming of a scourge upon the camp, "in consequence of the fractious and unruly spirits" that had appeared among them.

This warning was made good a few days later, when the cholera appeared in the camp with such virulence that thirteen men died before its ravages were stayed. Smith remained in camp through it all, and did what lay in his power to relieve suffering and make the visitation add to the hold he already had upon his followers. He made attempts at cure by "the laying on of hands and prayer," but as no miracle was wrought in response, he abandoned the effort, declaring that he had learned "by painful experience" that "when the Great Jehovah decrees

---

* "This was the commencement of a controversy between the Prophet and his High-Priest which was not settled till some time after their return to headquarters, at Kirtland, when the former underwent a formal trial on divers serious charges, before his priests, honorably acquitted, and the latter made to acknowledge that he had been possessed of several devils for many weeks." From the above account, "Mormonism and the Mormons," p. 115.

destruction, man must not attempt to stay His hand."

When the advance onward was resumed Smith discovered that exciting times and uncertain results awaited him if he persisted until a collision with armed enemies was precipitated, and that an overpowering force could be raised against him. Many of those who followed him were full of faith that a miracle would be wrought to give them victory in all cases, but Smith had reason for grave doubts upon that point. He soon came to the conclusion that a diplomatic retrogression from his high ground of defiance was needed to help him out of the position he had assumed.

When within a few miles of Liberty, Clay County, a deputation from the body of citizens who had already collected called on Smith and asked him the meaning of his warlike array. On his response, they very decidedly warned him that any overt act on his part would get himself and his followers into trouble. They showed him that the people of several counties were acting in concert, and that the consequences of any action on the part of his followers would be upon his own head.

The Prophet saw that the time had come to fight or back down, and that the former course would give him more risk and danger than he had bargained for. But another course would lay him open to the charge from his followers that he had disobeyed the heavenly orders under which they had come forth. He found a way out of the dilemma. He had an "annex" to his first revelation, soon after the deputation left, which declared that they "had been tried even as

Abraham was tried, and the offering was accepted by the Lord; and when Abraham received his reward they would receive theirs." In short, the war was at an end, and the promise of spoliation of their enemies was postponed until such time as the case of Abraham was taken up for consideration. The army of Zion, as Joseph had called his troops, was disbanded.* Such as could get home and wished to, departed for the East, but the main body remained and became afterward a part of Nauvoo. Each received a formal discharge from General Wight, and that was all he did receive from Smith or any one else. Not a cent of the money that had been given the Prophet as treasurer ever saw its way back to the pockets of the men who gave it.

Smith and his soldiers had been warmly received by the homeless refugees in Clay County, and the supplies of food and clothing they had brought were doubly welcome. The Prophet and his lieutenants went to work with vigor, and soon established the discouraged and chaotic community upon a new basis, and gave courage and hope where only fear and despair had before existed. On July 9th, Joseph started upon his return trip to Kirtland, reaching home on August 2d.

* Brigham Young never lost sight of his old companions-in-arms in this bloodless foray. Years afterward, at the close of each Mormon conference in Salt Lake City, he would call together the remnants of "Zion's army," with their families, and entertain them with a feast; speeches, songs, and "campfire" memories served to enliven the occasion.

IX.

FAR WEST AND NAUVOO.

THE exiles who had been so relentlessly driven across the Missouri into Clay County, were for a time allowed to rest in peace, and make some attempt to repair their broken fortunes. But the causes that had led to their persecution upon one side of the river, were soon at work upon the other, although no overt act against them occurred until in June, 1836, when they were formally requested by the residents of Clay to move still further on. The demands and replies were similar in purpose and temper to those already heard in Jackson County, and the final result was of a like character. Disposing of their possessions at such figures as they could command, the wanderers once more turned their faces toward the north, and in the semi-wilderness that afterward became Caldwell County, founded the town of Far West.

While the hostility of their old enemies was by no means appeased, nor the popular fear of Mormon designs removed, a season of comparative quiet ensued, in which their settlement grew in size and business, until at one time its population reached into the thousands. Log and frame houses were erected, as if by magic, shops and factories built, and schools opened. An air of thrift and a spirit of industry were everywhere apparent. It was in this young and energetic community that Smith and Rigdon found welcome and safety at the termination of their hurried flight from Kirtland, in January, 1838.

The Prophet had saved from the Kirtland wreck his dream of a great city, and almost immediately ordered such measures as would create in Far West that which had proved impossible in Ohio. A map was constructed after the Kirtland plan, surveys made, and in the centre of the proposed town a grand square laid out, upon which a second temple was to be erected.

Work upon the building was commenced in the summer of 1838, and ceremonies of consecration performed on July 4th. The structure was carried forward, until the walls were two feet high, when the storm of persecution and anger once more broke forth, and the third temple dream of Joseph came to an untimely end.*

Smith was as active in the new home as he had been in the old. In April he published a revelation commanding the Saints in the East to join their brethren in the West. On May 18th he directed the founding of a new city, several miles from Far West, to be called Adam-Ondi-Ahman, or " The Valley of

---

* " All that remains of this temple to-day is a depression in the earth three or four feet deep, the size of the original excavation, and some fragments of crumbling walls. Only one building remains in the city, said by some of the older settlers to have been occupied by Smith and his first wife. It is on a slight eminence, of log and frame, one and a half stories high, contains four rooms, has a large fire-place, and chimney of rude home-made bricks. It is now occupied as a farm-house. Two or three of the buildings of Far West were hauled to Kingston after they were abandoned by the Mormons, and are still in use there as shops and dwellings."—Judge William A. Wood, in *Magazine of American History*, July, 1886.

God, in which Adam placed his children." * Among
the commands issued in rapid succession was one re-
quiring the Saints to give the surplus of their property for the construction of a temple, for the founding of Zion, for the support of the clergy, and for the
payment of the debts of the presidency; another establishing a permanent ten per cent. income tax;
and still another prohibiting the sale of spirituous
liquors in Far West.

Yet the course of authority here, as in Ohio, was
full of thorns for the Prophet's feet. Internal dissensions that struck at the very root of Smith's
power, had found their way into the church at Far
West. None but extreme measures were possible
on his part, and he proved himself equal to the emergency. Oliver Cowdery and Martin Harris were cut
off from the church, while Orson Hyde and others †

---

* Extract from "Mormonism Unveiled; or, The Life and Confessions of the late Mormon Bishop, John D. Lee," page 91:
"Adam-on-Diamond (the popular pronunciation of the word) was at
the point where Adam came and settled and blest his posterity,
after being driven from the Garden of Eden. This was revealed to
the people through Joseph Smith, the Prophet. The temple-block,
in Jackson County, Missouri, stands on the identical spot where
once stood the Garden of Eden. When Adam and Eve were driven
from the Garden, they travelled in a northwesterly course until
they came to a valley on the east side of Grand River. There they
tarried for several years, and engaged in tilling the soil. . . . . On
the top of this range of hills Adam erected an altar of stone, on
which he offered sacrifice unto the Lord. There was at that time
(in 1838) a pile of stones there, which the Prophet said was a portion of the altar on which Adam offered sacrifice. Although these
stones had been exposed to the elements for many generations of
time, still the traces remained to show the dimensions and design
of the altar."

† In the concluding pages of the original edition of the Book of

apostatized and used their influence to fan into new flame the hatred and suspicious fear already smouldering in Gentile breasts. Thomas B. Marsh, no less

Mormon may be found the certificate of three men,—Oliver Cowdery, David Whitmer, and Martin Harris,—who made express declaration that they had seen the plates from which the book had been translated: "And we declare with words of soberness that an angel of God came down from heaven, and he brought and laid before our eyes, that we beheld and saw the plates, and the engravings thereon," with more to the same effect. Following this is another certificate of the same character, signed by eight witnesses, among whom were John Whitmer, Joseph Smith, Sr., and Hyrum Smith. The fate of the three first named in their connection with Mormonism is remarkable. All left the church at about the period of trouble above described. Oliver Cowdery went to Richmond, Ray County, Missouri, where he died on March 3, 1850. He never repudiated the Mormon faith as originally adopted and practiced, but, on the contrary, defended it on his death-bed. Trouble occurred between Smith and himself, as early as 1837, caused, according to the declarations of the latter, by the Prophet's selfish disposition and desire to gain the possessions of others. David Whitmer decided, in 1838, to cut loose from the church, having no liking for the course things were then taking, and proceeded also to Richmond, which he made his home, and where he died on January 25, 1888. He was a useful and respected member of the community, and a faithful believer in Mormonism to the end, declaring during the last few hours of his life, "I want to say to you all, the Bible and the record of the Nephites (the Book of Mormon) *is true*, so you can say that you have heard me bear my testimony on my death-bed." Whitmer always claimed to have the original manuscript of the Book of Mormon in his possession, refusing all offers made for it by the Salt Lake Mormons—whose claims and practices he repudiated. The third of the three, Martin Harris, had made repeated efforts to gain advancement in the church, but Smith had no further need of him now that his money was gone, and finally answered his demands and threats by expelling him from the church. He was afterward offered a restoration, which he declined, although still holding to his faith in Mormonism. He deserved far better treatment than he received. With property and

a personage than the President of the Twelve Apostles, also seceded, and united with others in publicly charging Smith and the Mormons with many crimes and misdemeanors—treason against the State, conspiracy with the Indians, counterfeiting, cattle stealing, immorality, and other offences of less degree.

While the Mormons would have been justified in attempting such defense as was possible to these charges, they did not content themselves with the exercise of that right, but repeated the mistakes that had been the main cause of their troubles in Jackson County. Their boldness grew with their numbers, and their defiance increased with their prosperity. Their arrogant claims of spiritual superiority, and confession of a purpose to ultimately possess all that land, stirred up the old enmity, which was by no means allayed when Sidney Rigdon, on July 4th of this year of trouble, preached a sermon that was full of vengeance and death, not only to the Gentiles, but to all who dissented from the doctrine of fire and the sword that he enunciated. Brigham Young, in speaking of this episode in after-years, said:[*] " Elder Rigdon was the prime cause of our troubles in Missouri, by his Fourth of July oration"; while another Mormon [†] referred to it as " a flaming speech, which had

reputation gone, the wife of his youth forever sundered from him, and faith in those about him shattered, he returned to Ohio, and lived in Painesville, where, as rumor declares, he was sought out by an agent of Brigham Young, who gave him money with which to go to Utah, where he ended his days in peace. He died at Clarkston, Cache County, Utah, on July 10, 1875, at the age of ninety-three.

[*] " Times and Seasons," vol. v., p. 667.
[†] The apostle Woodruff. " Times and Seasons," p. 698.

a tendency to bring persecution upon the whole church, especially the head of it." The text was from Matthew v. 13: "If the salt have lost its savor, wherewith shall it be salted? It is thenceforth good for nothing, but to be cast out and to be trodden under foot of men."

The significant passage in this address—which has passed into history as "Sidney's Salt Sermon"—was as follows:

"We take God and all the holy angels to witness this day that we warn all men, in the name of Jesus Christ, to come on us no more forever. The man, or the set of men, who attempts it, does so at the expense of their lives; and the mob that comes on to disturb us, it shall be between us and them a war of extermination, for we will follow them till the last drop of blood is spilled, or else they will have to exterminate us; for we will carry the seat of war to their own houses and their own families, and one part or the other shall be utterly destroyed. Remember it then, all men!"

The exasperation caused by this impolitic outburst; political contests in which the Mormons took a vigorous part, and sowed the seed of new and fruitful enmities; quarrels among individuals of the opposing factions; collisions of armed Mormons and Missourians equally well armed, in which life was lost and property destroyed; the calling out of the State militia—these events followed each other in rapid succession.* That deep blame lay upon both sides is a conclusion easily proved by the facts; but a relation of all that occurred during these direful days of Far

* Appendix C.

West, would be a profitless task, and, in the main, foreign to the purpose of this sketch.

The one important result of it all was the arrest, on October 31st, of Joseph Smith, Lyman Wight, Hyrum Smith, Sidney Rigdon, Parley P. Pratt, and a number of Mormons of lesser degree, who were taken to Independence, and afterward to Richmond, where they were lodged in jail upon various charges, among which were treason against the State, and murder—men having been killed in a number of the collisions between the Mormons and the troops.* The lack of any substantial grounds upon which a conviction could be had, is clearly shown in the course now pursued by the authorities, as Smith would have been brought to a speedy trial, and punished to the full extent of the law, if it could have been done without committing an outrage upon justice. The prisoners were held in Richmond till April, 1839, when they were indicted upon the charges of treason, murder, theft, and arson. They asked for a change of venue to Marion County. The request was granted, but Boone rather than Marion designated.

---

* "Document containing the Correspondence, Orders, etc., in relation to the Disturbances with the Mormons; and the Evidence given before the Hon. Austin A. King, Judge of the Fifth Judicial Circuit of the State of Missouri, at the Court-house in Richmond, in a Criminal Court of Inquiry, begun November 12, 1838, on the trial of Joseph Smith, Jr., and others, for High Treason and other crimes against the State. Published by order of the General Assembly. Printed at the office of the Boon's Lick Democrat, Fayette, Missouri, 1841." Page 97: "State vs. Joseph Smith, Jr., Hiram Smith, Sidney Rigdon, Parley P. Pratt, Lyman Wight, [and forty-eight others] who were charged with the several crimes of high treason against the State, murder, burglary, arson, robbery, and larceny."

As they were being conveyed to the seat of Boone County, the sheriff solved a vexatious problem for the authorities by allowing the prisoners to make their escape. As the main body of the Mormons had now left the State, public feeling was so far allayed, that the departure of Smith and his companions caused little excitement and no general protest.*

While Joseph and Hyrum were being carried away by the officers of the law, and ruin and death threatened from every side, the Mormons naturally turned for help and leadership to Brigham Young. His cool head, sound judgment, and steady nerves were of far more practical benefit at this crisis of affairs than all the revelations of Smith, or the eloquence of Rigdon or Pratt. To remain in Missouri was impossible. A deliberate plan of extermination had been announced

---

* From "Document" above quoted, page 157: "A change of venue was granted by our said court at said April term, to Jos. Smith, Jr., Lyman Wight, Hiram Smith, Caleb Baldwin, and Alex. McRay, in all the foregoing cases in which they are parties, to the circuit court of Boone County, in this State, the last named defendents being in the custody of the Sheriff of Daviess County, who was commanded by our said court to convey the said defendents to the jail of said county of Boone, and the said Sheriff returned the several orders of commitment into our said court, at the next ensuing term thereof, with a certificate of the escape of the said Joseph Smith, Jr., Lyman Wight, Hiram Smith, Caleb Baldwin, and Alex. McRay endorsed thereon. And writs of capias were issued against all the other defendents in the foregoing indictments, immediately after the finding of the same, and they were all returned at the next succeeding term of our said court without any service, none of the aforesaid defendents being found in the county of Daviess, and the said causes were all continued until the next succeeding December term, 1839, at which time a nolle prosequi was entered in each of the above causes, except those in which a change of venue, as aforesaid, were taken."

by so high an authority as the Governor of the State, and all classes of citizens had shown by their works * a grim purpose of carrying that policy into effect. Young rallied about him such men as could act as well as advise, and a speedy and permanent departure from the inhospitable soil of Missouri was agreed upon. An asylum had been offered by the people of Quincy, Illinois, and that point was selected as the haven toward which the church should direct itself. The burden of travel was once more resumed, and forsaking their homes at Far West, as they had those in Clay County and in Zion, the faithful band journeyed across Eastern Missouri, put the broad Mississippi between themselves and their old enemies, and with such courage and hope as their faith could give, began the building of a new habitation in a new land.

Young had been compelled to flee for his life from Far West, in February, and proceeding to Quincy, where the majority had preceded him, worked day and night to restore order, inspire confidence, and relieve distress. The condition of the exiles was pitiable in the extreme. Their property had been de-

* On October 27, 1838, Governor L. W. Boggs, in an order to General Clark, who had charge of the State troops operating in Caldwell County and vicinity, used these words : " The Mormons must be treated as enemies, and must be exterminated, or driven from the State, if necessary for the public peace—their outrages are beyond all description." Above "Documents," page 61. General Clark, in an address delivered to the Mormons at Far West, on November 6th, made use of the following remarkable language : " The Governor has commanded me to exterminate you, and not to permit you to remain in the State ; and had you not delivered up your leaders, and executed the conditions of our treaty, you would have been massacred, you yourselves, and your families ; and your houses would have been reduced to ashes."

stroyed or confiscated, and the land they had reclaimed and improved in Caldwell County, became a total loss.

Smith was permitted to again meet with his driven and disheartened followers at their temporary refuge in Quincy, on April 26, 1839. He was welcomed as one given back from the grave, and hope and courage made their appearance in his company. With the Prophet of the Lord once more among them, the devout were persuaded that Heaven's favor was not altogether withdrawn, and that at last the long-delayed promises were to be fulfilled.

For a few succeeding years of wonderful growth and prosperity it indeed seemed as if that belief had its foundation upon a sure resting-place. In Nauvoo, "the place beautiful," that soon arose as by magic, and was filled with thrift and the works thereof, the dream of a great city seemed sure of realization; and for a time there fell upon it no shadow of the tragedy and ruin in which it should end. The inner history of this strangely created and ill-fated town, if written with reference to all that was accomplished or attempted within it, would touch upon the borders of romance. Much of that history the world will never know, as it was buried in the graves of the chief actors therein.

There was need of resolution and prompt action upon the part of the Mormon leaders, if they would hold their following together, and prevent the breaking up of the church under misfortunes that might well have shaken the boldest, and unsettled the faith of the most devout. That need was fully supplied. Immediate preparations were carried forward for the founding of yet another Mormon capital. After various proffered sites had been examined, a selection was made in a bend of the Mississippi River, in Hancock County, some sixty miles above Quincy. The situation was one of natural beauty and advantage, the soil fertile, and adapted to the growth of various products, with the prairie stretching away as far as the eye could reach. The ground was undulating, and the point chosen as the immediate site of the city was bounded upon three sides by the river. A small settlement called Commerce, containing only a few rude houses, had already been commenced upon it.

On May 1st, a purchase was made by Smith, in behalf of the Mormon Church, of a tract of land, for which he paid fourteen thousand dollars. The groundwork of the city was speedily laid out, the name Commerce giving place to Nauvoo—a word furnished by Smith, who explained its meaning as "A beautiful site," conveying, at the same time, the idea of repose. The persecution by the Missourians had one result by no means intended—sympathy for the Mormons had been excited through the North and East, their missionaries were given hearings that would otherwise have been denied, and many pilgrims were soon wending their way toward Nauvoo. So rapid was the city's advance that by June, 1840, it contained two hundred and fifty buildings, with many more in course of construction. The wisdom displayed in the choice of its location was made still further apparent when the builders found a few feet below the surface a vast bed of limestone suitable for their purpose, so that all the needed material of that character was quarried within the limits of the city itself. Within a short period, steam saw-mills, a steam flour-mill, a tool-factory, foundry, and a manufactory for chinaware, were in busy operation. A steamboat owned by the Mormons made its appearance upon the Mississippi, giving means of transportation from Nauvoo to points above and below. Many of the dwelling-houses were small, and of wood, with more imposing structures scattered here and there among them. The plan of the city was similar to that proposed at Kirtland, and afterward at Far West, with wide streets crossing each other at right angles. The dimensions of Nauvoo were four miles by three in its widest measurements, narrowing as it approached the river.

Smith learned wisdom with age and experience, and the freedom with which revelations were issued in the early days, was cautiously restricted in these times of enlarged responsibility and world-wide attention. The decrees of Heaven, as sent through Joseph, were restricted to measures of importance, and issued only when some work of moment was in contemplation, some rebellious or doubting Mormon to be persuaded, or an especial favor granted or promised. One of the most important messages of which the Prophet was ever unburdened, was issued on January 19, 1841, when Nauvoo had gained a fair start in a prosperous career, and was giving promise of the more important things yet to come. It was a revelation of general direction and blessing, confirming some things already done, directing the beginnings of others, promising rewards to certain men whose faith may have needed stimulation, and speaking with grim meaning to such as had openly rebelled.

Beginning with the assuring annunciation that Joseph Smith, Sr., the first Patriarch of the church, whose earthly race had now been run, was sitting in honor at Abraham's right hand, the revelation proceeded directly to the consideration of material things by commanding the immediate erection of a hotel. The structure was to be "such an one as my servant Joseph shall show to them; upon the place which he shall show unto them also. And it shall be a house for boarding, a house that strangers may come from afar to lodge therein." The orders as to the manner of construction and finances were explicit, and left little to the officials of the church except obedience— a prime virtue of Mormonism from the days of Palmyra to those of Salt Lake. "And now I say unto you, as pertaining to my boarding-house which I have commanded you to build for the boarding of strangers, let it be built unto my name, and let my name be named upon it, and let my servant Joseph and his house have place therein from generation to generation." This advantageous provision for his family and himself was by no means left dependent by the Prophet upon the love and faith of his followers, but made a good claim in law—it being distinctly stated in the charter under which the building was erected, that as Smith had furnished the land upon which the house was to be built, a suite of rooms in said house should be set aside by the trustees for his use.*

* From "An Act to incorporate the Nauvoo House Association," approved by the Illinois General Assembly, February 23, 1841 : "Section 10. And whereas Joseph Smith has furnished the said association with the ground whereon to erect said house, it is further declared, that the said Smith and his heirs shall hold by perpetual succession a suite of rooms in the said house, to be set

Express directions were given in the revelation that George Miller, Lyman Wight, John Snider, and Peter Haws should form a society and receive stock subscriptions; no one man to subscribe less than fifty dollars nor over fifteen thousand, and no one to be accepted unless he paid cash down. Nor was any one to be enrolled among the stockholders who was not a member of the Mormon Church. Special orders were given Vinson Knight, William Marks, William Law, and others, that they should subscribe according to their means.

The command was also given—now for the fourth time,—that a temple should be erected. That at Kirtland had been already sold under the sheriff's hammer, and was in the hands of the enemy. The foundation commenced with such flourish of promises and outpouring of prophecies at Zion was weed-grown and forgotten. A heap of rubbish marked the site at Far West. A new plea and promise found incorporation in this fourth command—that a dedicated temple should be erected in which might be performed baptism for the dead.* The directions in this case were as minute as in the others, and Smith's orders were to be followed in everything: " And I will show unto my servant Joseph all things pertaining unto

apart and conveyed in due form of law to him and his heirs by said trustees, as soon as the same are completed."

* This seems to have been an ingenious device for hastening the building's erection. The new doctrine announced that the living might be baptized for the salvation of the dead who had died out of Mormonism But as this could be done only in a consecrated temple, one can see how great a leverage was secured for labor upon the ignorant, who would gladly give of their means to release their friends from torment.

this house, and the priesthood thereof; and the place whereon it shall be built."

The revelation having thus disposed of the building question, proceeded to promote Hyrum Smith to the position of Patriarch, left vacant by his father's death; warned Sidney Rigdon to humble himself, to become counsellor to Joseph, and renounce his purpose of removing his family to the East; declared that if Robert D. Foster "will obey my voice" he must "build a house for my servant Joseph according to the contract which he has made with him"—a neat stroke of diplomacy on the part of Smith that probably saved him the expense of a lawsuit; and proceeded to the appointment of a large company of apostles, high-priests, and missionaries. In this wholesale apportionment of honors Brigham Young was made President of the Twelve Apostles, in place of Thomas B. Marsh, who had renounced Mormonism and become one of its bitterest foes.

That portion of the "Book of Doctrines and Covenants" of the Mormon Church which belongs to Nauvoo, contains but a few recorded revelations that can be traced with certainty to Smith. In March of the year last named he uttered one which ordered the Saints in Iowa to build a city upon the river bank across from Nauvoo to be christened "Zarahemla." In July one was published which declared that Brigham Young need travel abroad no more, that he had well earned a rest, and should henceforth "stay at home and take care of his family." One more, and only one, of these unique utterances will we quote—that delivered a short period before his death, in which he gave the following formula for distinguishing a good angel from a bad: "When a messenger comes, saying he has a message from God, offer him your hand, and request him to shake hands with you.

"If he be an angel, he will do so, and you will feel his hand. .... If it be the Devil as an angel of light, when you ask him to shake hands, he will offer you his hand, and you will not feel anything: You may therefore detect him."

As has been remarked in an earlier portion of this work, Smith was a natural adept in politics, and now that he had control of the votes of at least three thousand men [*] he was not slow to turn that power to the use of the church and himself. Even in 1840 his influence had reached a point where he could not be safely ignored by the political parties in any event, and certainly not in a close election. An illustration of that point is clearly given in Nicolay and Hay's "Life of Lincoln," where we find this statement: "In the same letter (to Congressman Stuart, in March, 1840) Mr. Lincoln gives a long list of names to which he wants documents to be sent. It shows a remarkable personal acquaintance with the minutest needs of the canvass: This one is a doubtful Whig; that one is an inquiring Democrat; that other a zealous young fellow who would be pleased by the attention; three brothers are mentioned who 'fell out with us about Early and are doubtful now'; and finally he tells Stuart that Joe Smith is an admirer of his, and that a few documents had better be mailed to the Mormons."

The Mormon power in the local elections of Han-

[*] At one election in Nauvoo only six votes were cast in opposition to Smith's wishes.

cock County was absolute, and the Congressional district of which Nauvoo was a part may well be placed in the same category. By the coming election it might be left to Smith to give the final vote in the choice of a Governor of the State. The influence which he would thus wield is well described by J. H. Beadle, in his admirable work: *

"For the first time since its organization, the Whig party had a fair prospect of carrying the State and the nation, but Illinois was doubtful. If Henry Clay should again be the nominee of the Whigs, Kentucky, Louisiana, and other Southern States were considered certain for that party, and in certain very probable contingencies, Illinois would turn the scale one way or the other. It was quite certain the Mormons would, by 1844, give the casting vote in Illinois, and Joe Smith had perfect control of the Mormon vote. . . . . The Harrison campaign of 1840 was in full tide, and the politicians gathered thick around Joe Smith."

The Mormon leader shrewdly made sure of his reward before committal to either side. After secret consultations with prominent party leaders, and a conference with his advisers at Nauvoo, he was delivered of a revelation directing that the church should support the Whig ticket, which was elected. In payment for this service the Whigs in the Illinois Legislature made haste to grant the Mormons a special charter for their new city, in which were conveyed powers to an almost unlimited extent. The Mormons dictated the provisions of that remarkable document, and at a church conference, Smith, Doctor J.

* "Life in Utah." By J. H. Beadle, Philadelphia, 1870, p. 68.

C. Bennett, and R. B. Thompson were directed to prepare a charter which should fulfill their purposes, and place the whole city government absolutely in Mormon control. They did so, and Bennett was deputized to proceed to Springfield, and see it safely through the Legislature. He found his task one of uncommon ease, neither Democrat nor Whig caring to oppose his desire, lest the Mormon vote should be driven over to the other side to permanently remain.

When the desired charter was reported to the Assembly by the judiciary committee which had it in charge, with a recommendation for its passage, the party leaders crowded upon each other in their haste to vote in the affirmative. Not a dissenting vote was cast; and in that one act the Legislature of Illinois did more to foster a spirit of ambition and arrogance on the part of the Mormon leaders, and to hasten and intensify the bitter quarrels already upon their way, than was ever done by any act of Joseph Smith, or the bloodiest outrage by any Mormon or Missourian in the dark days of Independence and Far West. The politician saw only the small advantage of the day, and gave no thought of the evil seed he was sowing, to be garnered in the blood and disorder of the future.

The charter for Nauvoo was passed on December 16, 1840. It conferred almost unlimited powers, the language employed being as follows: " The City Council shall have power and authority to make, ordain, establish, and execute, all such ordinances, *not repugnant to the Constitution of the United States or of this State*, as they may deem necessary for the peace, benefit, good order, regulation, convenience, and cleanliness of said city." So wide was this grant of power, that the Mormons, at one time, felt justified in the claim that under it they could pass laws in opposition to those of Illinois! The officials allowed were a mayor, a vice-mayor, four aldermen, and nine councillors. A municipal court was organized, with the mayor as chief-justice, and four aldermen as his associates. This strangely-constituted and highly-centralized judicial body could not only issue writs of habeas corpus, but could try the sufficiency of those issued by other courts, and even go on and try the original cause of action—an arrangement by which Smith and his followers more than once profited.

The Mormons were not slow to make use of this plenitude of power, and eventually went so far as to establish a recorder's office at Nauvoo, in which alone could transfers of land be recorded; and also an office for the issuing of marriage licenses — a direct ignoring of the rights and perquisites of the county in which Nauvoo was situated. The municipal council at one time proceeded so far along the line of audacity as to petition Congress to set the city aside as a territory until Missouri should make good the losses she had caused the Mormons to suffer; and that the mayor of the city be given the power to call in and use the United States troops whenever he should feel the need of protection for himself or his followers.

Governor Ford refers to that remarkable document in the following words: *

"The powers conferred were expressed in language at once ambiguous and undefined, as if on purpose to

* "History of Illinois," p. 265.

allow of misconstruction. The great law of the separation of the powers of government was wholly disregarded. The mayor was at once the executive power, the judiciary, and part of the Legislature. The common council, in passing ordinances, were restrained only by the Constitution. One would have thought that these charters (the city, the Legion, and the Nauvoo house) stood a poor chance of passing the legislature of a republican people, jealous of their liberties. Nevertheless, they did pass unanimously through both houses. Messrs. Little and Douglas managed with great dexterity with their respective parties. Each party was afraid to object to them, for fear of losing the Mormon vote, and each believed that it had secured their favor.

"A city government under the charter was organized in 1841, and Joe Smith was elected mayor.* In this capacity he presided in the common council, and assisted in making the laws for the government of the city, and as mayor, also, he was to see these laws put into force. He was *ex officio* judge of the mayor's court, and chief-justice of the municipal court, and in these capacities he was to interpret the laws which he had assisted to make. The Nauvoo Legion was also organized, with a great multitude of high officers. It was divided into di-

* From this, the conclusion would be reached that Smith was elected first mayor of Nauvoo, which was not the case. The charter was passed in December, 1840, and on February 1, 1841, John C. Bennett was elected to that office, and received a commission as justice of the peace from Governor Carlin, in which was the following reference to that fact: "Know ye, that John C. Bennett, having been duly elected to the office of mayor of the city of Nauvoo, in the county of Hancock, I, Thomas Carlin," etc., as above related.

visions, brigades, cohorts, regiments, battalions, and companies. Each division, brigade, and cohort had its general, and over the whole, as commander-in-chief, Joe Smith was appointed lieutenant-general. . . . . Thus, it was proposed to re-establish for the Mormons a government within a government; a legislature, with power to pass ordinances at war with the laws of the State; courts to execute them, with but little dependence upon the constitutional judiciary; and a military force at their own command, to be governed by its own laws and ordinances, and subject to no State authority but that of the Governor."

X.

AT THE HIGH-TIDE OF POWER.

THE city government of Nauvoo was promptly organized, and among the chosen officials we find many leaders in the old Kirtland days. John C. Bennett,* an Ohio physician, who had removed to Illinois, became quartermaster-general of the State; and then joined the Mormons, and was elected mayor, with Joseph Smith in the position of vice-mayor.

---

* This remarkable person seems to have captivated the Mormons by his ability and address, and was rapidly advanced from one position of authority to another. In the same month that saw his elevation to the chief municipal office of the city, he was made major-general of the Nauvoo Legion, second only in command to Smith; was soon afterward elected chancellor of the Nauvoo University; and during the illness of Sidney Rigdon became a temporary member of the First Presidency. He also held the office of Master in Chancery for Hancock County, under personal appointment from no less a person than Judge Stephen A. Douglas. He afterward forsook the church, declaring that he had only joined it for the purpose of discovering its secrets, and exposing them, and became one of Smith's most determined and outspoken enemies. Governor Ford's opinion of the first mayor of Nauvoo is expressed with considerable frankness: " This Bennett was probably the greatest scamp in the Western country. I have made particular inquiries concerning him, and have traced him in several places, in which he has lived before he had joined the Mormons— in Ohio, Indiana, and Illinois—and he was everywhere accounted the same debauched, unprincipled, and profligate character. He was a man of some little talent, and had the confidence of the Mormons, and particularly that of their leaders."—" History of Illinois," p. 263.

In addition to the charter for the city, the Legislature also granted one for the formation of the Nauvoo Legion; another for the incorporation of the Nauvoo Agricultural and Manufacturing Association, with a capital stock of one hundred thousand dollars —its object being the promotion of agriculture and the manufacture of flour, lumber, etc.; and still another for the building of the Nauvoo House, with a capital stock of one hundred and fifty thousand dollars.

The city government was soon busy with matters of internal policy, and no lack of energy was displayed in meeting all questions as they arose, and disposing of them in accordance with what seemed to be for the best interests of the city and the church. Among the first measures acted upon was the creation of the University of Nauvoo, in which the children of the Saints were to be given an education that should ground them well in the Mormon faith. Another of the early steps taken was the passage of an ordinance to prevent the sale of whiskey in amounts less than one gallon, or of other spirits less than one quart—a step considered in those days as a long advance toward prohibition of the liquor traffic.

The Nauvoo Legion, to which incidental reference has been already made, occupied an unique position, forming upon one hand a part of the general militia of the State, and serving upon the other as a military police force under the direct control of the municipal officers of Nauvoo—in other words, the church. The formation of the Legion in the manner described was a part of the ill-advised and unseemly bid for Mormon support made by the politicians of Illinois, and proved no small factor in arousing the fear and jealousy with which the Gentile portion of Hancock County had already come to regard their neighbors at Nauvoo. These troops were under control of no State officer except the Governor himself, which in fact took it out of the militia except in name. The courts martial of the Legion were to be formed altogether of its own officers. It was composed of divisions, brigades, and regiments, and was in fact a Mormon army concealed in the guise of State troops, and yet so illy hidden that the enemies of the church could well persuade their hearers that it was a perpetual insult and menace to the people and boded no good for the peace and prosperity of Illinois. The stories of intended Mormon aggressions were revived, and the Legion with its showy uniform, good equipment, and boastful parades, was cited as proof of the darkest and deepest plots to which imagination could give creation.

Suggestions of this character found their way into public print, and gained general belief. An " officer of the United States army "[*] who claimed to have visited Nauvoo in its palmy days thus describes a parade of the Legion, which he witnessed:

"Yesterday was a great day among the Mormons. Their Legion, to the number of two thousand men, was paraded by Generals Smith, Bennett, and others,

[*] This letter was published in the New York *Herald*, under date of "City of Nauvoo, Illinois, May 8, 1842," and was signed "An Officer of the U. S. Artillery." As it was largely devoted to the praise of "Major General Bennett," and the service he was doing the Mormons by abiding with them, I suspect the pen of none other than Bennett himself. It is given in full (on page 155) in Bennett's anti-Mormon book, referred to hereafter.

and certainly made a very noble and imposing appearance. The evolutions of the troops directed by Major-General Bennett would do honor to any body of armed militia in any of the States, and approximates very closely to our regular forces. What does all this mean? Why this exact discipline of the Mormon Corps? Do they intend to conquer Missouri, Illinois, Mexico? It is true they are a part of the militia of the State of Illinois by the charter of their Legion; but then there are no troops in the States like them in point of enthusiasm and warlike aspect, yea, warlike character. . . . . They have appointed Captain Bennett, late of the Army of the United States, Inspector-General of their Legion, and he is commissioned as such by Governor Carlin. This gentleman is known to be well skilled in fortification, gunnery, ordnance, castramentation, and military engineering generally, and I am assured that he is now under pay derived from the tithings of this warlike people. I have seen his plans for fortifying Nauvoo, which are equal to any of Vauban's."

That the Mormon leaders had some purpose of their own in all this preparation, or at least desired their followers to believe they had, is vouched for on eminent Mormon authority. Bishop John D. Lee,[*] who was executed in Utah on March 23, 1877, for the Mountain Meadows Massacre, wrote a history of his life while in jail, in which he says: "At the conference in April, 1840, the Prophet delivered a lengthy address upon the history and condition of the Saints. . . . . 'When the right time comes, we will go in force and take the whole State of Missouri. It be-

[*] "Mormonism Unveiled." By John D. Lee, p. 110.

longs to us as our inheritance.' .... The people were regularly drilled and taught military tactics, so that they would be ready to act when *the time* came for returning to Jackson County, the promised land of our inheritance."

The year 1841 was one of hard labor blessed with abundant prosperity for the church, and all its plans and undertakings seemed to thrive. The command for the erection of a temple had been cheerfully received, and the work almost immediately entered upon. The corner-stone of this imposing and ambitious structure was laid on April 6, 1841, the eleventh anniversary of the founding of the Mormon Church, amid a pomp and show of power that was in striking contrast to the crude and impromptu ceremonies at the first temple in Zion, or even the more elaborate services in Kirtland and Far West in later years. The means and men at Smith's command, with all their wonderful increase, had not grown more rapidly than his ambition, or his desire to occupy a large place in the public view. The occasion was one of pride to the proud, and of thankfulness to those who accepted the prosperity of the day as a gift from God to His chosen church. The preparations had been carefully made, and no untoward or ill-omened event occurred to mar the joy and happiness that had taken possession of all Nauvoo.

At an early hour of the beautiful spring morning, the Legion, to the number of fourteen companies, in the full strength and panoply of war, was drawn up in line, and word conveyed to its General that it awaited his commands. Escorted by an elegantly arrayed and mounted staff, Smith galloped along the crowded streets, where uncovered thousands stood ready to receive him with cheers. It was naturally a moment of pride to the well-digger's son; and those who had seen him in the early days of poverty and contempt, could indeed feel that he had been wonderfully prospered, whether by an especial providence of God, or the happy evolution of circumstances. Met by a martial band, and saluted by the thunder of cannon, he moved rapidly to the grand-stand that had been erected for his special use.

When he reached it, the first event upon the well-arranged programme was introduced. A number of ladies drove up in carriages and presented the Legion, through its General, with a stand of colors. Joseph responded in a speech characteristic of the occasion and himself, and then handed the flag to General Bennett, with the usual suggestions as to the uses to which it should be put, and the care with which it should be guarded. The band again filled the air with music, the guns added their deep bass, and the Legion proudly marched before Smith in review.

A procession was formed, and a line of march taken to the site of the temple, the foundation walls of which had been already laid. The singing of hymns, an hour's sermon from Rigdon, and dedication and prayer by the Prophet, were the main features of the occasion. The first of the corner-stones laid in place, that at the southeast, was blessed by Smith, who represented the first presidency; the president of the high-priests laid that at the southwest; the high council that at the northwest; and the bishops that at the northeast.*

---

* From *Times and Seasons*, vol. ii., p. 380: "However anxious we are to portray the grandeur and majesty of the celebrations, the

The site of the temple was on a hill that commanded a view of the Mississippi on one hand, and the rolling country on the other. It was a location of rare natural beauty, and calculated to call attention to the consecrated structure as the traveller should come to Nauvoo either by boat or overland. Its material was a polished white limestone, nearly as hard as marble. It was calculated that its cost, when completed, would be in the neighborhood of one million dollars. The manner in which it was viewed by Mormon eyes can be learned from the following, penned by W. W. Phelps,* when it was well under course of erection:

"The temple is up as high as the caps of the pilasters, and it looks majestic. . . . . This splendid model of Mormon grandeur exhibits thirty hewn-

union and order which every way prevailed, we are confident we shall come very far short of doing them justice. For some days prior to the sixth, the accession of strangers to our city was great, and on the wide-spread prairie, which bounds our city, might be seen various kinds of vehicles wending their way from different points of the compass to the city of Nauvoo, while the ferry-boats on the Mississippi were constantly employed in wafting travellers across its rolling and extensive bosom. . . . . At length the long-expected morn arrived, and before the king of day had tipped the eastern horizon with his rays, were preparations for the celebration of the day going on. . . . . The assembly then separated with cheerful hearts, and thanking God for the great blessings of peace and prosperity by which they were surrounded, and hearts burning with affection for their favorite and adopted State. It was indeed a gladsome sight, and extremely affecting, to see the old revolutionary patriots who had been driven from their homes in Missouri, strike hands and rejoice together, in a land where they knew they would be protected from mobs, and where they could again enjoy the liberty for which they had fought many a hard battle."

* *Times and Seasons*, p. 759.

stone pilasters, which cost about three thousand dollars apiece. The base is a crescent new moon; the capitals, near fifty feet high; the sun, with a human face in bold relief, about two and a half feet broad, ornamented with rays of light and waves, surmounted by two hands holding two trumpets. . . . . The inside work is now going forward as fast as possible. . . . . The temple is erected from white limestone, wrought in superior style; is one hundred and twenty-eight feet by eighty-three feet square; near sixty feet high; two stories in the clear, and two half-stories in the recesses over the arches; four tiers of windows, two gothic and two round. The two great stories will each have two pulpits, one at each end, to accommodate the Melchizedek and Aaronic priesthoods. . . . . The fount in the basement story is for the baptism of the living, for health, for remission of sin, and for the salvation of the dead, as was the case in Solomon's temple, and all temples that God commands to be built. . . . . The steeple of our temple will be high enough to answer for a tower—between one hundred and two hundred feet high. But I have said enough about the temple; when finished it will show more wealth, more art, more science, more revelation, more splendor, and more God than all the rest of the world."* The same

---

* Fate did not deal kindly with this great and costly structure. On the 19th of November, 1848, it was seriously injured by fire; and when, in 1850, it was about to be rebuilt and used for school purposes by the colony of Icarians, into whose possession it had passed, a severe tornado completed the work of the flames, and left it little more than a heap of ruins. "There now remains," says the Hancock *Patriot*, in May, 1850, "nothing of the gigantic

writer describes the other public buildings at Nauvoo, at that time, as the Seventies Hall, the Masonic Hall, and Concert Hall, "all spacious, and well calculated for their designated purposes."

The Joseph Smith of Kirtland was also the Joseph Smith of Nauvoo, and the returning prosperity of the church was reflected in his bearing and the means by which he made his own shoulders bear as few of the burdens of life as the circumstances surrounding him would allow. If we can safely accept the testimony of one, he "revelled in luxury, played the gentleman and the Saint, hospitably entertained his friends, and became exceedingly popular in the church and outside world." An intelligent Englishman who paid a visit to Nauvoo, and not only heard Smith preach, but conversed with him in private, describes him as "a person of rude manners, fond of low jocularity, but sharp, and of great power in the pulpit."

In conversation, at the Prophet's house, the visitor asked which of the Trinity had appeared to him, on the occasion of the first revelation.

"It was the Father," was the response, "with the Son on His right hand, and He said, 'I am the Father, and this being on my right hand is my Son, Jesus Christ.'"

"There was nothing in his appearance," wrote the visitor, in description of Smith, "to indicate any aberration of intellect, or that he gave himself to any

---

work of the Mormons, except the west face, strongly united by its sides to another wall in the interior part and surmounted by an arch; between the two walls at the north and south are the two towers, or seat, of the staircases."

great degree of mental abstraction. My conclusion was that he was an impostor."

As at Kirtland, Smith was still a part of everything, and nothing could be done without his knowledge, if not with his consent. "It was the policy of Joseph Smith," says John D. Lee, who was a resident of Nauvoo at the time,* "to hold the city lots in Nauvoo at a high price, so as to draw money from the rich, but not so high as to prevent the poor from obtaining homes. The poor who lost all their property in following the church were presented with a lot free, in the centre of the city. . . . . All classes, Jews and Gentiles, were allowed to settle there—one man's money was as good as another's."

He pursued such a policy that none in the city might purchase real estate to sell again but himself; permitted no one but himself to have a license for the sale of spirituous liquors; and in many ways undertook to regulate and control the business of the Mormons.

The growth of the city and church was largely accelerated by the addition of converts from the old world. The Mormon creed had been first preached in England in 1837, by missionaries under the direction of Orson Hyde and Heber C Kimball. In 1840 the first company of emigrants, to the number of forty, left Liverpool under direction of Brigham Young, then president of the English mission. On September 7th of the same year another vessel, with two hundred converts on board, left the same place, and the whole company were eventually safely added to

* "Mormonism Unveiled," p. 109.

the Mormon flock in Nauvoo. In explanation of one reason by which Mormonism grew so rapidly in the early days, it may be noted that the accessions from foreign lands alone reached a total of thirty thousand eight hundred and fifty-four by 1859; the years 1840 to 1844, adding them as follows: 1840—240; 1841—1,135; 1842—1,614; 1843—769. By 1843 the sect in England alone had reached ten thousand.

The prosperity of the Mormon city naturally attracted the attention of the old enemies across the river, and led to constant threatenings and new endeavors for the revival of old grudges, and the setting in motion of legal charges already made. The initiative in this putting of words into acts occurred in the fall of 1841, when the Governor of Missouri made formal requisition upon the Governor of Illinois for the arrest and surrender of Smith, who had never been tried upon the indictments recited heretofore. The first part of the demand was complied with. The Prophet was taken into custody without resistance, but steps were immediately taken to prevent his transfer to the dangerous soil of Missouri. Application was made to the home courts for a writ of habeas corpus, which was promptly granted, and Smith was soon released and returned to his friends by Stephen A. Douglas, who then occupied a seat upon the bench. Other attempts of like character were made from time to time, but as none of them resulted in conviction or even trial, no reference to them is needed, except as showing the spirit of deep hostility and permanent enmity that was increasing with each passing day, between the Mormons and the unbelieving world about them.

In the early days of May, 1842, General Bennett resigned his office of mayor, and Smith was promptly elected to the place, Hyrum Smith becoming vice-mayor. The Prophet may be regarded at this point as having reached the culmination of his career, and gained a plenitude of power far beyond his wildest dreams. The spiritual and temporal head of a church numbered by tens of thousands, and established in almost every State in America, as well as in portions of Europe; the chief municipal and judicial officer of a great city in which his wish was the law; General of an army obedient to his slightest word and sworn to do his bidding; chief editor of the *Times and Seasons*, the organ of the Mormon Church; absolute dictator of the movements and almost of the thoughts of those who constituted the membership of his church; with a fame known from one end of the land to the other; with hundreds of missionaries everywhere preaching him as the favored of the Most High; and sought eagerly by the leaders of the two great political parties, who flattered and praised him that they might win his support—is there wonder that his judgment should at times be led astray, and that he should hope for even greater things in the years to come?

The closing portion of 1841 and the early months of 1842 may be regarded as the high-tide of Mormon prosperity in Illinois, and as the season of peaceful sunshine that preceded the storm.

After John C. Bennett retired from his office and withdrew from the church, there grew up a deep bitterness and hatred between Smith and himself. Whatever its cause, and how much of unfairness or wrong may have been done upon either hand, the results were of a damaging and dangerous character to the church, and the feud had much to do with what afterward occurred. There was outward peace upon his departure, and the church and its organ spoke fair words concerning him*; which were recalled and replaced with the most bitter denunciation when it was known that his purpose was to wage war upon Mormonism in all possible ways, at all times and in all

---

* Extract from a revelation given Joseph Smith, Jr., on January 19, 1841: "Again, let my servant, John C. Bennett, help you in your labor, in sending my word to the kings and people of the earth, and stand by you, even you, my servant, Joseph Smith, in the hour of affliction, and his reward shall not fail if he receive counsel; and for his love, he shall be great; for he shall be mine if he does this, saith the Lord. I have seen the work he hath done, which I accept, if he continue; and I will crown him with blessings and great glory."—*Times and Seasons*, vol. ii., p. 425. And again: "General Bennett's character as a gentleman, an officer, a scholar, and physician, stands too high to need defending by us." —*Times and Seasons*, vol. ii., p. 431. When Bennett prepared to withdraw from the Mormon Church, he was given the subjoined documents:

"MAY 17, 1842.

"BROTHER JAMES SLOAN: You will be so good as to permit General Bennett to withdraw his name from the church record, if he desire to do so, and this with the best of feelings towards you and General Bennett.   JOSEPH SMITH."

"In accordance with the above I have permitted General Bennett to withdraw his membership from the Church of Jesus Christ of Latter-Day Saints, this 17th day of May, 1842; the best of feelings subsisting between all parties.

"JAMES SLOAN,
"General Church Clerk and Recorder."

When Bennett made war upon the church, this certificate was replaced by a bull of excommunication, and a severe attack upon his character record, and motives.

places. His attacks were open and direct. He found ready entrance to the leading journals of the land, and for a time the Mormon Church filled a large share of public attention. He charged treason and treasonable purposes upon the Mormon leaders, made grave attacks upon the personal character of Smith and those directly associated with him, and cited so much of fact in his denunciation as to lead an excited and hostile community to accept his whole story as the truth. His charges were taken up and repeated in all corners of Missouri and Illinois, gaining in power and coloring as they went, until many honest and intelligent men began to believe that Nauvoo was a second Sodom, and a foul spot that it would be patriotism to blot out.

Not content with his letters and interviews in the public press, Bennett published a book,* in which all his charges were repeated, with much from Howe and other anti-Mormon writers of the day. The mood in which these exposures were received by the public can be judged somewhat from the following, which appeared editorially in the New York *Sun* of August 5, 1842:

"We watch the further movements of the Mormon expounded, and the anti-Mormon expounder, with

---

* "The History of the Saints; or, An Exposé of Joe Smith, and Mormonism." By John C. Bennett; Leland & Whiting, Boston, 1842. This work is one of the curiosities of anti-Mormon literature. It contains full-page portraits of Generals Smith and Bennett in uniform, and is made up of a vast amount of documents and other material "pitchforked" together in the most amazing confusion—a condition of things explained by its author in the declaration, "I have been more solicitous about the matter than the manner of it."

some degree of anxiety, as affording a thorough explanation to the philosophy of fanaticism, whose victims we so frequently find recorded in the history of civilization. . . . . The rule of our male Cassandra, our modern Jacob—a combined Prophet and Patriarch—could not last forever. He has degenerated from the religious moralist and priest into the lowest grades of chicanery and vice; he stands before us a swindler of his community, an impious dictator over free will, and now in his most glaring and even hideous aspect—a libertine, unequalled in private life—a Giovanni of some dozens of mistresses, and these acquired under the garb of prophetic zeal. . . . . The state of these revelations, although not contained in the Book of Mormon, or viewed by the divine inspiration of Joe's stone spectacles, will soon assume the settled principles of truth, and must bear conviction to the misled and ill-treated sect."

The Louisville *Journal,* then under editorial control of George D. Prentice, in its issue of July 23, 1842, voiced the general feeling of the West in the following words: " This exposition, as far as we have read it, is one of the most startling things of the kind we ever saw. Moreover, it is deeply interesting to the public. Joe Smith is generally regarded as a mere miserable fanatic; but although he may be a fanatic, he is something more; he is the Prophet and the commander-in-chief of thirty thousand Mormons, all of whom regard him as a leader sent from heaven, and look upon his commands as emanating from the Most High. Backed by his multitudinous and deluded hosts, he already attempts to control the politics of Illinois, and defies both the civil and military authorities of that State to call him to account for anything that he has done or may do."

The storm had so increased in volume and power, and the threats of legal prosecution on the part of Missouri had grown so loud, that in September the Prophet found it convenient to hide himself for a time, doubtless proceeding to some small Mormon settlement where he knew there was no danger of betrayal. From this covert he issued several addresses to his people, of which the following may be taken as a characteristic sample: " Forasmuch as the Lord has revealed unto me that my enemies, both in Missouri and this State, were again in the pursuit of me; inasmuch as they pursue me without a cause, and have not the least shadow or coloring of justice or right on their side, in the getting up of their prosecutions against me; and inasmuch as their pretensions are all founded in falsehood of the blackest dye, I have thought it expedient and wisdom in me to leave the place for a short season, for my own safety and the safety of this people. I would say to all those with whom I have business that I have left my affairs with agents and clerks who will transact all business in a prompt and proper manner, and will see that all my debts are cancelled in due time, by turning out property, or otherwise, as the case may require, or as the circumstances may admit of. When I learn that the storm is fully blown over, then I will return to you again."

Following the above were minute directions as to how the records should be kept of those who might desire baptism for the salvation of their unbelieving dead. He was very explicit in these instructions, as the books thus kept at Nauvoo would be opened on the judgment day, and a clerical error might be of serious moment to some poor soul whose passage had been paid into the Kingdom.

In May, 1843, there occurred an incident that was unfortunate for the Mormons, whether they were connected with it or not.

As Governor L. W. Boggs, of Missouri, was sitting by his window he was shot at, and very narrowly escaped instant death. The attempted crime was immediately fastened upon O. P. Rockwell, a well-known Mormon, and Smith charged with being the promoter of the deed—a charge in support of which some very strong and pertinent evidence has been produced. The two were promptly indicted in the Missouri courts, and a requisition for their arrest and conveyance to Missouri obtained. When the papers were served there was an instant resort to habeas corpus. The writ was granted, and then tried by the municipal court of Nauvoo. Of course the prisoners were discharged. It is needless to say that the shooting and the bold act of the Nauvoo court added so much fuel to the already increasing flame.

An attempt had been made after Smith's return to the Mormons at Quincy to enlist the national government in their behalf, that they might receive redress for their losses in Missouri. At a church conference Rigdon and others were commissioned to go to Washington, and lay their complaints before the President. During the summer of the same year Smith himself made a like journey, and was allowed to personally lay his case before Van Buren. He received no encouragement from that source, and none from

Congress, the reply in each case being that as Missouri was a sovereign State the matter of her obligations to her citizens was no question for the consideration of the general government. Not yet rebuffed, the Mormons gravely made out a bill of one and a third million dollars, which was sent to Washington as a claim for indemnification, but no response was received and the matter was allowed to drop. This journey East, contact with the life of the capital and the suggestions it contained, and above all, the free and frequent proofs of political power he had given through his control of the solid Mormon vote, had directed Smith's ambition into a new channel, and caused him to make one of the greatest mistakes of his life. He was gravely announced in 1844 by the newspaper organ of the church, as a candidate for President of the United States.

No one can for a moment suppose that he had any serious hope or expectation of an election, and the small gain to his personal vanity which was the only recompense he could secure by this movement, was nothing when compared with the ridicule brought upon the church and himself, and the weapon placed in the hands of those who were preaching the dangers that must flow from any further satisfaction of the Prophet's ambition. The announcement of his candidacy was made in the *Times and Seasons*, in the following language: "This question arises, whom shall the Mormons support?—General Joseph Smith, a man of sterling worth and integrity, and of enlarged views; a man who has raised himself from the humblest walks of life to stand at the head of a large, intelligent, respectable, and increasing society, that has spread, not only in this land, but in distant nations; a man whose talents and genius are of an exalted nature, and whose experience has rendered him every way adequate to the onerous duty. Honorable, fearless, and energetic, he would administer justice with an impartial hand, and magnify and dignify the office of chief magistrate of this land."

The article from which the above has been extracted, refers, with some sarcastic bitterness of spirit, to the various charges against the Mormons, long since floating through the country:

"Gentlemen, we are not going either to 'murder ex-Governor Boggs,' nor a Mormon in this State, 'for not giving us his money'; nor are we going to 'walk on the water'; nor 'drown a woman'; nor 'defraud the poor of their property'; nor 'send destroying angels after General Bennett to kill him'; nor 'marry spiritual wives'; nor commit any other outrageous act this election, to help any party with; you must get some other person to perform these kind offices for you in the future. We withdraw."

Smith entered upon his campaign with his usual earnestness and audacity. He ordered his missionaries and ministers all over the country to advocate his claims. On February 7th he issued an address, entitled "Views of the powers and policy of the Government of the United States," which opens with this remarkable piece of bombast: "Born in a land of liberty, and breathing an air uncorrupted with the sirocco of barbarous climes, I ever feel a double anxiety for the happiness of all men, both in time and in eternity."

In that document he opposed slavery; also imprisonment for minor offences, so long as " the duellist, the debaucher, and the defaulter for millions, and other criminals, take the uppermost rooms at feasts, or, like the bird of passage, find a more congenial clime by flight." He declared it to be the duty of public officers to "ameliorate the condition of all "; quoted from the inaugural addresses of nearly all the Presidents; and made use of quotations in a half-dozen languages, to show the depth of his learning. He ended the jumble—for no other word describes it—with the following curious mixture of politics and religion:

"When the people petitioned for a national bank, I would use my best endeavors to have their prayers answered, and establish one on national principles, to save taxes, and make them the controllers of its ways and means; and when the people petitioned to possess the territory of Oregon or any other contiguous territory, I would lend the influence of a chief magistrate to grant so reasonable a request, that they might extend the mighty efforts and enterprise of a free people from the east to the west sea, and make the wilderness blossom as the rose; and when a neighboring realm petitioned to join the Union of the sons of liberty, my voice would be, 'Come!' yea, come Texas, come Mexico, come Canada; and come all the world; let us be brethren, let us be one great family, and let there be a universal peace. Abolish the cruel custom of prisons (except certain cases), penitentiaries, courts martial for desertion; and let reason and friendship reign over the ruins of ignorance and barbarity; yea, I would, as the universal friend of man, open the prisons, open the eyes, open the ears, and open the hearts of all people to behold and enjoy freedom, unadulterated freedom; and God, who once cleansed the violence of the earth with a flood, whose Son laid down His life for the salvation of all His Father gave Him out of the world, and who has promised that He will come and purify the world again with fire in the last days, should be supplicated by me for the good of all people.—With the highest esteem, I am a friend of virtue, and of the people,

"JOSEPH SMITH."

The address was printed in the leading newspapers of the land, and the comments upon it, while various, ran in a vein of good-natured ridicule, with occasional serious declarations that Mormonism was becoming a menace to the people. Other movements on the part of Smith gave new ground for the feeling of alarm among his immediate neighbors. He asked Congress for authority to raise one hundred thousand volunteer troops for the ostensible purpose of protecting American citizens on their way to Texas, Oregon, and other frontier points; and even went so far as to ask for the rank of General in the United States army. People remembered Aaron Burr, and asked each other where the ambition of the Mormon Prophet would end. Meanwhile, he was none the less bold in his claims of heavenly favor, and we hear him in the conference of that year (1844) declaring that "The Great Jehovah has always been with me, and the wisdom of God will guide me at the seventh hour. I feel that I am in more immediate communion with God, and on a better footing with Him than

I have ever been in my life; and I am happy to appear among you under these circumstances."

Another needless act of folly on the part of Smith at this critical juncture was his correspondence with Henry Clay, and the impudent and unseemly manner in which he addressed that eminent and venerable man. In November, 1843, he had addressed a letter to the Kentucky statesman, the purport of which was contained in this question, "What (if elected) will be your rule relative to us (the Mormons) as a people?"

Mr. Clay immediately responded in the only strain proper or even possible to one in his position as the chosen candidate of a great party. In a letter full of courtesy, he declared that, while he could make no pledges, he felt that the Mormons "in common with all other religious communities," "ought to enjoy the security and the protection of the courts and the laws."

This response did not guarantee such consideration, nor contain such flattering reference to his power as Smith desired, and after waiting six months, on May 13, 1844, he addressed another letter to Mr. Clay, which no gentleman could have written, and that was insolent, coarse, and too worthless for quotation. The tenor of the whole production may be guessed from a brief extract, in which he declares Mr. Clay "a blackleg* in politics, begging for a chance to shuffle yourself into the Presidential Chair, where you might deal out the destinies of our beloved land for a game of brag." To this tirade Mr. Clay, it is needless to say, made no reply.

* The language of the gambler so plentifully used in the above was an added insult to Mr. Clay, and doubtless intended as such.

The joy of the Mormons over Smith's method of conducting his presidential campaign was such that on May 17th they gave him a formal ovation, and finally in the excess of their enthusiasm he was lifted upon the shoulders of sturdy men, and carried bodily through the streets. One month later all that was left of the man, his follies, his ambitions, and his claims of spiritual power, was likewise borne aloft through the streets of Nauvoo, amid the sound of weeping, and with funeral plumes stirring the silent air about his murdered form.

XI.

DOWNFALL AND DEATH.

THAT the Mormon Church could long hold peaceable possession of the land it had purchased and the city it had built on the eastern bank of the Mississippi, had become impossible at this stage of events, and the only question to which it could with profit address itself, was whether it had defense against the storm that darkened about its horizon. The enemies who had so fruitfully multiplied in recent days had a purpose that stopped only at expulsion or extinction, and in their ranks were many who had abandoned the church and were anxious to advance all possible measures of revenge. John C. Bennett did not stand alone in his denunciations and exposures. By his side were William Law, once councilor to Smith; Wilson Law, an ex-general of the Nauvoo Legion; Dr. R. D. Foster, a man of wealth; Francis and Chauncey Higbee, with others of lesser note who had deserted the church for reasons of their own, or been cut off and cast out for causes involved in the carrying out of its policy. This hostile coterie found ready aid among the people of Hancock and Brown Counties for any scheme they might inaugurate against the common enemy at Nauvoo. The selfish policy of the Mormons in throwing their vote in whatever direction the gain of the moment suggested, had produced its natural result, and both Democrat and

Whig had come to look upon them as uncertain allies and unscrupulous enemies; while many who had been their outspoken friends two years before had come to regard them with suspicious fear, if not yet with open and avowed hostility. The orthodox churches of Illinois stood in solid phalanx against the new doctrine that had won such marvelous advance in a decade; while the moral sense of the community was shocked by the stories long since afloat of gross immoralities on the part of the Mormon leaders.* In short, Nauvoo, in these spring days of 1844, rested upon a powder-magazine that might at any hour explode and send it and the church into a ruin beyond repair.

The support made secure by these allied forces gave new boldness to those in the forefront of attack, and a movement was made in June that of necessity brought affairs to a crisis. Law, Foster, the Higbees, and other apostate Mormons, decided upon the establishment of a newspaper organ in the very stronghold of Mormonism, the avowed purpose of which was to make war upon the leaders of the church.† The *Nauvoo Expositor* was arranged for,

---

* See Appendix D.

† From "History of Hancock County, Illinois," by Th. Gregg, Chicago, 1880, page 302: "In the meantime the seceders were not idle. Law boldly denounced the Prophet from the stand in the city; while the others were busy among the people in and out of the city. The prospectus for the newspaper was circulated extensively, and received with much comment. Its title was to be the *Nauvoo Expositor*, and its purposes as set forth in the prospectus were the 'Unconditional Repeal of the City Charter.—To correct the abuses of the Unit Power.—To advocate Disobedience to Political Revelations,'—in short, to oppose the Prophet Smith, and correct

and its first and last number made its appearance on June 7th. Its motto was, "The Truth, the whole Truth, and nothing but the Truth"; and while it boldly attacked Smith and his immediate associates, it yet professed belief in the divine origin and essential truth of the Mormon creed.

This solitary issue was indeed a broadside. In addition to the recapitulation of charges already openly made in the general newspaper press, it contained the affidavits of sixteen women who charged Smith with immoral conduct, or attempts upon their virtue. The sheet was hardly upon the street before Smith and his friends were in motion to welcome it with such vengeance and punishment as his almost absolute power made possible. The City Council was summoned by fleet messengers, and upon its assembling the offending paper was read, and the course to be pursued discussed with such calmness as the feelings of those who had been attacked would permit.

the abuses of which he was claimed to be the cause. The paper was issued under date of June 7th. It had for its editor Sylvester Emmons, and the names of William Law, Wilson Law, Charles Ivins, Francis H. Higbee, Chauncey L. Higbee, Robert D. Foster, and Charles A. Foster as its publishers. In a literary point of view, it exhibited no decided talent. It had evidently been prepared in hurry and excitement, and with no attempt at artistic arrangement. About half its reading matter was selected. Of its original contents, five or six columns were occupied with a 'Preamble, Resolutions, and Affidavits of the seceders from the Church of Nauvoo,' giving reasons for their action, and making charges against Smith and his adherents. A number of editorial articles followed, couched in strong language, but not remarkable for ability or point. The confessed aim and purpose of this sheet were to expose the enormities practiced by the Prophet and his followers at Nauvoo."

It was indeed a dire dilemma in which the church found itself. The continuation of the publication meant open rebellion within the Mormon capital, exposure of much that might otherwise be hidden, unpunished contempt and defiance, and a breaking down of the centralized spiritual authority by which the Prophet held so many diverse and incongruous elements together. Bold measures, on the other hand, meant renewed outcry and added grounds of attack from the increasing bands of enemies about.

A member of that City Council, the Apostle John Taylor, has described the situation as judged from the Mormon point of view: "They felt," he writes,* "that they were in a critical position, and that any move made for the abating of that press would be looked upon, or at least represented, as a direct attack upon the liberty of speech, and that, so far from displeasing our enemies, it would be looked upon by them as one of the best circumstances that could transpire to assist them in their nefarious and bloody designs. Being a member of the City Council, I well remember the feeling of responsibility that seemed to rest upon all present; nor shall I soon forget the bold, manly, independent expressions of Joseph Smith on that occasion in relation to this matter. He exhibited in glowing colors the meanness, corruption, and ultimate designs of the 'Anti-Mormons'; their despicable characters and ungodly influences, especially of those who were in our midst; he told of the responsibility that rested upon us as guardians of the public interest, to stand up in the defense of the in-

---

* "The City of the Saints." By Richard F. Burton, New York, 1862, p. 520.

jured and oppressed, to stem the current of corruption, and, as men and Saints, to put a stop to this flagrant outrage upon this people's rights.

"He stated that no man was a stronger advocate for the liberty of speech and of the press than himself; yet, when this noble gift is utterly prostituted and abused, as in the present instance, it loses all claim to our respect, and becomes as great an agent for evil as it can possibly be for good; and notwithstanding the apparent advantage we should give our enemies by this act, yet it behooved us, as men, to act independent of all secondary influences, to perform the part of men of enlarged minds, and boldly and fearlessly to discharge the duties devolving upon us by declaring as a nuisance, and removing this filthy, libellous, and seditious sheet from our midst. The subject was discussed in various forms, and after the remarks made by the mayor every one seemed to be waiting for some one else to speak. After a considerable pause, I arose and expressed my feelings frankly, as Joseph had done, and numbers of others followed in the same strain; and I think, but am not certain, that I made a motion for the removal of that press as a nuisance. This motion was finally put and carried by all but one; and he conceded that the measure was just, but abstained through fear."

The measure under which action was to be taken, as finally decided upon, was as follows: "Resolved by the City Council of the city of Nauvoo, that the printing-office, from whence issues the *Nauvoo Expositor*, is a public nuisance; and also all of said *Nauvoo Expositors* which may be or exist in said establishment; and the mayor is instructed to cause said printing establishment and papers to be removed without delay, in such manner as he shall direct."

The designated official, in the person of Joseph Smith, lost no time in seeing the council's order carried out. The papers, the presses, and office fixtures of the doomed *Expositor* were carried into the street, and burned. This result was not attained without opposition on the part of those whose property was being destroyed. "The printing-press and the grocery of Higbee & Foster," writes John D. Lee,* "were declared nuisances, and ordered to be destroyed. The owners refused to comply with the decision of the city council, and the mayor ordered the press and type destroyed, which was done. The owner of the grocery employed John Eagle, a regular bully, and others, to defend it. As the police entered, or attempted to enter, Eagle stood in the door, and knocked three of them down. As the third one fell, the Prophet struck Eagle under the ear, and brought him sprawling to the ground. He then crossed Eagle's hands, and ordered them to be tied, saying that he could not see his men knocked down while in the line of their duty, without protecting them."

This bold attack upon free speech, the liberty of the press, and the rights of private property, was heralded throughout the land, and met by an almost unanimous expression of condemnation from press and people alike. The anti-Mormon newspapers of the immediate section made this action of Smith and his council the basis of repeated and vehement on-

---

* "Mormonism Unveiled," p. 153.

slaughts upon the church, and the feeling of the people was soon at a white heat. Meetings of citizens were called at various points, in which speeches were made and resolutions adopted,* denouncing the outrage of the suppression, in no measured terms. The crisis of Nauvoo had indeed come, and all its powers and resources were to be put to an immediate test.

The owners of the *Expositor* made prompt appeal to the laws of the State, in the hope that by some chance enough power had been withheld from the city council of Nauvoo under its remarkable charter, to give them redress. On June 11th a writ was issued by a justice of the peace of Carthage, ordering the arrest of several leading Mormons, on the charge of riot and the destruction of property. Among those named were Joseph and Hyrum Smith, the mayor and vice-mayor of Nauvoo, John Taylor, and W. W. Phelps. As soon as the Carthage constable had placed the parties named under arrest, a writ of habeas corpus was sworn out before the municipal council of Nauvoo, and the prisoners taken from the constable's custody and set at liberty.

This final defiance of the laws of the State and its officers could have but one effect. The people of

* The feeling of the people can be judged somewhat from the following, which was adopted at an immense mass-meeting at Warsaw, and afterward indorsed by a similar gathering in Carthage:

"*Resolved*, That the time, in our opinion, has arrived when the adherents of Smith as a body should be driven from the surrounding settlements into Nauvoo. That the Prophet and his miscreant adherents should then be demanded at their hands, and if not surrendered, a war of extermination should be waged to their entire destruction, if necessary for our protection.

"*Resolved*, That every citizen arm himself, to be prepared to sustain the resolutions herein contained."

Hancock County, while invoking the aid of the chief Executive of the State on the one hand, determined to act for themselves on the other. Armed bands of men were formed, and an immediate attack upon Nauvoo threatened. Smith realized his danger, and calling the officers and men of the Legion about him, admonished them of their sworn allegiance to the church and himself, and declared that the city would be defended at all hazards.

Compelled by the crisis of affairs to take action of some character, Governor Ford proceeded to Carthage, from whence he sent a message to Smith and the council, asking an explanation of the troubles that had arisen.

Confronted thus by the chief executive authority of the State, and feeling danger in the air all about them, the leading Mormons decided upon a temporary absence from Nauvoo, in order that the tempest might somewhat subside, and a way out of their difficulties present itself. But this decision was soon abandoned, and the conclusion reached that all who were under question of the law, should go to Carthage and meet whatever charges had been lodged against them.*

---

* If we may accept the testimony of Bishop John D. Lee, Smith actually left the State, and voluntarily came back into danger: "Higbee, Foster, and others . . . . got out writs for the arrest of Joseph and others, and laid their grievances before the governor. Joseph, knowing the consequences of such a move, concluded to leave for the Rocky Mountains, and lay out a country where the Saints would not be molested. He crossed over into Iowa, with a few faithful friends with him. These friends begged him to return and stand his trial; that the Lord had always delivered him, and would again. He told them that if he returned he would be killed,

At an early hour of the morning, Joseph, Hyrum, and other members of the council, accompanied by a party of devoted friends, set out from Nauvoo on horseback. While en route they were met by an aide-de-camp of the Governor, who bore a demand from that official for the immediate surrender of the State arms then in the hands of the Legion. The whole party returned to the Mormon capital, the demand was complied with, and evening had arrived before Carthage was reached. The small town was filled with militia under the Governor's command, and crowds of excited people whom the stirring scenes of the day had called in from the surrounding country. Those upon whom accusation rested because of participation in the destruction of the *Expositor* office, appeared before a local magistrate and gave bail in the sum of five hundred dollars each, to appear before the next session of the county court.

The natural expectation of the Mormons that their

> but that if he went away he would save his life, and the church would not be hurt; that he would look out a new country for them; that the governor had also advised him to do so. These old grannies then accused him of cowardice, and told him that Christ had said He would never leave His brethren in trouble. He then asked them if Emma (his wife) wished him to return. They answered "Yes.' He then said it was all light before him, and darkness behind him, but he would return, though he felt like a sheep being led to the slaughter. The following day he crossed the river again to Illinois. He kissed his mother in particular, and told her that his time had come, and that he would seal his testimony with his blood. He advised his brother Hyrum not to go with him—that he would be a comfort to the churches when he, the Prophet, should be gone. Hyrum said, 'No, my brother, I have been with you in life, and will be with you in death.' "—" Mormonism Unveiled," p. 154.

voluntary appearance in the stronghold of their foes, and formal submission to the demands of the law, would end in their dismissal to their homes for the present, was rudely dispelled when two men named Spencer and Norton appeared before a justice of the peace and swore out warrants for the arrest of Joseph and Hyrum on the charge of treason against the State—the alleged offense having been committed on June 19th, when the Legion had been called together in order to meet any danger that might arise. They were committed to jail. Their friends hurriedly communicated with Governor Ford, who expressed his regret that new troubles had arisen, but advised them to let the law take its course. On the following morning, June 26th, in response to a request from the Smiths, he paid them a visit in jail, and there was an extended conference, which ended in nothing. In the afternoon the prisoners were brought again before the justice, and after some parleying as to legal jurisdiction, were granted until noon on the following day for the securing of witnesses. They were then remanded to jail, and went straight from the court-room to the place that on the morrow was to witness a cruel attack and bloody death.

There have been many accounts written of these final scenes in the life of the Mormon Prophet and his brother, and many explanations, arguments, and apologies advanced by those who had a part therein or stood so near that some portion of the blame was laid upon them. With the greater portion of that literature we have nothing to do. All parties agree to the main facts of the murder, and with those only is this narration concerned.

Governor Ford has bequeathed us a voluminous account of his part in the final tragedy,* and the steps by which it was brought about. "The force assembled at Carthage," he writes, "amounted to about twelve or thirteen hundred men, and it was calculated that four or five hundred more were assembled at Warsaw. .... I ordered the troops to be disbanded, both at Carthage and Warsaw, with the exception of three companies, two of which were retained as a guard to the jail, and the other to accompany me to Nauvoo. .... Having made these arrangements, we proceeded on our march, and arrived at Nauvoo about four o'clock of the afternoon of the 27th of June. As soon as notice could be given, a crowd of the citizens assembled to hear an address which I proposed to deliver to them. .... A short time before sundown we departed on our return to Carthage. When we had proceeded two miles, we met two individuals, one of them a Mormon, who informed us that the Smiths had been assassinated in jail, about five or six o'clock of that day. The intelligence seemed to strike every one with a kind of dumbness. .... It was many days after the assassination of the Smiths before the circumstances of the murder became fully known. It then appeared that, agreeably to previous orders, the posse at Warsaw had marched on the morning of the 27th of June in the direction of Golden's Point, with a view to join the force from Carthage, the whole body then to be marched into Nauvoo. When they had gone eight miles, they were met by the

---

* "History of Illinois."

order to disband; and learning, at the same time, that the Governor was absent at Nauvoo, about two hundred of these men, many of them disguised by blacking their faces with powder and mud, hastened immediately to Carthage. There they encamped at some distance from the village, and soon learned that one of the companies left as a guard had disbanded and returned to their homes; the other company, the Carthage Grays, was stationed by the Captain in the public square, a hundred and fifty yards from the jail, whilst eight men were detailed by him, under the command of Franklin A. Worrell, to guard the prisoners. A communication was soon established between the conspirators and the company; and it was arranged that the guard should have their guns charged with blank cartridges, and fire at the assailants when they attempted to enter the jail. General Deming, who was left in command, being deserted by some of his troop, and perceiving the arrangement with the others, and having no force upon which he could rely, for fear of his life retired from the village. The conspirators came up, jumped the slight fence around the jail, were fired upon by the guard, which, according to arrangement, were overpowered immediately, and the assailants entered the prison, to the door of the room where the two prisoners were confined, with two of their friends who voluntarily bore them company. An attempt was made to break open the door; but Joe Smith, being armed with a six-barrelled pistol, furnished by his friends, fired several times as the door was bursted open, and wounded three of the assailants. At the same time several shots were fired into the room, by some of which John Taylor received four wounds, and Hyrum Smith was instantly killed. Joe Smith now attempted to escape by jumping out of the second-story window; but the fall so stunned him that he was unable to rise, and, being placed in a sitting posture by the conspirators below, they dispatched him with four balls shot through his body."

The actual events at the jail after the farce of overpowering the guards and taking possession by a show of force, had been enacted, have been graphically described in brief compass by one whose opportunities for information were excellent, whose fairness cannot be questioned, and whose ability to distinguish the true from the false is of the highest order: * "Smith and his brother had been that day removed from their cells, and given comparative liberty in a large, airy room on the first floor above. This afternoon they were receiving the visits of two Mormon brethren, Richards and Taylor. They heard the row at the door and the rush on the stairs, and instinctively barred their door by pressing their weight against it. The mob fired at the door. Hyrum Smith fell, exclaiming, 'I'm a dead man.' Taylor crawled under the bed with a bullet in the calf of his leg. Richards hid himself behind the door in mortal terror. . . . . Joe Smith died bravely. He stood by the jamb of the door and fired four shots, bringing his man down every time. He shot an Irishman named Wills, who was in the affair from his congenital love of a brawl, in the arm; Gallagher, a Southerner from the Mississippi bottom, in the face; Voorhees, a half-grown

* "The Mormon Prophet's Tragedy." By John Hay, *Atlantic Monthly*, December, 1869, p. 669.

hobbledehoy from Bear Creek, in the shoulder, and another. . . . . Smith had two loaded six-barrelled revolvers in his room. . . . . The four shots which I have chronicled, and two which had no billet, exhausted one pistol, and the enemy gave Smith no time to use the other. Severely wounded as he was, he ran to the window, which was open to receive the fresh June air, and half leaped, half fell, into the jail yard below. With his last dying energies he gathered himself up, and leaned in a sitting posture against the rude stone well-curb. His stricken condition, his vague wandering glances, excited no pity in the mob thirsting for his life. They had not seen the handsome fight he had made in the jail; there was no appeal to the border chivalry—there is chivalry in the borders, as in all semi-barbarous regions. A squad of Missourians who were standing by the fence levelled their pieces at him, and, before they could see him again for the smoke they made, Joe Smith was dead."

The last few hours of life that were given to the doomed man, who had travelled so long and devious a road from the Palmyra log-cabin only to meet grim death in Carthage jail, were of necessity full of fear and heaviness. He was utterly in the hands of his enemies, guarded by men who had themselves threatened his life, and could not for a moment be depended upon to interpose themselves between the prisoners whom it was their duty to protect, and any who might seek their lives. In popular opinion, and in the due process of law, there was small hope of favor; and any attempt at violent rescue at the hands of armed men from Nauvoo, could only end in death to many, and bring on a civil war that would drench Hancock County in blood, lay the Mormon capital in ashes, and drive the church an outcast from the region that only a few years before had opened arms and given it welcome. There was but one possible course—to wait with such hope and courage as could be summoned, for whatever punishment or deliverance fate might already have set upon its way.

Of those closing hours, Apostle John Taylor, who was present, has written an account,* which may be taken as true, so far as it relates to matters unconnected with the purposes or actions of the foes outside. "I do not remember," he declares, "the names of all who were with us that night and the next morning in jail, for several went and came. . . . . There was also a great variety of conversation, which was rather desultory than otherwise, and referred to circumstances that had transpired; our former and present grievances; the spirit of the troops around us, and the disposition of the Governor; the devising of legal and other plans for deliverance; the nature of testimony required; the gathering of proper witnesses; and a variety of other topics. . . . . At another time while conversing about deliverance, I said, 'Brother Joseph, if you will permit it and say the word, I will have you out of this prison in five hours, if the jail has to come down to do it.' My idea was to go to Nauvoo, and collect a force sufficient, as I considered the whole affair a legal farce, and a flagrant outrage upon our liberty and rights. Brother Joseph refused. Elder Cyrus Wheelock came

* "The Martyrdom of Joseph Smith." By Apostle John Taylor. This whole story is reprinted in "The City of the Saints," p. 517.

in to see us, and when he was about leaving drew a small pistol, a six-shooter, from his pocket, remarking at the same time, 'Would any of you like to have this?' Brother Joseph immediately replied, 'Yes, give it to me'; whereupon he took the pistol, and put it in his pantaloons pocket. . . . . The report of the Governor having gone to Nauvoo without taking the prisoners along with him caused very unpleasant feelings, as we were apprised that we were left to the tender mercies of the Carthage Grays, a company strictly mobocratic, and whom we knew to be our most deadly enemies. . . . . Some time after dinner we sent for some wine. It has been reported by some that this was taken as a sacrament. It was no such thing; our spirits were generally dull and heavy, and it was sent for to revive us. I believe we all drank of the wine, and gave some to one or two of the prison guards. We all of us felt unusually dull and languid, with a remarkable depression of spirits. In consonance with those feelings I sang the following song, that had lately been introduced into Nauvoo, entitled 'A Poor Wayfaring Man of Grief':

> A poor wayfaring man of grief,
>   Hath often crossed me on my way,
> Who sued so humbly for relief
>   That I could never answer nay.
>
> I had not power to ask his name,
> Whither he went, or whence he came;
> Yet there was something in his eye
> That won my love, I know not why.
>
> .   .   .   .   .   .
>
> Then in a moment to my view
>   The stranger started from disguise;

> The tokens in his hands I knew;
> The Saviour stood before mine eyes.
>
> He spake—and my poor name he named—
> 'Of me thou hast not been ashamed;
> These deeds shall thy memorial be;
> Fear not; thou didst them unto me.'"

"The song," continues Taylor, "is pathetic, and the tune quite plaintive, and was very much in accordance with our feelings at the time, for our spirits were all depressed, dull, and gloomy, and surcharged with indefinite ominous forebodings. After a lapse of some time, Brother Hyrum requested me again to sing that song. I replied, 'Brother Hyrum, I do not feel like singing'; when he remarked, 'Oh! never mind; commence singing, and you will get the spirit of it.' At his request I did so. Soon afterward I was sitting at one of the front windows of the jail, when I saw a number of men, with painted faces, coming round the corner of the jail, and aiming toward the stairs."

The Apostle's description of the attack is vivid, and does not materially differ from those already given. As Hyrum fell he cried, "I am a dead man," and spoke and moved no more. As he fell Joseph leaned over him, and in tones of deep and sad sympathy exclaimed, "Oh! my poor, dear brother Hyrum!" "While I was engaged in parrying the guns," his narration continues, "Brother Joseph said, 'That's right, Brother Taylor; parry them off as well as you can.' These were the last words I ever heard him speak on earth."

Their work of murder completed, the assassins left the town and made haste to Warsaw and other points from whence they came. The people of Carthage waited in silent fear for the sudden vengeance they were sure would befall them from Nauvoo. But it came not. The blow had fallen with such force that every emotion except grief and apprehension was driven from the minds of the Mormons, who prepared to receive their dead with such honors as befitted their rank in the church. The Legion stood under arms from ten in the morning until three in the afternoon, when the funeral cortège appeared on the Carthage road and was escorted to the Mansion House, amid lamentation and weeping from the thousands who believed that Joseph had been in truth a prophet of the Lord, who had now sealed his mission in his blood. An oration was pronounced by Dr. Richards, while addresses were delivered by others who counselled peace, and asked their hearers to leave vengeance to God alone, and trust that in His hands justice would at last be done.

Even the lifeless body of the fallen Prophet could not escape the ambition of the leaders of the church, nor be safe from the sacrilege of those who had pursued him with such relentless purpose to the death. "The interment of the mortal remains of the Prophet and the Patriarch was attended to with proper solemnity," we are told on authority, to which, for many years, the Mormon records were open,* "and a sorrowing multitude accompanied the mourners to the burial-place; but there was a sequel to the public services which the people never knew. The bodies of Joseph and Hyrum were not in that funeral pro-

* "Rocky Mountain Saints," p. 174. Its author, T. B. H. Stenhouse, was for twenty-five years a Mormon Elder and missionary.

cession; they were reserved for private interment. It was believed that sacred as the tomb is always considered to be, there were persons capable of rifling the grave in order to obtain the head of the murdered Prophet for the purpose of exhibiting it, or placing it in some phrenological museum—the skull of Joseph Smith was worth money. This apprehension, in point of fact, proved true, for the place where the bodies were supposed to be buried was disturbed the night after the interment. The coffins had been filled with stones, etc., to about the weight which the bodies would have been. The remains of the two brothers were then secretly buried the same night by a chosen few, in the vaults beneath the temple. The ground was then levelled, and pieces of rock and other *débris* were scattered carelessly over the spot. But even this was not considered a sufficient safeguard against any violation of the dead, and on the following night a still more select number exhumed the remains, and buried them beneath the pathway behind the Mansion House. The bricks which formed the pathway were carefully replaced, and the earth removed was carried away in sacks and thrown into the Mississippi. If this last statement is true, the bodies must have been removed a third time, as, since writing the above, the author has it on unquestionable authority that they now repose in quite a different place. Brigham Young has endeavored to obtain possession of the remains of the Prophet, that they might be interred beneath the temple at Salt Lake. It is stated by Brigham, that Joseph, like the son of Jacob, made the request that the Saints when they went to the Rocky Mountains should carry his bones with them. The family of Joseph maintain that the Prophet never expressed any such desire, but said very much to the contrary. It is affirmed that previous to Joseph's death, he predicted that the church would be scattered, and saw that the time might come when Brigham Young would lead the church; and that if he did, he would lead it to perdition. He told his wife, Emma, to remain at Nauvoo, or if she left, to go to Kirtland, and not to follow any faction. To have given the bones into Brigham's charge would have been to confirm the Saints in the Rocky Mountain Zion, to which the Smith family are decidedly opposed. The remains of the martyrs are destined for Zion in Missouri."

With the death of Joseph Smith, the initial era of Mormonism may be said to have come to an end. The strong hand with which Brigham Young put aside all claimants for the succession; relegated the Prophet's son and brothers to inferior places in the church; gave Sidney Rigdon over to excommunication and the mercy of Satan, and took matters into his own control and saved the church from disintegration and extinction; the season of peace that for a time fell upon Nauvoo; the yet greater storm by which it was followed; the final expulsion; the sad and weary pilgrimage across the plains; and the undreamed-of power and glory of after-days,—* these are moving scenes in this great drama of a false religious growth, but do not belong to that inceptive epoch that has been chronicled herein.

Those who sought to destroy Mormonism by the

---

* Appendix E.

cowardly attack on Carthage jail, gave it a far more powerful ally than Rigdon, or Young, or Smith himself could have given it in decades of missionary preaching. The halo of a martyrdom had descended upon it; and of all the works performed by Joseph Smith for the system of which he was the foundation and the head, none could reach even a portion of the power, and influence, and vitalizing force that lay in the legacy of his bloody death.

XII.

THE SCATTERED FLOCK.

WHEN Sidney Rigdon found himself cast out of the fold, and given officially over to the buffetings of Satan for a thousand years, that once-powerful leader gathered about him such as would heed his call, and led them eastward to Pennsylvania, where he made a vain attempt to found a church of which he should be the spiritual and temporal head; but they fell from him one by one, some going into the orthodox churches, some into infidelity and others back to the fold of which Young had become shepherd. William Smith, the Prophet's brother, piloted a few to Northern Illinois; Elder Brewster gathered a group of stragglers in Western Iowa; Bishop Heddrick, a like following in Missouri; and Bishop Cutler, in Northern Iowa; but leadership, opportunity, and money were wanting, and all came to naught. Lyman Wight was followed to Texas by a company of some size. The authority of Young was recognized until the promulgation of polygamy, when it was repudiated; and on Wight's death the faction went slowly to pieces.

Joseph Smith, the eldest son of the Prophet, remained with his mother at Nauvoo after the exodus of the main body of the church to the West. In 1851, a number who had scattered through Iowa, Illinois, and Missouri, gathered in solemn conclave, and made formal declaration that they had been instructed in a revelation from God to refuse the leadership of Young, who was not the "divinely appointed and legitimate successor of Joseph Smith, and as being the promulgator of such false doctrines as polygamy, Adam-God worship, and the right to shed the blood of apostates." No special result followed this gathering, until in 1860, when the Joseph Smith of the third generation became president of the Reorganized Church of Jesus Christ of the Latter-Day Saints—the name officially adopted. The old temple at Kirtland came recently under control of the organization,* and after repairs and renovation, wit-

---

* By the courtesy of Harley Barnes, Esq., of Painesville, the seat of Lake County, in which Kirtland is situated, I am able to furnish the following brief account of the fortunes of the old temple. The temple property, consisting of the building and nearly two acres of land, was conveyed to Joseph Smith, Jr., as president of the church, on May 5, 1834; and again by deed dated January 4, 1837, the former deed being considered illegal. It was again deeded April 10, 1837, by Smith to William Marks, and on February 11, 1841, by said Marks, to Smith as sole trustee in trust for the church. It was next ordered sold by the Probate Court of Lake County, on application of Henry Holcomb, administrator of Joseph Smith, then deceased, for the payment of the decedent's debts. The property was sold under this order to William L. Perkins, on April 19, 1862. On the same day it was conveyed by Mr. Perkins to Russel Huntley. On February 17, 1873, Mr. Huntley conveyed it to Joseph Smith (the president of the Reorganized Church) and Mark H. Forscutt, both of Plano, Illinois. On August 18, 1879, an action was commenced in the Lake County Common Pleas Court by the Reorganized Church, against Lucius Williams, Sarah F. Videon, Joseph Smith, Mark H. Forscutt, "The Church in Utah of which John Taylor is president, and commonly known as the Mormon Church," and "John Taylor, president of said Utah Church"—a proceeding to quiet title and obtain legal possession of the temple property. No defense was made; and on February 23, 1880, Judge L. S. Sherman delivered a decision in which he de-

nessed, on April 6, 1883, a grand reunion of Mormon pilgrims, from the West and elsewhere. The organization and government of the Reorganized Church are patterned after those of the early days; while polygamy is specially condemned as a joint device of Satan and Brigham Young. "We number," wrote President Smith, under date of Lamoni, Iowa, December 15, 1884,* "approximately 18,000,† and are scattered from Maine to New Mexico, Oregon to Florida; some in England, Wales, Denmark, and Australia, and Society Islands. Our largest numbers are in Iowa, Missouri, Illinois, Nebraska, Kansas, California, and Utah, respectively. We have maintained

---

clared that "The Church in Utah, the defendant, of which John Taylor is president, has materially and largely departed from the faith, doctrines, laws, ordinances, and usages of said original Church of Jesus Christ of Latter-Day Saints, and has incorporated into its system of faith the doctrines of Celestial Marriage and a plurality of wives, and the doctrine of Adam-God worship, contrary to the laws and constitution of said original Church"; and the court further found that the plaintiff, the Reorganized Church, was "the true and lawful continuation of and successor to," the said original church; and was, in law, entitled to "all its rights and property." The sale ordered by the Probate Court, above described, was therefore declared to have been illegally made, and the title declared to be "vested in the heirs of said Joseph Smith, in trust for the legal successor of said original church."

* "A Solution of the Mormon Problem." By John Codman, New York, 1885, p. 23.

† Mr. H. A. Stebbins, secretary and recorder of the Reorganized Church, in answer to a request for information on the part of the author, writes, under date of Lamoni, Iowa, February 21, 1888, that at this date there are upon the church records the names of between twenty and twenty-one thousand members, who, with others in various parts of the country not thus recorded, will bring the membership up to a total of from twenty-two to twenty-five thousand.

a mission in Utah since 1863, with from one to a dozen men there. We number between 800 and 1,000 in Utah. There are members in Idaho, Montana, Colorado, and Arizona. We have been persistent to the extent of our means [to win Mormons from polygamy], and have kept from two to five elders in the missionary field in Utah for the last five years."

Among those who attempted to wear the mantle of the Prophet, in the troubled days of 1844, was James Jesse Strang, whose subsequent "Mormon Kingdom," on the Beaver Islands of Lake Michigan, has become one of the strange and unique things of American history. This remarkable episode of Mormonism has been overlooked in the larger and more important operations of Salt Lake; yet in interest and romance it cannot be surpassed by any act in that great drama of ambition and superstition. The following account * of this bold attempt and early failure to found a kingdom on American soil, is well worth reproduction in this connection:

"Far out in the deep blue waters of Lake Michigan, about forty-five miles from the Straits of Mackinac, stands Big Beaver Island, the largest of a scattering group, famous for having been the seat of an heretical sort of autocracy, styling itself the Kingdom of the Mormons, ruled over by a potentate designated as King Strang. Although the rise and progress of this kingdom, its final downfall and the expulsion of its people from the island was an eventful and a woeful chapter in the annals of the polygamous sect, one might read whole libraries of Mormon literature with-

* "An American Kingdom of Mormons." By F. D. Leslie; in *Magazine of Western History*, of Cleveland; April, 1886, p. 645.

out learning that such an institution ever existed. This discrepancy or omission in Mormon history is due to an antagonism which sprang up between Strang and Brigham Young, completely alienating the one from the other. James Jesse Strang received his appointment as elder from Joseph Smith, founder of the faith, March 3, 1844, only one week after his baptism into the communion of the Mormon Church, and was, on June 19th following, vested with authority to establish a branch nucleus at his home in Burlington, Wisconsin. Joseph Smith having been mobbed and murdered at Carthage jail, June 27th of the same year, Strang, although less than five months a member of the Mormon Church, advanced his claims to the mantle of the martyred leader and pushed them with vigor. His principal title was an ambiguous clause in the letter of Smith clothing him with the powers referred to, which he readily construed into a declaration nominating himself as the prelate's successor in case that dignitary should succumb to the ominous dangers then threatening him. . . . . According to the will of God revealed to Joseph Smith, Strang gathered up his votaries and planted a Stake of Zion on White River, Wisconsin, naming the place Voree, now known as Spring Prairie. A Mormon organ, entitled the Voree *Herald*, was started and schools were established, the community living in common. As Smith had done before him, the Prophet now proceeded to fortify himself in his position by publishing feigned interviews with God and bringing forth tables from the earth bearing what he claimed to be divinely inspired inscriptions. Eighteen metallic slabs, curiously carved, which Strang pretended to have discovered in the banks of the White River, he christened Plates of Laban. It was claimed with the most positive and solemn assurance that they were written before the Babylonian captivity. Strang's divine library consisted of the Bible, recognized as the supreme authority, the Book of the Law of the Lord, composed of the Prophet's translations of the characters on the Plates of Laban; the Book of Mormon and Smith's Book of Doctrines and Covenants.

"Such was the prosperity of the community that its founder conceived the idea of permanently establishing and perpetuating the happiness of the sect by planting a kingdom on Big Beaver Island, where his people would be further removed from the 'invidious Gentiles,' and where his acts would not be so openly visible to the eyes of the authorities. This plan was carried into execution in 1847. And without license, reason, or excuse, and in open defiance of the law, Strang proclaimed himself king. The Voree *Herald* was issued as the *Northern Islander*, under the editorship of the king. A well-equipped printing-house was established, and for a time a daily edition of the *Islander* was published. Having settled his people on the island, where his policy could be carried out to better advantage than in the midst of hampering Gentiles, Strang assiduously directed his entire attention to the government of his kingdom. His authority was supreme. His commands were not given as a species of ukase, but were claimed to be absolute and indefeasible. His subjects were obedient and quiescent so long as his rule promoted their prosperity without being particularly offensive. How much they respected the compact when the administration of affairs became unsatisfactory will shortly be seen. The king not only conducted personally the civil and ecclesiastical business of his realm, but found time to regulate in a minute and meddlesome manner its secular concerns. The communistic principle was abandoned and individuals were allowed to hold titles to their lands. The Israelitish tithe of one-tenth was assessed for the support of Church and State, no other taxes being levied for Mormon purposes. Some of his enactments respecting temporal affairs were very stringent, well calculated to preserve manhood, sobriety, and peace. According to authority, the probity of which there is no reason to question, the use of intoxicating liquors, tobacco, tea, and coffee was prohibited, and gaming and betting were not permitted. 'Prostitution and lewdness were discountenanced alike in both sexes,' writes one of Strang's wives, ' and it was as necessary for a man to be careful of his reputation as for a woman.' Pursuing she says: 'They were very strict in all that regulated society, morals, and religious observances, and absolute obedience was enjoined. The seventh day was set apart as the Sabbath, and every one physically able was required to attend church upon that day. Schools were organized and flourished, and intellectual culture encouraged. The women were required to wear bloomers.' In a State possessing the right of autonomy, such a governmental fabric would look plausible enough.

" But Strang did not enjoy a reign of uninterrupted peace and prosperity. His kingdom, though insular, was not removed beyond the power of its enemies to assail. The islanders and fishermen—a rough, lawless set, whose ill-will was not a good thing to incur—were bitterly opposed to the advent of the Mormons, and did their best to prevent them from obtaining a foothold. There arose at once a distinction between Mormon and Gentile, and the inimical tendencies of the two classes soon ripened into a deadly and implacable hatred. A warfare of plunder was constantly kept up. The odiousness of the despised sect rendered impartial judgment on the part of the general public impossible. In this condition of affairs, in the midst of a marauding and unscrupulous class of itinerant fishermen and skippers, it is highly probable that both Mormon and Gentile had depredations charged to them of which they were not guilty. The buccaneer infesting the lakes at that day could have had no better opportunity of plundering both saint and pagan without being likely to bring suspicion and punishment upon his own head.

"It is a well-authenticated fact that the crafty king had the high-handedness to prostitute the power of civil law to foster Mormonism and wreak vengeance on his enemies. In the fall of 1852 he became an independent candidate for the State Legislature, and was elected by Democratic votes. He filled the position with ability. During the winter following he organized the county of Emmet and introduced a bill to admit it, which was passed. This county embraced Beaver Island, and St. James was chosen as the county-seat. He had now the power of the State law to serve him in the promulgation of his doctrines. . . . . The authorities, having for some time kept Strang and his confederates under distrustful surveillance, determined at length to put an end to his presumptive kingdom. By order of District Attorney George C. Bates, the United States steamer *Michigan* was sent to St. James, and Strang, together with several of his colleagues, was arrested on a warrant charging him with trespassing on public lands, stealing timber, counterfeiting, mail robbing, and other crimes. They surrendered peaceably and were taken to Detroit. In June, 1851, they were arraigned before Judge Ross Wilkins, of the United States district court, and a jury. In his violation of the law, Strang had so shrewdly evaded it in technicalities that the evidence against him was insufficient. But there were internecine forces at work to accomplish the downfall of his kingdom. The majority of his subjects were not Mormons at heart, and did not hold their institution sacred any more than they regarded the king as their valid sovereign. Strang's first downward step was the introduction of polygamy, which he at first pretended to disfavor to such an extent as to pronounce a terrible curse upon those practicing it, and which his votaries, be it said to their credit, looked upon with aversion and abhorrence. Plural marriages were few. Strang, himself, had only four wives. From the time he publicly recommended polygamy, the difficulty of insubordination and disrespect became serious. The 'petticoat rebellion' is a somewhat ludicrous example of his meddlesomeness, and of the instrumentality of the women in consummating his ruin. As before stated, Strang had adopted the bloomer style of dress for the women. Many disgusted females rebelled against the uncouth pantalets and returned to the interdicted long skirts. Strang's threats were sufficient to compel acquiescence in the majority of insubordinates, but a few of the more resolute told him with indignation that they would not submit to his interference in domestic affairs, and defied him to force the use of the unfeminine bloomers upon them. The husbands of the rebellious women were, in pursuance of the ecclesiastical law, excommunicated. Among the latter were Dr. H. D. McCulloch, of Baltimore, Maryland, Thomas Bedford and Alexander Wentworth, leaders in the conspiracy that undermined the king. A series of tantalizing lawsuits was instigated against Bedford, and one against McCulloch, to vex them and exemplify Strang's power over the subservient magistrates who were his tools.

"One night Bedford was seized by seven armed men and fiendishly whipped. For three nights thereafter he watched Strang's house, but found no opportunity of taking revenge on the author of the outrage. Bedford, Wentworth, and McCulloch, the triumvirate of sedition, then agreed upon the murder of the king, but it was thought advisable to defer the execution of the design until the arrival of the United States steamer *Michigan*. On June 15, 1856, the *Michigan* cast anchor in the harbor of St. James, and while Strang was on his way to interview the captain, Bedford and Wentworth shot and mortally wounded him. He was removed to Voree, where he died July 9th, following. Bedford and Wentworth were, by the arbitrary intervention of the officers of the *Michigan*, taken to Mackinaw on board that steamer, where they were lionized as heroes who had rid the world of an hitherto invincible monster. If they ever received any punishment it was slight.

With the assassination of Strang, the Mormon kingdom collapsed. During the latter part of his reign, the king's power was so enervated, and his security rendered so precarious by civil strife, that he entertained few hopes of the institution surviving his demise, and on his death-bed advised the Mormons to emigrate. There being no ties of cognation, sympathy, or common belief to bind them together, except perhaps their hatred of the fishermen, they began at once to quit the island for various places. But their enemies would not let slip so rare an opportunity of wreaking vengeance on their heads. Chartering a vessel, a large mob of desperadoes from the neighboring islands and the mainland sailed for St. James. With remorseless brutality the remaining Mormons, several hundred in number, mostly women and children, were driven by force and arms aboard a propeller bound for Milwaukee, only a few hours being given them to collect their portable property, the greater part of which was left behind. The predatory gang then proceeded to plunder the effects of the ejected colony, giving as an excuse for their spoliation that the property was to indemnify them against losses sustained at the hands of marauding Mormons. The immunity of these lawless invaders from justice was a matter of course, in a community so prejudiced against the Mormons, whose chief offense seems to have been in their inappropriate appellation—since Mormonism is now synonymous with polygamy. The miserable outcasts landed in various places, but mostly in Milwaukee."

APPENDIX.

A.

SOLOMON SPAULDING.

So long as a mystery hangs over the origin of the Book of Mormon, so long will the name of Solomon Spaulding be associated with a creed which was formulated years after his death, and with a church of which he never heard. The claim put forward with such certainty by some, and denied with equal vigor by others, that it was upon a heavy and else forgotten romance of his that the Mormon book was founded, has rescued him from oblivion, and made him one of the unsolved enigmas of the century. Fate has indeed reserved him to a unique fame, so different from that to which his natural aspirations turned. The story may be briefly told, although volumes have been devoted to it. Mr. Spaulding was born in Ashford, Conn., in 1761; graduated at Dartmouth College in 1785; became a minister of the Congregational Church; preached for a while, and then because of ill-health gave his time to mercantile pursuits; failed, and in 1809 removed to Salem—now Conneaut—Ohio, where he made another business venture that was no more successful than the first. With enforced leisure upon his hands, and a strong literary faculty that demanded use, he wrote much; taking as his theme the prehistoric inhabitants of America, and making his imagination furnish that information which the then discovered facts of Archæology did not supply. In 1812, in the hope that a publisher might be found for what he had written, he removed to Pittsburgh, and took his manuscript to the printing-office of Rev. Robert Patterson, to see if arrangements could not be made to that end. As he had no means of his own, and as the publisher could see no chance of success for the venture, the "Historical Romance" upon which his hope had been built, was not given to the world. Broken in spirit and health, poor in pocket, and with old age approaching, he removed to Amity, Washington County,

Pennsylvania, where he died within two years. There, recently, a visitor who felt that life had not dealt altogether fairly with the poor old man, and that history had not always been considerate in the use of his name, went into the deserted little graveyard, and under the moss of a crumbling stone, discovered this inscription, and rescued it from an early oblivion :

IN MEMORY OF
SOLOMON SPAULDING, WHO DEPARTED THIS LIFE
OCTOBER 20TH, A.D. 1816.
AGED 55 YEARS.

Kind cherubs, guard the sleeping clay,
Until the great decision day,
And saints complete in glory rise
To share the triumphs of the skies.

The claim is put forth, and supported by a great deal of direct if not conclusive evidence, that the manuscript of the Spaulding book was left in Patterson's printing-office; that Sidney Rigdon came into possession of the original or a copy ; that he was thrown into connection with Joseph Smith ; and that chance, circumstances, deep cunning, a keen eye to the main chance, and a public anxious to be duped by any religious vagary that might present itself, performed the rest. Many witnesses have been placed on record as deposing that parts of the Book of Mormon are identical with the romance of Solomon Spaulding, as read to them by the author during the long leisure of winter, in pioneer days. An analysis of the testimony pro or con. is foreign to the purpose of this book ; but those who have the desire to pursue the matter to the limits of all information now extant, are referred to the following works, devoted entirely to this phase of Mormon history : The pamphlet publication, written by the son of the Robert Patterson above referred to, " Who Wrote The Book of Mormon," by Robert Patterson, Pittsburgh, 1882 ; and " New Light on Mormonism," by Mrs. Ellen E. Dickenson, New York, 1885.

B.

MARTIN HARRIS AND CHARLES ANTHON.

Rev. Mr. Clark, in " Gleanings by the Way," pp. 222 to 238, lets a flood of light in upon this episode of Mormonism : " It was early in the autumn of 1827" (quoting Mr. Clark's personal experience) "that Martin Harris called at my house in Palmyra, one morning about sunrise. His whole appearance indicated more than usual excitement, and he had scarcely passed the threshold of my dwelling before he inquired whether he could see me alone, remarking that he had a matter to communicate that he wished to be strictly confidential. Previous to this I had but very slight acquaintance with Mr. Harris. He had occasionally attended divine service at our church. . . . . I invited him to accompany me to my study, where, after having closed the door, he began to draw a package out of his pocket with great and manifest caution. Suddenly, however, he stopped, and wished to know if there was any possibility of our being interrupted or overheard. When answered in the negative, he proceeded to remark that he reposed great confidence in me as a minister of Jesus Christ, and that what he had now to communicate he wished me to regard as strictly confidential. He said he verily believed that an important epoch had arrived. . . . . The whole thing appeared to me so ludicrous and puerile, that I could not refrain from telling Mr. Harris that I believed it a mere hoax, got up to practice upon his credulity, or an artifice to extort from him money; for I had already, in the course of the conversation, learned that he had advanced some twenty-five dollars to Jo Smith as a sort of premium for sharing with him in the glories and profits of this new revelation. . . . . My intimations to him in reference to the possible imposition that was being practiced upon him, however, were indignantly repelled. . . . . He then carefully unfolded a slip of paper which contained three or four lines of characters, as unlike letters or hieroglyphics of any sort as well could be produced were one to shut up his eyes and play off the most antic movements with his pen upon paper. . . . . My ignorance of the characters in which this pretended ancient record was written, was to Martin Harris new proof that Smith's whole account of the divine revelation made to him was entirely to be relied on. . . . . He was so much in earnest on this subject, that he immediately started off with some of the manuscripts that Smith furnished him, on a journey to New York and Washington, to consult some learned men to ascertain the nature of the language in which this record was engraven. . . . . The Rev. Dr. Coit, rector of Trinity Church, New Rochelle, Westchester County, N. Y., hearing that the Mormons in that place . . . . were claiming the patronage of Professor Anthon's name in behalf of their notions, took the liberty to state the fact to him, and ask in what possible way they had contrived to associate him with themselves. In reply to this inquiry Professor Anthon wrote the letter above referred to [first published in *The Church Record*] which we here insert:

"'NEW YORK, April 3, 1841.

"'REV. AND DEAR SIR:—I have often heard that the Mormons claimed me for an auxiliary, but as no one until the present time has ever requested from me a statement in writing, I have not deemed it worth while to say anything publicly on the subject. What I do know of the sect relates to some of their early movements; and as the facts may amuse you, while they will furnish a satisfactory answer to the charge of my being a Mormon proselyte, I proceed to lay them before you in detail. Many years ago, the precise date I do not now recollect, a plain-looking countryman called upon me with a letter from Dr. Samuel L. Mitchell, requesting me to examine and give my opinion upon a certain paper, marked with various characters, which the doctor confessed he could not decipher, and which the bearer of the note was very anxious to have explained. A very brief examination of the paper convinced me that it was a mere hoax, and a very clumsy one too. The characters were arranged in columns like the Chinese mode of writing, and presented the most singular medley that I ever beheld. Greek, Hebrew, and all sorts of letters more or less distorted, either through unskilfulness, or from actual design, were intermingled with sundry delineations of half-moons, stars, and other natural objects, and the whole ended in a rude representation of the Mexican zodiac. The conclusion was irresistible that some cunning fellow had prepared the paper in question, for the purpose of imposing upon the countryman who brought it, and I told the man so, without any hesitation. He then proceeded to give me a history of the whole affair, which convinced me that he had fallen into the hands of some sharper, while it left me in great astonishment at his own simplicity. [Professor Anthon here repeats the story of the golden plates, as told by Smith and repeated by Harris.] On my telling the bearer of the paper that an attempt had been made to impose on him and defraud him of his property, he requested me to give him my opinion in writing about the paper which he had shown to me. I did so without hesitation, partly for the man's sake, and partly to let the individual "behind the curtain" see that his trick was discovered. The import of what I wrote was, as far as I can now recollect, simply this, that the marks in the paper appeared to be merely an imitation of various alphabetical characters, and had, in my opinion, no meaning at all connected with them. The countryman then took his leave, with many thanks, and with the express declaration that he would in no shape part with his farm, or embark in the speculation of printing the golden book. [Professor Anthon here describes a second call, at a later date, and his refusal to accept a copy of the newly-published Book of Mormon, or have anything to do with it.] That the Prophet aided me by his inspiration in interpreting the volume, is only one of the many amusing falsehoods which the Mormonites utter relative to my participation in their doctrines. Of these doctrines I know nothing whatever, nor have I ever heard a single discourse from any one of their preachers, although I have often felt a strong curiosity to become an auditor, since my friends tell me that they frequently name me in their sermons, and even go so far as to say that I am alluded to in the prophecies of Scripture! If what I have here written shall prove of any service in opening the eyes of some of their deluded followers to the real designs of those who profess to be the apostles of Mormonism, it will afford me a satisfaction, equalled, I have no doubt, only by that which you yourself will feel on this subject.

"'I remain very respectfully and truly, your friend,

"'CHARLES ANTHON.

"'REV. DR. COIT,
"'*New Rochelle, N. Y.*'"

C.

THE DANITES.

The dark deeds of the "Danites" belong properly to the days of Salt Lake, but that the organization already existed in Missouri and there performed its bloody work, seems to be proved, in spite of Joseph Smith's emphatic denial. When Thomas B. Marsh, the chief of the Twelve Apostles, left the Mormon Church, he made an affidavit, under date of October 24, 1838, before Henry Jacobs, a justice of the peace for Ray County, Missouri, in which he used the following words: "They have among them a company, considered true Mormons, called the Danites, who have taken an oath to support the heads of the Church in all things that they say or do, whether right or wrong." To this Orson Hyde, at that time at war with the Church, added his testimony, in a like oath, in which he said: "The most of the statements in the foregoing disclosure I know to be true; the remainder I believe to be true." John Hyde, also an apostate Mormon, in his "Mormonism," p. 104, says: "When the citizens of Carroll and Davis Counties, Missouri, began to threaten the Mormons with expulsion in 1838, a death society was organized, under the direction of Sidney Rigdon, and with the sanction of Smith. Its first captain was Captain 'Fearnot' alias David Patten, an apostle. Its object was the punishment of the obnoxious. Some time elapsed before finding a suitable name. They desired one that should seem to combine spiritual authority with a suitable sound. Micah iv. 13 furnished the first name, 'Arise, and thresh, O daughter of Zion; for I will make thy horn iron, and thy hoofs brass; and thou shalt beat in pieces many people; and I will consecrate their gain unto the Lord, and their substance unto the Lord of the whole earth.' This furnished them with a pretext; it accurately described their intentions, and they called themselves the 'Daughters of Zion.' Some ridicule was made at these bearded and bloody 'daughters,' and the name did not sit easily. 'Destroying Angels,' came next; the 'Big Fan' of the thresher that 'should thoroughly purge the floor,' was tried and dropped. Genesis xlix. 17 furnished the name that they finally assumed. The verse is quite significant: 'Dan shall be a serpent by the way, an adder in the path, that biteth the heels, so that his rider shall fall backward.' The 'Sons of Dan' was the style they adopted; and many have been the times that they have been *adders in the path, and many a man has fallen backward, and has been seen no more.* At Salt Lake, among themselves, they ferociously exult in these things, rather than seek to deny or extenuate them." Were testimony needed to prove the existence of this body, it could be produced in abundance. John D. Lee, the Mormon bishop, in his Confessions, on p. 57, says: "At the same conference (that of 1838) another organization was perfected, or then first formed— it was called the Danites. The members of this order were placed under the most sacred obligations that language could invent. They were sworn to stand by and sustain each other. *Sustain, protect, defend,* and *obey,* the leaders of the Church under any and *all circumstances unto death;* and to disobey the orders of the leaders of the Church, or divulge the name of a Danite to an outsider, or to make public any of the secrets of the order of Danites, was to be punished with death. And I can say of a truth, many have paid the penalty for failing to keep their covenants." For more light upon this subject see the little work "Brigham's Destroying Angel; being the Life, Confessions, and Startling Disclosures of the Notorious Bill Hickman, the Danite Chief of Utah," written by himself, with explanatory notes by J. H. Beadle, New York, 1872.

D.

POLYGAMY.

That the plural-wife system had no part in the Mormon doctrine of early days, is a matter of evidence and record, as it is commanded in a revelation that a man shall have only one wife, and cleave unto her. Polygamy may, therefore, be regarded as an outgrowth of the enlarged powers and opportunities of later days. When Bennett, the Higbees, and other members of the Mormon Church apostatized at Nauvoo, and made their furious attacks upon the whole Mormon scheme, one of their main points of argument was that the system of spiritual wifehood was already in secret practice, and that under the guise of celestial marriage, Smith and other leaders of the Church were living in adultery with scores of women. Addressing a public ready to believe that Mormonism was a cloak for the covering of any abomination known to man, they had no difficulty in securing belief for their charges; turning against the Church the whole moral and religious sentiment of the country. The revelation commanding polygamy was first published in the *Deseret News Extra*, of Salt Lake City, on September 14, 1852; although given, as the Church claimed, to Joseph Smith at Nauvoo, on July 12, 1843. The sons of Smith, and the members of the Reorganized Church of Latter-Day Saints, deny not only the charges of Bennett *et al.* as to the Prophet's immoral practices, but all reputed connection of his with the revelation itself; claiming that the latter was a device invented by Young to defend his own practices, and cunningly given on the authority of Smith that it might carry greater weight with the Church. "The Mormon history relates," says Mr. Beadle, in "Life in Utah," p. 337, "that when the full force of the new covenant was perceived the Prophet was filled with astonishment and dread. All the traditions of his early education were overthrown, and yet he felt that it was the work of the Lord. In vain he sought to be released from the burden of communicating the new doctrine to the world, and at length obtained permission to keep it secret, as yet, from all but the Twelve Apostles, and a few other leading men. As the hour approached when he was to meet them in council, horror and fear of what might be the result, overcame him, and he hastily mounted his horse and fled from the city. But a mighty angel met him on the road, stood in the way with a drawn sword, and with awful voice and offended mien, bade him return." Whether the work of Smith or Young, the revelation was not announced to the Church until on August 29, 1852, when Brigham made it public, and preached a sermon commanding obedience to its requirements—paving the way for others by himself becoming eventually the possessor of nineteen wives. The effect upon the people of Utah was not marked, as they only now saw the open doing of what they had long known in secret, but elsewhere it became an immediate damage to the Church, and the forerunner of many ills in the future—of which the recently passed Edmunds law, and the prosecutions and convictions thereunder are not the least. "In England, especially," says Mr. Beadle, in continuation of the above, "the demoralization was fearful; hundreds after hundreds apostatized, whole churches and conferences dissolved; talented knaves in many instances, finding in this the excuse for going off without surrendering the money-bags which they held. The missions entirely disappeared in many parts of Europe, and even in America, thousands of new converts who had not gone to Zion turned away and joined the Josephites, Gladdenites, Strangites, and other sects of recusant Mormons." The practical and theological sides of the system are thus briefly condensed by the same author—who has resided in Salt Lake City for a number of years, and made of Utah Mormonism a practical study: "Of their theology as it relates to polygamy, but little need be added. It is so thoroughly grafted into and interwoven with their whole system, that at no point can one be touched without attacking the other. Polygamy is not, as recusant Mormons assert, a mere addition by Brigham Young to the original faith; it is a necessary and logical outgrowth of the system. If Mormonism be true, their polygamy is right; for 'pre-existence of the soul,' 'progression of the gods,' and all other peculiarities of the system, depend by a thousand combinations and inter-relations upon the plurality system. A man's or woman's glory in eternity, is to depend upon the size of the family for a woman to remain childless is a sin and calamity, and she cannot secure 'exaltation' as the wife of a Gentile or an apostate; her husband's rank in eternity must greatly depend upon the number of his wives, and she will share in that glory whatever it is. All this points unerringly to polygamy. Hence, also, the last feature of this complex and unnatural relationship known as 'spiritual wives,' which is to be understood as follows: Any woman, having an earthly husband of whose final exaltation she is in doubt, may be 'sealed for eternity' to some prominent Mormon, who will raise her and make her a part of his final kingdom. . . . . By 'marriage for the dead' living women are sealed to dead men, and *vice versa*, some one standing proxy for the deceased. ; . . . So a man may have a wife 'for time' who belongs to some man already dead 'for eternity,' in which case all the children will belong to the latter in eternity, the living man merely 'raising up seed unto his dead brother.' To such lengths of vain imaginings may a credulous people be led by artful impostors."

E.

THE MORMONS OF SALT LAKE.

There were many claimants for the position of prophet and president made vacant by the death of Joseph Smith, but, as in many other cases, he who was wise enough to claim the least, eventually received the most. William Smith claimed the succession because he was the prophet's brother; Sidney Rigdon began to have visions and dream dreams, and announced himself as the chosen one; James Jesse Strang advanced his right, under special commission from Joseph; while Lyman Wight, Gladden Bishop, John E. Page, and others, began to feel the spirit of prophecy, and announced themselves as ready to take the lead. But Brigham Young, advancing no special plea of spiritual direction, and depending upon that strong common-sense that aided him in so many emergencies, came home to Nauvoo as rapidly as possible, took matters into his own hands, and by his courage and address saved the society and the Church from going to pieces. He caused the Twelve Apostles, of whom he was head, to issue on August 15th an "Encyclical letter to all the Saints in the world," and on October 7th a general council was held at Nauvoo. Under his advice it was decided that for the present the government should be in the hands of the Twelve, which lodged the chief executive power in the strong hands of Young. Rigdon's claims were derided, while he, and those who had sided with him, were cut off from the Church and sent forever adrift. Young addressed himself with energy to the repair of the shattered fortunes of the Saints, hastened the completion of the temple, and used his best endeavors to keep peace with the hostile elements now ranged all about the fold. But the enmity was too deep and lasting to wear easily away. The politicians of Illinois had no further hope from the Mormon vote, and accordingly the General Assembly repealed the charter of Nauvoo. Warned by the signs of the times, the Mormon leaders decided to emigrate to some place in the far West. In 1846 a number emigrated to Council Bluffs, Iowa; while those who remained behind were driven from Nauvoo by force, and compelled, in a large measure, to abandon their homes and possessions. Meanwhile men had been sent forward to the Valley of the Great Salt Lake, in Utah; and as their report was favorable, Young gathered up all who would trust themselves to his guidance, and led them across the hills and plains to a place that in those days was far beyond the confines of even such semi-civilization as that of Missouri and Iowa. Salt Lake City was founded, and the barren wilderness was made to blossom as the rose. The weaker brethren who had remained behind, came on in numbers, while great accessions were received through the labors of missionaries who had been sent abroad. In March, 1849, a State was organized, under the name of Deseret, the "land of the honey-bee." A legislature was chosen and a constitution framed, and an application made to the General Government for admission to the Union. The plea was refused, but as a compromise, the country occupied by the Mormons was, in 1850, organized into the Territory of Utah, and Brigham Young appointed Governor. A United States court for the Territory was organized and judges appointed, but were not allowed to exercise their functions when they arrived at Salt Lake. Young was suspended, and Colonel Steptoe, of the United States army, appointed in his stead. A conflict between the Government and Mormons was carried on—in which armed forces on both sides confronted each other at times—until 1858, when the Mormons submitted to Federal authority, on condition that all past offenses against the Government should be pardoned. On the conclusion of the war of the Rebellion a Federal governor was again appointed, and in 1871 a law was passed declaring polygamy to be a criminal offense; although the statute was for a long time a dead letter. Young remained the head of the Church, an absolute autocrat in matters spiritual and temporal, until his death on August 29, 1877. He left a fortune of two million dollars, and nineteen wives and fifty-six children. He was succeeded in office by Elder John Taylor, who remained at the head of the Church until his death in the summer of 1887. Since then no formal choice of a successor has been made. From the time that the newly-formed Republican party in its first national platform adopted in 1856 referred to "those twin relics of barbarism, polygamy and slavery," to the present, many efforts have been made by the Government and people to limit the power and influence of the Mormon Church, and avert the dangers its existence and growth so surely threatened. An estimate of the strength of the Mormon organization may be given as follows: The population of Utah, at the last enumeration, was 147,000, of whom 125,000 are Mormons; but as adherents of the Church are scattered all over the world, it is impossible to arrive at a just idea of their numerical strength. They have of late years made considerable progress in Idaho, Arizona, Colorado, Montana, Wyoming, and Washington Territories, and their number in the United States outside of Utah cannot fall much below 27,000. In Europe they have also many adherents, and their number the world over cannot be less than 213,000.

www.ingramcontent.com/pod-product-compliance
Lightning Source LLC
Chambersburg PA
CBHW032105230426
43672CB00009B/1646